AUTOMATED INFORMATION RETRIEVAL IN LIBRARIES

**Recent Titles in
The Greenwood Library Management Collection**

Strategic Marketing for Libraries: A Handbook
Elizabeth J. Wood, with assistance from Victoria L. Young

The Smaller Academic Library: A Management Handbook
Gerard B. McCabe, editor

Operations Handbook for the Small Academic Library
Gerard B. McCabe, editor

Data Bases for Special Libraries: A Strategic Guide to Information Management
Lynda W. Moulton

Time Management Handbook for Librarians
J. Wesley Cochran

Academic Libraries in Urban and Metropolitan Areas: A Management Handbook
Gerard B. McCabe, editor

Managing Institutional Archives: Foundational Principles and Practices
Richard J. Cox

Automated Information Retrieval in Libraries

A MANAGEMENT HANDBOOK

Vicki Anders

The Greenwood Library Management Collection

GREENWOOD PRESS
New York • Westport, Connecticut • London

Library of Congress Cataloging-in-Publication Data

Anders, Vicki.
    Automated information retrieval in libraries : a management handbook / Vicki Anders.
        p. cm. — (The Greenwood library management collection, ISSN 0894-2986)
    Includes bibliographical references and index.
    ISBN 0-313-27361-8 (alk. paper)
    1. Information retrieval. 2. Libraries—Automation—Management.
I. Title.   II. Series
Z699.A63   1992
025—dc20   91-44401

British Library Cataloguing in Publication Data is available.

Copyright © 1992 by Vicki Anders

All rights reserved. No portion of this book may be reproduced, by any process or technique, without the express written consent of the publisher.

Library of Congress Catalog Card Number: 91-44401
ISBN: 0-313-27361-8
ISSN: 0894-2986

First published in 1992

Greenwood Press, 88 Post Road West, Westport, CT 06881
An imprint of Greenwood Publishing Group, Inc.

Printed in the United States of America

The paper used in this book complies with the Permanent Paper Standard issued by the National Information Standards Organization (Z39.48-1984).

10 9 8 7 6 5 4 3 2 1

Contents

Illustrations	vii
Preface	ix
1. Automated Information Retrieval: Integrating the Options	1
2. Operations of an Automated Information Retrieval Service	41
3. Finance and Budget	77
4. Staff	105
5. End-User Services	131
6. Databases and Vendors	169
7. The Technology: Hardware and Software	197
8. Planning for the Future	215
Index	245

Illustrations

1. Search Request Form — 58
2. Search Log — 59
3. Ready-Reference Log — 60
4. Automated Statistics and Records — 62
5. Sample Statistics — 64
6. End-User Worksheet — 147
7. End-User Appointments and Logs — 148

Preface

It was not so many years ago that automated information retrieval meant exclusively online searching by librarian intermediaries. Books and articles on the subject discussed dealing with a handful of online vendors, training librarians to be search analysts, and how to afford it. Searches were performed on tiny Texas Instruments Silent 700 terminals at 300 baud and were printed on thermal paper that curled like an ancient scroll and quickly faded to a uniform and barely legible grey. It was state-of-the-art technology. Graduating to 1,200 baud was astonishing.

End-users entered the picture in the 1980s. Although I had performed ready-reference searches for a couple of years previously, it was the end-users who expanded my contact with automated information retrieval. I was the bibliographic instruction librarian at the time, and spent a good many hours developing slide-tape shows, written manuals and computer-assisted instruction programs to teach end-users how to use BRS/After Dark. I spent many more hours standing at their shoulders explaining which key to punch, the difference between AND and OR, and how to get the computer to print citations. It was the first time I ran into this phenomenon: No matter how many manuals the end-user has read or how many demonstrations the end-user has seen, as soon as the end-user sits down at the keyboard the question comes up,"Now what do I do?" End-users have searched BRS/After Dark and Knowledge Index at Texas A&M University's Evans Library since 1982, and the question is still asked by the majority of new users. But enough have figured it out that end-users now account for 75 percent of the library's total online connect hours. I have been the manager of the library's automated information retrieval service for several years now, and I hear the question every day.

In 1986 Evans Library installed several CD-ROM databases; in 1990 Wilson database tapes were loaded with the library's NOTIS online public access catalog. The automated information retrieval picture has changed considerably since the early days of the 300 baud TI terminal.

This book attempts to illuminate the total picture of an integrated automated information retrieval service by showing how online, ondisk, and locally loaded databases work together to serve search analysts, librarians, and end-users. The book is intended for the managers of the services who deal with the day-to-day details of providing mediated searches, discretionary searches, and end-user searches, or for those managers who are considering adding a new service, and for library management personnel who want a review of the automated information retrieval options and the procedures and costs involved in providing them. Automation of one sort or another consumes more and more of library budgets and library staff each year, and new developments in the technology and techniques of automated information retrieval constantly change the delivery of information services. It is important to understand all the options available, how they affect each other and how they affect the library in general, in order to select the right configuration of options for any one library.

Selective annotated reference sections follow each chapter and should be used as guides to additional reading. I have tried to include books of collected readings, either of reprinted articles or original contributions, because they bring together a variety of viewpoints in one convenient package. Case study articles illustrating unique solutions to particular problems, articles showing a good research design or methodology that can be repeated and tested in a local environment, literature reviews, and surveys that illustrate how a variety of libraries are using and applying automated information retrieval have been selected for inclusion. Very few articles published prior to 1980 are listed unless they are landmark articles much cited in the literature. An American bias is very noticeable. References within the text of the chapter lead the reader to articles about the point being discussed; these articles may not necessarily draw the same conclusion that I have in the text.

I am aware that "compact disc" and "optical disc" use the letter C instead of the letter K, but I have deliberately chosen to spell the word *DISK*. I have chosen the word "ondisk" to provide a distinction from "online" searching and to refer to the portable databases designed to be mounted on a local microcomputer; thus it includes CD-ROM, optical disks, and laser disks, and can be extended to include those databases distributed on floppy disks and intended to be loaded on the capacious hard disks of microcomputers.

I wish to thank the Faculty Academic Study Program of Texas A&M University for the grant of a Faculty Development Leave allowing me the time to research this book. Thanks are also due to my colleagues in the Reference Division of Evans Library who have lived through many changes and additions to their duties and responsibilities brought on by changes and additions to the automated information retrieval services we offer. They have served as the guinea pigs in many research projects. Special thanks go to Dr. Kathy Jackson, an enthusiastic supporter and promoter of automated information retrieval.

AUTOMATED INFORMATION RETRIEVAL IN LIBRARIES

1

Automated Information Retrieval: Integrating the Options

WHAT IS AUTOMATED INFORMATION RETRIEVAL

Sitting at his terminal in his crowded office late at night, Professor Smith finds just the reference he needs in the library's OPAC (online public access catalog) in that portion of the OPAC where the commercially produced database INSPEC is loaded. He checks the local holdings and discovers that the journal he wants is not in the library's collection. "Rats!" he says, and although he has done it many times before he has to ask for onscreen help to remember how to place an interlibrary loan request via his office computer. Once the onscreen form is filled in and transmitted by E-mail to the library's interlibrary loan office he sighs and briefly regrets the intolerable bother and delays just to get this one article in his hands. The next morning an interlibrary loan clerk prints out the latest batch of requests waiting on the office computer, and as is the practice of interlibrary loan clerks everywhere, checks them against the library's online catalog just to be sure they are legitimate, and then checks the journal titles against a bibliography of online full-text journals. Professor Smith's journal is there along with a few others. The clerk sends an E-mail message consisting of the appropriate interlibrary loan requests to the Automated Information Retrieval Service Office where it is received by the service coordinator, who notes that there are not so many this morning and decides to do them herself right away. She signs on to the full-text databases and downloads the appropriate articles, signs off, does a little manipulating of the downloaded records to link them to the appropriate interlibrary loan requests and the accounting system, then hits the "send" button. The downloaded articles are now in the memory of the campus mainframe computer linked to several microcomputers and terminals all over campus, including Professor Smith's computer where it waits until he comes in at noon, turns on his computer, and finds the article he requested. Instead of recalling the good old days when he had to walk over to the library, check a card catalog, fill out an interlibrary loan form by hand and carry it to the interlibrary loan office, then wait for days or weeks for the article to appear, Professor Smith grumbles to himself, "Now, why couldn't the library have gotten this to me last night?"

This is not a scene from the year 2000; it is possible, and it is happening today, including Professor Smith's attitude. Automated information retrieval is defined in this text as computerized access to commercially available databases. Therefore, the locally loaded version of INSPEC and the online database of full-text journals fall within the definition, because both are accessed by computer and both are commercially produced, but the library's online catalog of holdings, being locally produced, does not.

A generation has passed, yet librarians still refer to automated information retrieval as "new" technology, when in fact, as early as 1964 computerized searches in batch mode were available on the MEDLARS database produced by the National Library of Medicine. In the early 1960s, abstracting and indexing services began replacing standard typesetting machines with computerized phototypesetting. The purpose was to produce printed indexes faster and cheaper, but the by-product—a machine-readable tape—had a life of its own. In the early years the machine-readable tape could be batch searched, whereby a number of search requests were loaded at one time and allowed to run, and the resulting printouts were handed over to the requesters some hours or days or even weeks later. There was no interaction with the database; a search strategy could not be modified except as part of another batch to be run later. Faster, more powerful computers and reliable telephone networks created the conditions that made online, interactive searching from remote terminals possible. In 1972 DIALOG began commercial operations with just three databases; by 1975 many academic and research libraries in the United States had instituted automated information retrieval services, and a landmark one million remote searched were performed in that year.

By the early 1980s some abstracting and indexing database producers were making their machine-readable tapes available for lease. Libraries could mount the tapes and searching software on mainframe computers that could be accessed by local users. A locally loaded database cut out the middleman vendors and thus cut out connect time charges. Some leased databases require citation charges to be paid as a royalty to the database producer in addition to the lease charge. Locally loaded databases were and still are an expensive option. Also in the early 1980s, Knowledge Index and BRS/After Dark made several databases available for searching on user-friendly systems by end-users.

In 1986 databases on optical disks and compact disks became widely available. Like their online counterparts, these are large databases run by powerful search engines, but they are moderately user-friendly and thus designed for end-users, and like locally loaded databases they have no connect time charges and no citation charges unless the library imposes them. Although they can be expensive to purchase, the per-search cost of a popular CD-ROM database is quite low compared to the online version. Neufeld and Cornog (1986) and Williams (1977) detail the history of automated information retrieval.

In the early 1990s there are literally thousands of databases available, and some of them are available in all the forms mentioned above: online, online for end-users, locally loaded as a leased tape, or locally loaded as an optical disk. A library may have any combination of these forms depending on the clientele served and the service philosophy of the library. The budget greatly influences how much and what kind of searching will be done, and the organization of the library will affect the organization of the automated information retrieval service. This chapter discusses the options available and describes the typical setting of the different options, their operation, environment, clientele, and use. Finally, the chapter describes the impacts of automated information retrieval services on the library and on each other. First, some definitions are necessary.

What Is a Search?

A search is defined as the access to a database or databases necessary to answer a question. A patron wanting the full bibliographic details for an ERIC document so far identified only as ED123 456 can be answered by accessing the ERIC database and typing the character string ED123 456, and printing the single retrieval in bibliographic format. If the online version of ERIC is searched, the cost is a couple of dollars and a couple of minutes for the answer to the patron's question. Many searches are far more complex and require the formulation of a *search strategy*, a formalized model of the question written out in the style that the computerized database can accept. Several sources describe in detail the development of search strategies and the mechanics of online searching, including Gilreath (1984); Li (1985); Armstrong and Large (1988); and Vigil (1988). These should be used with caution because any guide to searching is out of date as soon as it is published, due to the improvements and upgrades the vendors add to their search engines.

For example, a veterinary medicine student needs to find information on the nutritional requirements of elderly cats. The *search analyst*, a librarian with special training in automated information retrieval, explains which databases are most likely to contain citations on the subject, and the patron selects two of them: the Commonwealth Agricultural Bureaux database, which includes Nutrition Abstracts and Index Veterinarius, and BIOSIS. Both databases are widely available through different vendors, and the search analyst decides to use the BRS system to compile a bibliography of sources. The first step is to analyze the question for the concepts it contains, like so:

CATS ELDERLY NUTRITIONAL

It has been decided to search two different databases, and the search analyst will therefore use *free-text* terms rather than the controlled vocabulary particular to a single database. Free-text searching finds words as they occur in any basic index field of a bibliographic citation—title or abstract or descriptors—whereas *controlled vocabulary* searching searches only in the descriptor field, and the descriptors are seldom the same in two different databases. The search analyst and the student requesting the search must put their heads together to make a list of synonyms for each of the concept groups, because different authors may use different words to describe the same thing. Author Smith may use "cats" and author Brown may use "felines." The search strategy expands to look like this:

CATS	ELDERLY	NUTRITIONAL
cat	old	nutrition
feline	older	diet
felines	geriatric	dietary
felis	mature	food
felidae	senile	feed
	aged	

Notice that singular and plural forms of words are listed as synonyms because computerized searching is quite literal and searches for character strings exactly as they are entered. Typing "cat" at the terminal keyboard will not normally retrieve "cats." However, the search analyst applies his or her special knowledge of automated information retrieval techniques to revise the list. For example, BRS has an automatic plurals option which, if it has been turned on, will retrieve "cats" when "cat" is typed. In order to avoid typing both "old" and "older", the search analyst revises the character string to read "old$2", using the BRS truncation technique to instruct the computer to search for the character string "old" plus up to two more characters if they exist. The search analyst could apply the same technique to the word stem "feli" by typing "feli$3" and thus avoid consuming online time by typing four variations based on the same word stem. The search analyst points out a possible danger here: searching for the scientific terms felis/felidae can retrieve information on lions, tigers, and other large undomesticated predators, and the patron has made it clear that his research relates to domestic house cats. However, in combination with the other concept groups, any such retrieval would probably deal with the nutrition or diet of elderly tigers, and the patron thinks there might be information of interest to him in such an article. They agree that it is better to leave the scientific terms in and possibly retrieve some citations outside the area of interest, rather than leave them out and possibly miss some relevant citations because the search strategy was too narrowly defined. The search strategy now looks like this:

CAT	ELDER$2	NUTRITIO$3
feli$3	old$2	diet$3
	geriatric	food
	mature	feed
	senile	
	aged	

Integrating the Options

Further discussion reveals that the patron wants only English language articles and only publications from the last ten years. The search analyst makes the appropriate notations on the search strategy worksheet after consulting the BRS Aid-Pages to see how the two different databases handle language and year limits. The search analyst explains how logical and positional operators such as AND, OR, NEAR, and WITH will be applied to the concept groups, and asks once again if there are any other terms the patron wants included or excluded from the search. There are not, and the search analyst says, "Let's go online"—the rallying cry of all enthusiastic search analysts.

From the terminal or microcomputer in the library, the search analyst places a long-distance call through a local packet-switching network such as Sprintnet or Tymnet to the BRS computer in Chicago, enters an account password and a security password, and then instructs the computer to open the appropriate database. The search strategy is typed as it was worked out on the search strategy worksheet, like so:

```
ENTER DATABASE NAME_:   caba
*SIGN ON        9:50:42         06/20/91
CABA 1972-MAY 1991 (9105)
BRS SEARCH MODE - ENTER QUERY
     1_:   feli$3
  RESULT         7620 DOCUMENTS
     2_:   old$2 or geriatric or mature or senile or aged
  RESULT         175994 DOCUMENTS
     3_:   diet$3 or food or feed
  RESULT         333882 DOCUMENTS
     4_:   1 and 2 and 3
  RESULT         47 DOCUMENTS
```

At this point, the search analyst prints the titles and descriptors of a few of the citations retrieved so that the patron can examine them to see if the search is retrieving the type of information needed. If not, the search can be refined by adding or subtracting terms or limiting terms to certain fields. Once the patron is satisfied with the samples retrieved, the full set can be printed either online (citations printed at the library terminal immediately) or offline (citations printed at the BRS site and sent to the library by mail). The search analyst then saves (stores temporarily in the BRS computer's memory) the basic search strategy, changes to the BIOSIS database, and executes the saved search. Once again the search strategy can be modified online if the sampled citations are not precisely what the patron wants. After the second set of prints has been ordered, the search analyst signs off and disconnects from the BRS computer and the telephone network.

This is one search. The same search could be performed by an end-user through the BRS/After Dark system, or it could be performed on the compact disk versions of the two databases. The process of accessing a database or databases to find the answer to a question constitutes a search.

Search Engine or Search Software or Search Protocols

In the sample search above, the BRS truncation symbol—$—and the positional operators such as NEAR or WITH, are examples of the commands that must be used when searching a BRS database. The truncation symbol used by a different vendor, such as DIALOG's question mark, cannot be used as the truncation symbol when searching BRS. SilverPlatter uses a different set of commands, as does ORBIT, as does UMI. Each vendor has a different set of commands that must be used when searching that vendor's databases, otherwise the system will not work properly. For example, if one uses the DIALOG truncation symbol while searching in a BRS database (such as 1- geriatric or aged or senile or mature or old?), the BRS computer interprets the ? entered at the end of the character string as the command to erase the entire line, which it does. It presents the searcher with the old prompt (1-). The searcher must reenter the character string and this time remember to use the correct truncation command, a very frustrating experience which has happened to practically every searcher. The truncation symbol is an example of a *search protocol*, an abbreviated command instructing the host computer to perform a particular function. *Search software* usually refers to the physical machine-readable tape or diskette that contains the program allowing a computer to perform the functions. *Search engine* refers to the system of commands and techniques and user interfaces unique to a particular vendor's products. In practice, the three phrases are used interchangeably as shorthand to say, "If one searches a SilverPlatter database, one must use SilverPlatter commands." The proliferation of search engines complicates the lives of searchers as it becomes more and more difficult to remember which system uses ? or $ or : or # as the truncation symbol, and which ones have automatic plurals.

Databases

Technically, just about any accumulation of alpha or numeric or symbolic characters can be a database. An address book or a recipe file can be considered a database. If the address book or recipe file is loaded on a floppy disk using database management software (DBMS; also called database management

Integrating the Options 7

system), it becomes a machine-readable file. In the context of this book, a *database* is machine-readable, computerized, automated, and has an associated search engine allowing the data to be retrieved, sorted, or otherwise manipulated, and is commercially produced by a publisher, association, government agency, or other organization with the intention of disseminating the information publicly, usually for a price. The last point—commercial production and distribution of the database—distinguishes the subject of this book from the many OPACs, locally produced ready-reference files, and computerized address books being compiled. There are several different types of databases:

1. *Bibliographic*—usually the machine-readable equivalent of an abstracting or indexing tool. A bibliographic database provides surrogate information, that is, citations to works such as articles or monographs rather than the text of works. These are the databases that have been available the longest and are used most often in libraries. ERIC is an example of a bibliographic database, produced by the Educational Resources Information Center and corresponding to the printed tools *Current Index to Journals in Education* and *Resources in Education*. A typical entry in ERIC and other bibliographic databases consists of a unique accession number; author, title, and publication information; descriptors or subject headings usually assigned as a controlled vocabulary; and an abstract, which in some databases is quite lengthy. Some databases may have coded fields to aid retrieval, such as the Biosystematic Codes in the BIOSIS (Biological Abstracts) database, or the event codes and product codes in the PTS (Predicasts Terminal System) databases. A bibliographic database can be quite small, containing only a few thousand entries, or so massive with millions of entries that it would be unwieldy to search and so has been split into smaller databases based on ranges of publication years. BIOSIS, CA Search (Chemical Abstracts), and MEDLINE (Index Medicus) are examples of these massive databases. Some bibliographic databases do not directly correspond to a single printed tool but combine two or more printed equivalents in one database. ERIC is an example; INSPEC is another, combining *Physics Abstracts, Electrical and Electronics Abstracts*, and *Computer and Control Abstracts*. Some bibliographic databases are available only in machine-readable form and do not have print equivalents, such as InfoTrac and other databases from IAC (Information Access Company).

2. *Full-Text*—the entire document, possibly excluding illustrations, stored in machine-readable form. The widespread use of computerized phototypesetting to produce printed journals, newspapers, and books also produces a machine-readable tape. Therefore, the possibilities for producing full-text databases are enormous, but not yet fully realized. Many major newspapers and a small percentage of journals are available in full-text. The first publicly available full-text files were the law databases provided by LEXIS and WESTLAW. Many reference tools such as the *Merck Index* and *Encyclopedia of Associations* are

available as full-text files. These are a kind of hybrid database, in that they are not intended to be printed or read as full-text in the same way that an article from an online newspaper might be printed out in full. Rather, the manipulating and sorting capabilities of the computer allow the retrieval of bits of data or the production of lists sorted in an order not possible in the printed tool. For example, one can get an alphabetical list of academic library directors from the *ALA Directory* in its online version in a matter of minutes, whereas this would be a very tedious task using the printed tool.

3. *Numeric*—in libraries, usually hybrid databases of text and numbers, primarily in the business or finance subject areas. Numeric ranges can be searched, for example to produce a list of companies with fifty to one hundred employees, or selected numeric data can be printed for a particular company, perhaps as a spreadsheet. Census data is another example of a numeric database. Since numeric databases are intended to be manipulated, sorted, and resorted, researchers prefer to search the databases themselves rather than try to explain what they want to an intermediary. Numeric databases can also be excellent for providing quick answers at the reference desk (Bellardo, 1986; Chen, 1984).

4. *Vendor*—the middleman in the automated information retrieval industry. Rather like a supermarket, the vendor acquires database tapes from the database producers, usually manipulates the data somewhat to fit the search engine unique to the vendor, and sells access to the databases mounted on the vendor's mainframe. Some vendors are also database producers. For example, DIALOG produces its *CHRONOLOG* as a printed journal and an online journal. Some database producers are the sole vendors of their databases, as WILSONLINE used to be for the Wilson databases until it began leasing its tapes to BRS in 1991. Individuals or organizations wanting access to databases must negotiate a contract with the appropriate vendor.

5. *Online*—accessing a remote database from a local terminal or microcomputer. OPAC (Online Public Access Catalog) terminals are usually hardwired, meaning the terminals located in the library are directly connected (wired) to the library's or parent organization's mainframe computer where the OPAC database is mounted. When accessing DIALOG or BRS databases, the connection is made by telephone, usually through packet-switching networks such as Sprintnet or Tymnet.

6. *Ondisk*—A CD-ROM or other optical disk database mounted on a local microcomputer, or possibly mounted on a LAN (local area network) linking several ondisk workstations.

7. *Locally Loaded Databases*—commercially produced databases on machine-readable tapes that have been leased from the database producer and mounted on a local mainframe computer with associated search software. The Wilson databases, INSPEC, GEOREF, COMPENDEX, and many others can be leased from the database producers. The contracts vary considerably; some require

per-citation charges, some base the rental rate on the number of terminals that can access the database. All are expensive.

8. *Automated Information Retrieval Service*—the unit, department, or division in the library that coordinates, manages, or otherwise interacts with all of the above.

THE AUTOMATED INFORMATION RETRIEVAL SERVICE

A library that provides online access for mediated searches or end-user searches, or has ondisk products, or any combination of automated information retrieval options must have a distinct unit or department that manages the service, and the service must have a manager/coordinator who is able to communicate and coordinate the interactions of library staff and vendors and the library clientele. Someone must be responsible for seeing that searchers are trained, contracts are signed, procedures for delivering service are in place, equipment works, and reports are written. Sources on the organization of an automated information retrieval department include Hoover (1979), Lamb (1981), McKinney and Mosby (1986), Auster (1986), Sieburth (1988), *Video to Online* (1983), and Watson (1983). These sources concentrate on mediated search services rather than describing all the options. Information on the duties and responsibilities of managing an automated information retrieval service can be found in Chapter 2 of this text. In around 80 percent of academic libraries, the service manager/coordinator is a reference librarian, the search analysts are reference librarians, and the automated information retrieval service is part of the reference department.

The organizational structure of the parent library strongly influences the organization of the automated information retrieval service. An organization of largely autonomous branch libraries will probably prefer autonomous automated information retrieval services in the major branches, with some central coordination of policies and fee structures. On the other hand, there may be a strong centralized administration where all management issues such as policy, publicity, billing, reporting, training, and vendor relations are handled, and searching is performed at the service points. A single, centralized service is another option; it can be integrated within the reference department, or it can be an entirely separate unit. There are advantages and disadvantages to each structure.

An automated information retrieval service integrated with the reference department is probably the easiest to establish, in that existing staff and facilities can be designated for the service. Clerical staff for directing telephone calls, typing, and other support functions can be shared. Reference librarians, already trained to answer questions and interact with the public, can provide a full range of reference services with the addition of automated information retrieval. Searching enhances a reference librarian's skills, in that the rigid logic of various search engines forces the librarian to parse and analyze thoroughly the question to be answered and the indexing techniques of the tools being queried. The librarian works with and interacts with the database rather than merely referring the patron to the index where the patron does the actual searching. A librarian familiar with both print and automated tools can make informed choices as to which is better suited to answer a particular question. Furthermore, a contract with a full-service vendor such as DIALOG greatly increases the number of reference tools available to the librarian, and these tools should not be denied to the reference staff by an organizational decision regardless of where, ultimately, the automated information retrieval service fits in the library's organization chart. If all reference staff are familiar with automated information retrieval, referrals to the service can be made with better precision, and for more hours than the service itself is available. It may be easier to justify hiring more reference librarians who have collateral duties as search analysts than it is to hire additional librarians whose sole function is searching. Finally, integrating the automated information retrieval service with the reference department avoids competition for staff, budget, facilities, and status.

If staff sharing is one of the major advantages of an integrated service, it can also be the major disadvantage. Unfortunately, searching is often an extra responsibility added on top of an already overburdened staff. Training and practice can take a good deal of time. One mediated search appointment takes at least an hour to interview the patron, formulate the search, execute the search, and deal with the paperwork after the patron has left. Two or three searches a day, plus desk duty, plus collection development duties and all the other responsibilities of reference librarians can become too much. Some librarians may not be comfortable with searching; others may have the skills but simply not be good searchers. (In such cases an integrated service is an advantage, since these individuals can be absorbed by the myriad other duties of a reference division.) If some librarians are trained as searchers and others are not, the staff may become polarized over a "status" issue: nonsearchers may feel that searchers are not carrying their weight at the desk or with other reference duties.

A separate centralized automated information retrieval service has several advantages over an integrated service, namely better visibility and greater technical skills. The individuals in the unit have clear job descriptions; it is possible to hire new people with higher qualifications and the specialized training in place, rather than plucking a reference librarian from other duties and sending him or her off to training sessions in the hope that the training will "take" and the motivation to be a good search analyst will develop. The staff of a separate unit is usually highly motivated, since the continuance of their jobs depends on their success as searchers. They develop an identification with the product they deliver, they care about the quality of the service, and their technical skills are constantly honed by full-time involvement in searching. The greater autonomy of a separate unit allows it to respond faster to changes—new technology or new searching techniques or changing clientele—and it makes planning for growth and change much easier than in an integrated service, where it may be months before every librarian is trained on a new system or has studied and understood the implications of a proposed change. An autonomous unit can devise its own publicity campaigns and manipulate its environment to make it more visible and attractive to its clientele.

The disadvantages of a separate unit are many. It must compete for budget and staff. A separate unit will undoubtedly be more expensive than an integrated unit. It must hire clerical staff rather than share staff with a reference division. A separate automated information retrieval service, disassociated from other public service points in the library, will always look for an online solution to a reference question even though it may not be the best solution, and if automated information retrieval is not integrated into reference services, the online solution may be ignored by or even unknown to the reference staff. This lack of referral or cross-reference between the services is built into the organizational structure, and it may also become deliberate if there are real or perceived differences in personal status between the two staffs, which can happen if the automated information retrieval service has a nicer office or higher salaries, or if access to automated information retrieval is denied to the reference staff.

A dispersed service is a logical solution if there are branch libraries or even separate service points in one library—a separate government documents division service desk, for example—although duplication of ondisk products, online contracts, and staff training can get expensive. Dispersion allows the development of greater expertise in particular subject areas or databases and allows access at the point where it is needed rather than shuffling patrons off in search of service at the main library or reference desk. A policy statement dividing responsibility for certain subjects or databases may be necessary, for instance, a policy stating that medical databases will only be searched at the medical library.

Whatever organizational structure is finally adopted, several points argue in favor of centralized coordination. A dispersed service needs central coordination to insure consistent policies, a consistent level of service, and consistent training of the staff delivering the service. Negotiating contracts with vendors, establishing policies, reporting activities and statistics consistently, and handling the budget are best managed by a central authority. If dispersed units are allowed to set their own fee structures, or if the quality of service is very different, dispersion becomes counterproductive. Patrons will shop around for the best fees or the best searchers. Finally, a central coordinator needs to keep all public service librarians informed of what the automated information retrieval service can do. In fact, all public service librarians should have some training allowing them to participate in automated information retrieval, if only to know when to recommend a search or a particular database, and how to make an informed choice between print sources and automated sources of information.

Making the Informed Choice: When to Choose the Automated Information Retrieval Option

Automated Information retrieval can seem like magic. From a database consisting of millions of citations—CA Search or BIOSIS, for example—a handful of specific citations can be retrieved in seconds. The same search through shelf after shelf of printed volumes is daunting and depressing if not impossible. The computer's ability to handle complex, multitopic searches, to limit or qualify a search by date or language or document type, and to search for words or phrases not encompassed by a controlled vocabulary, give it a decided advantage over equivalent print tools. There are many databases, especially in business and finance, that exist only because of the computer's facility for storing, searching, and updating, and therefore have no print equivalent. There are printed sources that are enhanced by the computer's ability to sort and resort the data contained in them in order to produce output not envisioned by the original print source. Directories are a good example, wherein entries in strictly alphabetical order in the print equivalent can be resorted in zip code order, or Standard Industrial Classification (SIC) number order, or ranked according to net profits. A contract with one or two of the major vendors greatly expands the library's reference collection by allowing on-demand access to seldom used tools that may be far too expensive to justify their purchase as print equivalents.

Computerized searching allows interaction with the data that is not possible with the printed sources. A question can be refined or asked in slightly different configurations until the desired data is retrieved. A question can be asked repeatedly of each new update to the database to provide SDIs—selective dissemination of information—either by using the vendor's SDI facility or by uploading stored searches at intervals from a local cache stored on a floppy disk. The output from a search can be downloaded and edited to suit an individual's needs. All of these factors give automated information retrieval a decided advantage over printed tools.

An interesting body of literature has grown up detailing the advantages and disadvantages of automated information retrieval and providing checklists to aid the decision-making process of whether to select it over a print search. Included in this body are Champlin (1985), Kibirige (1988), Piternick (1990), Reese (1988), Tenopir (1988), Thesing (1983), and Tobin (1983).

Automated information retrieval does have disadvantages. One of the greatest of these is the misconception people have regarding automated information retrieval and computers in general that leads them to believe that the computer is infallible. Computers may be infallible, but the people operating them are not. Students especially who use a computerized index are likely to believe that they have exhausted the possibilities, that the information they have found, or did not find, represents everything that is available. Students are quite likely to revise a perfectly good research topic if a computer search does not produce results; in other words, they will ask only those questions that the computer can answer. The common misconception applied to the *Readers' Guide to Periodical Literature*—that it indexes *everything*—is likewise applied to any computerized search; people believe that they have tapped into one huge superdatabase that includes everything. A search analyst can dispel this misconception in the mediated search interview, but during this procedure misunderstandings between search analyst and the patron, a poor search strategy, or even spelling errors can put a faulty printout into the hands of the patron who expects and perceives the information to be authoritative. Most people do not question the output of a computer.

The majority of computerized databases accessed in libraries produce citations, not facts. They produce citations to resources that may not be in the local collection and thus create demands that the local library cannot meet. Most bibliographic databases do not provide good coverage of the monographic literature or literature older than the early 1970s. Some subject areas—anthropology, archaeology, ancient history, and journalism, among others—simply are not represented by a database. Some questions are too broad to be asked of a computerized database. The freshman who needs to find "ten good citations on the federal deficit" cannot be helped by a database search because the computer cannot distinguish between good articles and bad ones, and the search would produce hundreds of citations. Such a question is far better served by a printed index where the student can browse citations listed under a controlled vocabulary subject heading to select the articles considered "good" or, more likely, get an idea of the breadth of the topic as it was initially phrased and so learn to refine the question and thus refine the answers. Browsing to uncover new or unknown aspects of a question or the surrounding disciplines is impossible or excessively expensive in a computerized search; computers suppress serendipity. A printed tool has no mechanical failures and very little downtime, and it is usually much easier to teach a person how to use the print version of an index than the computerized version.

There are intangible differences between print and automated versions of the same tool. A search of the same relatively simple topic in both print and automated versions of a source will produce different results. Two different people searching the same subject in the same automated database will produce quite different results in which no more than 40 percent of the output may be common to both (Cleverdon, 1984). A controlled vocabulary is no guarantee of consistency, since two different indexers will seldom select exactly the same set of index terms to describe the same article. The results of a search will be judged differently by different people; one researcher may judge 80 percent of a printout to be relevant, while another researcher working on the same subject may say 20 percent or less of the citations are relevant due to concepts that were not articulated during the search interview and that in fact the researcher may not be able to articulate—the "I'll know it when I see it" syndrome. That researcher who judged 80 percent of a printout containing one hundred citations to be relevant probably will not examine and read all eighty of the relevant citations and in fact will probably read fewer than half of them because the amount of knowledge gained with each successive article will diminish to the point where the effort expended to collect and read more papers is no longer worthwhile. This leads one to believe that those researchers who request a comprehensive bibliography actually can be satisfied with much less. End-users especially are inclined to print out far more citations than they intend to use, and their printouts become browsing lists from which they will select a few relevant articles, in much the same way as they would have used a printed index. These intangible factors make it difficult to judge when to prefer an automated source over a print source.

Nonetheless, there are certain factors that favor selecting automated information sources over print sources, as follows:

— The availability of an appropriate automated source or database for the subject to be searched, or the unavailability of a print source either because there is no print equivalent or it is not held in the local collection
— A complex, multiconcept question, or one that includes coded information best handled by a computer such as document type or language, or possibly "hedges" stored with the database
— Those questions that might be asked of a print source but are best answered by the computer's ability to find and sort the data—directory-type questions, for example—or extracting bits of data from a full-text source
— The most current information is needed
— The access point or terminology is not part of a controlled vocabulary
— The known data is not sufficient to access a print source; a common personal name, for example, or a garbled citation, no publication date known, a joint author, a corporate author
— An exhaustive search is needed, or one that would require the physical handling of many print volumes (an "exhausting" search, in other words)
— The information is needed immediately
— The patron prefers a computerized search

Cost can be a factor in deciding against an online search, but cost should not be used as an excuse to deny online sources when the question meets the criteria listed above. A manual search through print tools for a garbled citation, date unknown, is like gathering firewood to heat up the lunchtime leftovers when a microwave is available. In present practice, probably less than 5 percent of all questions asked at a reference desk will be answered by an automated information source, but for those 5 percent, much time and effort will be saved by preferring the automated solution (Hitchingham, 1984). All public service librarians must be able to recognize when automated information retrieval is appropriate, when it is possible, and when it is preferable.

THE SERVICE OPTIONS

There are several ways to integrate automated information retrieval into the services provided by a library. A mediated search service is the most frequent application, but it is certainly not the only option, and perhaps not the best option. A mediated service easily and quickly expands to encompass ready-reference searching at the reference desk, then the bibliographic instruction staff proposes to demonstrate online searching at graduate level classes or faculty meetings.

Statistics from the mediated search service show that two or three databases are used so often that the purchase of their CD-ROM equivalents can be justified. The options expand, like ripples in the water. The typical settings and procedures of the various options are described below.

A Mediated Online Service

A mediated search service accessing the major online vendors is the most familiar option in most libraries. Mediated means that there is an intermediary—a search analyst—between the ultimate consumer of the information and the database. The search analyst has special training in the use of vendors' search engines and databases that should allow the analyst to perform a search faster and more effectively, an important point when dealing with systems that cost a dollar a minute at the moderate end of the price range. Mediated search services are usually part of the reference department of a library and are also found in branch libraries and possibly at other service desks in a large library. The budget and the logistics of duplicating telephone lines and equipment and passwords are usually the determining factors in deciding how many search stations will be available.

The clientele of a mediated search service are those who desire a comprehensive search of the literature, those who are too busy to perform the task for themselves, or those who do not have the skills or the opportunity to perform searches for themselves. This usually means faculty and graduate students in an academic library. If the service charges a fee, undergraduates will seldom request a search. The clientele are usually researchers who are well-versed if not immersed in the subject to be searched, and they have high expectations of the service offered them. They expect the search analyst to be professional and skilled.

Procedures. Typically, a mediated search service operates on an appointment basis. The person needing information makes an appointment with a search analyst, usually of an hour's duration. At the beginning of the meeting the search analyst may need to explain how automated information retrieval works if the patron is new to the operation, to help the patron understand search strategy formulation and also to explain why the search analyst is asking so many questions and why automated information retrieval does not always produce the expected results. The analyst and the patron discuss a search strategy to settle on the concept groups and keywords that will be used, and the analyst suggests databases that should produce results. Once the appropriate databases have been selected, the analyst may use thesauri and other database-specific help tools to refine the search strategy.

Using a terminal or microcomputer, the analyst dials up the vendor's mainframe computer and begins typing the search strategy. As sets are combined the analyst may print browsing formats of a few citations so that the patron can see what is being retrieved by the search strategy and, if necessary, refine the search with more keywords or different combinations of concept groups. Once the patron is satisfied with the type of information being retrieved, the full results can be printed either online or offline, usually depending on how much money is involved and whether or not the patron is willing to wait a few days for the results.

Throughout the process, the patron has been interacting with the search analyst and with the database. The patron agrees to the search strategy and the selection of databases, modifies the search as it is ongoing, and decides which set of results to print and the format of the printout. The intermediary advises and instructs the patron, and translates the patron's wishes into a language the computer can understand until the patron is satisfied with the results and the search is complete. The search analyst signs off. Depending on the patron's familiarity with search output and the library, the analyst may need to explain the coding on the printout and how to find materials in the library or request materials through interlibrary loan. The search analyst will need to record some figures for statistics and other record-keeping purposes and may need to calculate a bill if the patron is to be charged for the search.

Advantages and Disadvantages. The major advantage of the mediated search format is the presence of the intermediary, the search analyst with special training for interacting with a vendor's search engine and a wide variety of databases quickly and effectively. If the search analyst is also a reference librarian, he or she probably has a wide knowledge of indexing and abstracting tools, the databases derived from them, and the indexing techniques they use. He or she has perhaps performed hundreds of searches and is not intimidated by the technology. The experienced search analyst quickly recognizes mistakes and knows how to correct them. One thing that continually astonishes patrons is how quickly a good search analyst can scan citations as they scroll up the screen; this is something that simply comes with experience, whereas inexperienced users can consume a great deal of online time and money merely reading the information displayed on the screen.

The patrons requesting a mediated search are given a private consultation lasting as long as an hour. This special attention is different from the anonymous and sometimes cursory assistance offered at a busy reference desk where librarians must rush through one question in order to get on to the next one and the one after that. The patron sees that his or her question is perceived by the search analyst as being important. The patron is flattered, and the status of the library and the librarian is enhanced.

Very little advance preparation is required from the patron, yet a mediated search teaches patrons a great deal about information management—the plethora of databases available and the importance of selecting the right tool, controlled vocabularies, thesauri, keywords and concepts, and the idea of formulating a search strategy before diving in. Unlike other attempts at library instruction, this teaching is taken to heart because it is presented at the exact moment the patron needs instruction, it produces immediate results, and its importance is enhanced by the atmosphere of a private consultation rather than being received in a classroom setting directed at several people.

The appointment for a private consultation can also be seen as a disadvantage of the mediated search format. Usually, appointments are only available during weekday office hours. Appointments usually mean that the service is not available on demand for the patron who drops in or needs information on an emergency basis, and search analysts must be scheduled to meet the appointments, which is sometimes seen as taking them away from other duties. The private consultation format can be intimidating both to the patron and to the analyst who is made nervous by the patron peering over a shoulder, watching every keystroke, and expecting the analyst to explain complex searching concepts while typing rapidly to avoid high online charges.

In order to make a wide variety of databases available for searching it may be necessary to negotiate contracts with several vendors. Depending on the type of contract negotiated, a library can pay a monthly or annual minimum fee for the right to access a vendor's databases, even though the service is used infrequently. Multiple vendors means multiple search engines that the analysts must learn and remember and practice to keep up their abilities. The more search engines used, the more difficult it is for search analysts to be proficient in all of them.

Mediated online searches offered during business hours are expensive. Most libraries have found that they must charge back to the patron the direct costs of the search—the online connect costs, telecommunication costs, and citation charges. Fees prohibit many patrons from using the service and they raise the expectations of those who are willing to pay. New or inexperienced patrons have high expectations of the service anyway, since they frequently expect the computer to perform miracles. Billing patrons and paying the bills from vendors increases the amount of paperwork the department must handle.

There is always the possibility of miscommunication between the patron and the analyst. The best search analyst cannot produce a good search if he or she does not understand what the patron wants. Search analysts can take a patron's question and rephrase it so that it fits the thesaurus terms or the databases available and no longer fits the patron's needs. This is especially true of vague questions, the broadly interdisciplinary ones or the philosophical "why" and "what if" questions that the search analyst tries to pin down with a few keywords neatly divided into four or five concept groups. In cases like this the patron would be better served by print tools and leisurely browsing, but the appointment has been made, and both the patron and the analyst are conditioned to expect results from the computer.

The Setting and Equipment. To complement the private consultation format of a mediated search, the ideal setting is a quiet office, tastefully decorated, in an accessible location with prominent signage to identify it to patrons. In practice, most libraries cannot afford the money or the space for anything approaching this ideal, and the search service is located in a fairly quiet corner of a larger office or in a cubicle delimited by temporary walls or other office landscaping. Nothing particularly fancy is actually needed. A searching area, where patron and analyst can sit down and discuss the topic, a desktop surface for writing and spreading out papers and tools, shelving for documentation, and the workstation consisting of a terminal or microcomputer with a modem and a printer, and a telephone line are all that are required. It should be a quiet area to allow concentration on the topic, and since printers are usually noisy it may be necessary to protect surrounding areas from the noise generated by the searching process. A mediated search service also needs office support equipment consisting of filing cabinets, a place to store supplies of forms, printer paper and ribbons or ink, and access to an office microcomputer, preferably one with a hard disk capable of storing a year's worth of statistics and searching records.

The service needs clerical support: telephone answering and appointment scheduling, billing if necessary, a place where patrons can come to pick up off-line printouts, and the support for recording statistics and producing reports. If more than one person searches, the search analysts will need desks apart from the searching area, and in fact the searching area or search station should not be one individual's "home base", since it may be needed for demonstrations or ready-reference searches conducted by staff other than the search analyst.

Large operations simply need more of the same. If multiple searches are conducted at the same time a few problems arise. Multiple passwords will be needed if it is likely that two analysts may be accessing the same vendor at the same time, otherwise the second analyst to attempt to log on will receive a "password in use" type of message and will have to wait until the first searcher completes the search and signs off. Multiple telephone lines will also be necessary, and these present a particular problem. The typical configuration of office telephones in which a single telephone instrument can receive or place calls on more than one line will not work with a modem or communications software because the modem cannot punch a button to select the desired line. Each modem must be connected to a single line jack. The only way around this problem is to use an acoustic coupler in which the telephone handset is settled into rubberized "mouse ears," and not all handsets are configured to fit the acoustic coupler. A modern, slimline telephone will not fit. Furthermore, acoustic couplers are more prone to line noise than modems directly wired to a line jack, and there is always the possibility that someone will punch the button for the line on which a search is being conducted, and interrupt the signal. A single telephone jack for each modem is the best solution, although it is expensive and can present wiring problems.

If more than one search is conducted in the same area, some provision for noise abatement and privacy must be made. Patrons may be reluctant to discuss their research topics if a stranger is likely to hear it. If searches are conducted in different locations in branch libraries or at separate service desks, it will be necessary to duplicate some of the documentation tools. It may be necessary to design and print different forms to be used at each of the different searching locations. Multiple searching locations require a hard look at the budget and continuous oversight by the service manager to be sure that policies and procedures are consistently followed at all the searching sites.

The Options. There are several variables that can be introduced into the mediated service setting. The most familiar—and the most controversial—of these is the question of whether or not to charge a fee. Online searching is expensive. Some libraries argue that their budgets will not stretch to cover the costs, and if online searching is to be offered at all it must be on a cost recovery basis. This is a compelling argument. Other libraries have found ways to stretch their budgets. While nearly every librarian supports the concept of free library service, exceptions are readily made for online searching because the cost is readily accounted. Once a search analyst sends the logoff command, the total cost of the search appears on the screen or the bottom of the printout. This is not true of other library services where the cost of buying, storing, and managing a collection of print tools in order to answer a patron's question is nearly impossible to total. Although the result—the answer to a patron's demand for information—is essentially the same, the online search has a price tag attached, which can be easily charged back to the patron.

Some have argued that offering free online searches will produce such a demand for the service to answer any and every trivial question that no amount of budget stretching can cover the unpredictable costs, but this can be obviated by the use of appointments as a prerequisite for a search. Most people will not go to the trouble of making and keeping an appointment for a trivial search, and those who do can be redirected to appropriate print tools during the search interview. Libraries that offer free service should have written policy statements that govern the conditions under which an online search will be undertaken, basically leaving the decision whether or not to use online services up to the librarian.

Another option that can be exercised is whether or not the patron must be present during the search. The patron is the best judge of the relevance of citations retrieved and the best authority on keywords to be searched, therefore his or her presence during the search is highly desirable. There are times, however, when the patron cannot or prefers not to be present, and there are search services and search analysts who prefer to do the actual online portion of the process without the patron's presence. The pre- and postsearch interviews and explanations can be conducted as usual, and the online search is conducted in private without interruptions. Several searches can be batched together, thus saving the online connect time consumed by logging on and logging off; or the searches can be performed during off-peak hours when rates are cheaper; or the search strategies can be typed and edited offline and uploaded, again saving some of the online connect costs. The patron's interaction with the database is lost, but these can be very efficient ways to conduct searches.

The number of vendors and databases offered varies from library to library. No one vendor offers access to every database, and, depending on the disciplines likely to be searched, some libraries have contracts with twenty or more vendors. This complicates the lives of search analysts who must remember several different search protocols, and drains budgets that must pay for training and documentation and minimum access fees for some of the vendors. A very specialized library may decide that it will not offer access to databases outside its specialty, even though many other databases are available through its contract with a particular vendor. Multiple searching locations in branch libraries can divide responsibilities for particular vendors or databases, although for the convenience of the patrons and library staff the main library probably should have access to all the vendors and databases searched by the branches. Some vendors offer services other than access to bibliographic databases such as SDI, or full-text databases, or access to document delivery services. The document delivery services may be seen as competition for the library's interlibrary loan service, which may or may not be welcome. Management decisions will have to be made as to which of the nonsearching services offered by vendors will be used.

A Fee-Based Service

A fee-based service is designed to provide full information retrieval and delivery to individuals or organizations not affiliated with the library's parent organization for a fee, based on full cost recovery of staff time, equipment, and supplies (Beaubien, 1987). It provides library service to those who have not otherwise paid support through fees or tuitions, to those who, unlike the academic faculty, are not accustomed to doing in-depth research, and to those who do not want to be taught how to use the library for themselves but prefer instead to have the work done for them. In other words, it serves the local community's businesses, industries, and research parks, users who can place a tremendous burden on the library staff with their demands for information to the detriment of the library's primary clientele. Automated information retrieval to provide customized bibliographies is only part of a fee-based service. Document delivery, photocopying from library resources, printing from full-text online sources, or ordering through document delivery services and interlibrary loan make up the other large part of a fee-based service; some services will also undertake to prepare brief reports answering questions from the library's reference tools.

Full cost recovery, and possibly a small margin of profit, make a fee-based service unique and present a unique set of problems. Cost accounting is not an activity librarians think about in an environment of free library service, and an attempt to track down the cost of answering a reference question can be eye opening. For this reason, fee-based services often have a staff entirely separate from the staff engaged in the library's primary operations, or may assign staff to the fee-based service for a certain percentage of time. Equipment such as microcomputers and modems, office space and overhead, and contracts with vendors must also be separated from the library's inventory and operating costs. Organizationally, a fee-based service is a step-child; it interacts with all the units in a library and most often reports to the director.

Procedures. A client submits an information request to the fee-based service either in person or otherwise. The fee structure of the service is explained to the client and an estimate of the cost of the information request is delivered to the client, who may be asked to sign a form agreeing to pay for the service. If an online search is part of the information request, the client may or may not be present during the search. In any case, the client's involvement in the process of tracking down the requested information is usually limited to delivering and clarifying the request.

The staff of the fee-based service does whatever is necessary to put the desired information into the client's hands, including automated information retrieval procedures, finding material, photocopying or otherwise reproducing material, and packaging the material in a format acceptable to the client. The staff keeps track of every minute and every transaction for billing purposes and perhaps adds a percentage to bring in a small profit. The information and the bill are delivered to the client.

Advantages and Disadvantages. A fee-based service is an excellent public relations tool that provides a needed service to local businesses and industries without putting an undue burden on the library staff. It can bring in additional revenue. It provides a way to serve people who cannot come to the library because they live in remote communities, to former students and faculty who have moved away, and to those who for one reason or another cannot get the service they need or want from a local library. Local businesses especially appreciate the service because it provides information rather than instructions on how to find the information for themselves, which is what they would usually get if they approached a busy reference desk. Furthermore, it demonstrates the value of information and library service by putting a price tag on them.

The price tag is the major disadvantage. A library contemplating initiating a fee-based service probably has no idea how much to charge for an information transaction, and a fee-based service may run for a year before it has a good grip on the costs involved and can provide an accurate estimate for an individual transaction. The bookkeeping alone will consume a full-time clerical staff position. In the first year of operation, the fee-based service will need to be funded by the library; the equipment must be bought and the salaries paid before the money starts coming in.

Staff is another problem. The most accurate accounting requires a separate staff whose every minute is devoted to the fee-based service and therefore can be billed to a customer. This can lead to an elitist attitude on the part of the fee-based staff and competition with the library staff for resources and reputation. Shared staff working a percentage of time in the fee-based service may develop the habit of providing a certain level of service for those who pay, and an entirely different level of service for those who do not. It is very difficult to integrate the two different outlooks involved in running a business and in working for a service organization. In one, the customer is always right and is paying for a quality product, and in the other the customer is frequently wrong or at least misinformed and may not even say "thank you" after demanding expert and professional help.

In some states, a fee-based service in a state- or tax-supported institution may be illegal (Josephine, 1989). The law may require a separate staff with separate job descriptions and separate accounting procedures. It is tempting to contemplate a service that pays its own way, but management should look carefully into local laws.

The Setting and Equipment. A fee-based service really needs a separate office as its headquarters and its own telephone lines. For one thing, this assures that the equipment and supplies are used exclusively by the fee-based service, and it provides consistent access for the paying clientele rather than requiring them to track down the "fee-based librarian" who may at that moment be working at a non-fee-based reference desk. If possible, the office should look as nice as the offices of its clientele. It should be easy to find and clearly marked with the service's name. Standard office equipment, an online workstation, and a photocopier are needed in the office. The forms and stationery should be distinctive and should not look like the library's. Publicity and other promotional material need a professional, well-designed look.

The whole environment of a fee-based service should emphasize its separateness from other library operations. There should be a written policy detailing the kinds and amount of support the established library will provide to the fee-based service and how competition for resources will be resolved. Careful accounting and clearly stated goals for cost recovery are essential. If a profit is made, the library must have clear rules on how the profit is to be handled, who may distribute it, and how. A nonprofit organization must examine the laws regulating not-for-profit institutions and stay within them.

Discretionary Use

The power of automated information retrieval should not be reserved for the patrons of a mediated search service or end-users. A single contract with one of the major online vendors vastly increases the resources of the library by making available on demand expensive or little-used reference tools that the library would not otherwise purchase. Library staff should be allowed to access these databases at their discretion and at library expense if doing so will facilitate or promote the pursuit of an answer to a question. Ready-reference use of online resources to answer questions is well established (Belanger and Emmick, 1986; Bonta, 1983; Brownmiller, et al. 1985; Hitchingham et al., 1984). Discretionary use also includes demonstrations performed by bibliographic instruction staff, training and practice time, and librarian research. With the exception of demonstrations, discretionary use means that the librarian, not the patron, decides if an automated information resource is appropriate. If a patron asks for automated information retrieval, he or she can be directed to the mediated search service or any end-user services available, unless the librarian feels that the question is appropriate for discretionary use.

Discretionary implies disorganized, but discretionary use should be under the supervision of the automated information retrieval service manager, who should see to the training, the policies and procedures governing discretionary use, the purchase and maintenance of equipment, the budget for discretionary use, and scheduling if any is required. Online access always has the potential of being disastrously expensive, so the manager must set clear rules and emphasize the "discretion" in discretionary use.

Integrating the Options 23

Training for discretionary use is a major responsibility of the service manager. If it is the library's policy to permit ready-reference use of online services, it follows that anyone who works at the reference desk should be trained to provide the service, including the paraprofessionals. This training can be effectively accomplished in-house rather than going to the expense and inconvenience of sending every reference staff member to vendor-sponsored training sessions. The manager should constantly emphasize that ready-reference means "quick and dirty" and reference staff are not expected and should not attempt to provide the same in-depth search as the mediated search service, and that therefore in-depth training is not necessary. The manager should provide basic training covering search strategies and search engines, and should see that staff maintain their searching skills and keep up with the policies governing discretionary use. Once librarians have these skills, they may want to apply them to their own research. The library will have to establish a policy stating whether or not librarians engaged in research activities of their own can conduct their own online searches and how these searches will be funded.

Procedures. A question is asked at the reference desk that the librarian believes can best be answered by an online database. The librarian goes online, prints the results, and hands the printout to the patron. Some explanation of the information on the printout is probably necessary, but once the patron is happily on his way the librarian quickly jots down a few figures in the ready-reference log book and turns her attention to the next question. Within a month the bill for the search is received and is paid from library funds.

The sticking point in the scenario above is knowing when to prefer online resources over a manual search. The policy and procedures manual should have a section on "Guidelines for Ready-Reference Use" to help librarians decide, with standards such as these:

A. A ready-reference search can use no more than two databases;
B. A ready-reference search can print no more than ten citations;
C. A ready-reference search must be brief, usually one to five minutes online, and must require no advance preparation such as consulting a thesaurus or extensive profiling of search strategies;
D. Appropriate topics that can be searched within the guidelines above include:
   1. Verifying garbled citations, especially when the date of publication is unknown;
   2. Names, addresses, and other directory-type information;
   3. Very recent publications are needed;
   4. Keywords to be searched are not part of a controlled vocabulary;
   5. The source is not available in the library, or is at the bindery or otherwise off the shelf. (The policy manual should specify whether or not online sources are always searched, at library expense, when the print sources requested by a patron are not in the library collection.)

These are the most common guidelines usually followed for ready-reference use. Depending on the clientele served and the types of questions frequently asked, libraries will want to amend or add to the list. One frequent amendment is the "disabling" of certain, very expensive databases that, due to their connect costs or printing costs, cannot be searched inexpensively no matter how short the search is, or databases that are already available to end-users either as locally loaded or ondisk products.

Record-keeping is essential if the manager is to oversee effectively the extent and costs of ready-reference searching. Separate passwords designated exclusively for ready-reference use simplify record-keeping because each password generates a separate invoice from the vendor. Accurate costs and statistics can be gleaned from these invoices. A simple log book at the reference desk should be maintained for checking against invoices to be sure the password has not been compromised and there is no unauthorized use of the password. Separate log book pages for each vendor simplify invoice verification.

It is important to make patrons aware of the difference between a ready-reference search performed at the librarian's discretion and an in-depth search that may require a fee. Certainly, the patron should not be left with the impression that the computer has found everything on the topic. Librarians should know when to refer patrons to other databases or to the mediated search service for an in-depth search. Also, librarians should be comfortable with the idea of saying "no" to a patron who demands a ready-reference search when one is inappropriate.

Demonstrations for groups and training or practice for library staff do not have the problem of immediacy inherent in a ready-reference search. One can plan ahead, make sure that the equipment is working and available, and prepare a search strategy that is guaranteed to work instead of producing a surprise result or no result. The costs can be kept down by using an ondisk product, an inexpensive online database, or one of the special teaching accounts some vendors make available, such as BRS's Instructor service or DIALOG's Classmate service. If bibliographic instruction staff are expected to demonstrate automated information retrieval products, they need fairly in-depth training and practice to insure that they are able to handle unexpected questions or problems.

Advantages and Disadvantages. All the advantages of automated information retrieval already discussed apply to discretionary use, especially in connection with ready-reference. Also, the reference collection is extended by the online sources and the status of the library and of librarians is enhanced by the presence of a computer terminal at the reference desk. Using an online source allows the librarian to put the answer in a patron's hands rather than merely pointing to an index that will lead the patron to the answer. This makes both the librarian and the patron feel good.

The cost of ready-reference is unpredictable and can be high, especially in the early months. Newly trained librarians may timidly refrain from going online, or may dive in enthusiastically and make expensive mistakes. The training and practice time for librarians and paraprofessionals can get very expensive in itself. In some libraries training has concentrated on teaching reference staff to recognize questions appropriate for ready-reference and then to refer the patron to the searching staff. This takes the "ready" out of ready-reference; furthermore, interaction with the databases is the best training for recognizing when an automated information retrieval solution is appropriate.

Some staff will always be uncomfortable with automated information retrieval, leading to uneven application of the option. Depending on which librarian is on duty, a patron may get a quick answer, a slow answer, or perhaps even no answer. Some librarians may come to rely too much on online sources; they tax the budget, they fail to instruct patrons of the existence and use of print sources, and they quickly run out of options if online searching does not supply an answer to the question. Training, frequent review and oversight, and close coordination with the head of the reference department alleviate these problems but will never completely eliminate them.

The Setting and Equipment. In order for ready-reference to be truly "ready," a terminal at the reference desk is required. Ideally this should be a multifunction microcomputer with communications software that allows easy logon to the various vendors by storing passwords and logon protocols. A forgotten password puts an immediate end to any attempt at ready-reference. The microcomputer can be configured to access local databases or the E-mail facility and bibliographic utilities such as RLIN or OCLC or OCLC's EPIC database, as well as the commercial database vendors. If it is left at the reference desk when the desk is unattended, some provision for security—both for the equipment and the passwords—must be made. Some documentation, such as database catalogs and quick guides, should be available at the terminal, but thesauri and detailed database guides are inappropriate for ready-reference. As mentioned before, record-keeping and log books should be simple so that staff do not spend a great deal of time recording searching activity.

The equipment for demonstrations and training presents a special problem. If groups are to be served, a large screen projection system is needed. If bibliographic instruction librarians provide demonstrations in classrooms, the equipment needs to be portable. None of this equipment is cheap. Here is a list of equipment that two sturdy people can carry to a classroom and can demonstrate all the options a library might have to offer:

— Portable PC, with 40MG hard disk, internal modem, internal CD-ROM drive
— Large screen projection system (a projection pad in a carrying case)
— A portable overhead projector.

There is a product available that combines the projection pad and overhead projector in one piece of equipment, but it is not very portable. Classrooms and indeed other places where the bibliographic instruction (BI) staff might be invited to demonstrate an online or ondisk product often have access to an overhead projector, so this piece of equipment may not need to be carried to the site. If an online demonstration is requested, it is essential to be sure that the right kind of telephone connection is available at the site.

A separate training room with sufficient equipment reserved for training would be lovely but also expensive. In practice, it may be necessary to schedule a piece of equipment designated for other use, such as the ready-reference terminal or mediated search equipment, for demonstration purposes.

End-User Online Services

End-users are a special case and are dealt with in a separate chapter. A brief review in this chapter indicates how end-user services are integrated into the automated information retrieval service that manages contracts with vendors, online equipment, budget, policies and procedures, and most importantly the impact of an end-user service on other automated information retrieval services. End-users are nonlibrarians performing their own searches on library equipment and library contracts. They can be students, faculty, staff, or local area users. BRS and DIALOG offer simplified search engines and reduced rates during non-business hours especially for end-users, or a library may prefer to use "gateway" services such as EasyNet to make online searching available to end-users.

Automated information retrieval service staff will be involved with preparing instructional materials, taking appointments, monitoring and assisting end-users, troubleshooting equipment and supplies, keeping records and gathering statistical information, and possibly billing and receiving money. The cost of an end-user online operation can be easily controlled by limiting the number of appointments available and the vendors or databases available to end-users. An end-user online operation should be centralized in one location accessible to the public. A separate room is ideal for providing security for the equipment and passwords and for controlling noise.

Procedures. A student needs a fairly in-depth search of a database, which is rather expensive through the mediated search service. The librarian at the reference desk explains that the student can search the database for himself at night when the rates are vastly reduced. The student makes an appointment to use one of the library's searching stations, then sits down with the instruction manual to figure out how the search is performed. The manual tells the student how to fill in a profiling sheet dividing the topic to be searched into keywords and concept groups, as well as what databases are available and how to select the appropriate ones. It should also explain how Boolean logic works and how to apply it according to the search protocols of the end-user system's search engine.

When the student arrives for the appointment, the end-user service staff reviews the student's profiling sheet, revises it if necessary, and answers any questions the student may have. Then the staff member signs on to the online system, selects the appropriate database, and turns the keyboard over to the end-user. The staff member is available to answer questions and get the end-user out of difficulties if any occur, but the keyboarding and decision making is done by the end-user. Eventually the end-user prints out a set of citations or other results. The staff member makes sure that the patron has logged off properly, performs any record-keeping, statistical, or billing functions required, and explains or clarifies the data on the printout if necessary.

Advantages and Disadvantages. End-user online searching during nonbusiness hours is inexpensive. Far more people can be served at less cost than a mediated service operating during business hours, thus taking a great deal of pressure off the mediated service. In fact, over time and if enough facilities are made available to end-users, the mediated service will experience a significant decline. End-users are almost invariably happy with the results of their searches, even though an experienced search analyst looking at those same results might be appalled at the "garbage" retrieved—the false drops, irrelevant citations, sloppy logic resulting in overlapping sets of citations, and the sheer number of citations printed.

Security for end-user passwords and equipment is a problem, since the service must be in an area accessible to the public. Thus, it is especially important to protect the passwords by changing them frequently or making them invisible. The end-user's expectations of online systems create disadvantages. The usual expectation that the computer is looking at everything and finding everything is especially misleading in an end-user environment. One of the most difficult messages to get across to end-users is the necessity of selecting a database, since most of them expect that there is only one superdatabase accessed by the computer. Also, there are significant gaps in the coverage of databases available in the non-business-hours online service to end-users, most noticeably in the geology and geophysics area. End-users invariably expect the citations they retrieve to be available to them in the library's collections, and since most end-users are students, the time delays inherent in interlibrary loan are unacceptable because the assignment is due tomorrow.

Setting and Equipment. One of the advantages of an end-user online service is that the equipment used by mediated searching during weekday business hours can be kept busy by end-users during nonbusiness hours and on weekends. More search stations may be needed if the library can afford to serve a large population of end-users, and certainly end-users consume far more printing supplies than a mediated service. Less documentation than the mediated service is needed since end-users are notoriously unwilling to read instructions, but if the end-user service is in the same location or area as the mediated service, the thesauri and database documentation will be available to those end-users who want to use them.

Ondisk Services

Commercially produced databases distributed on optical or compact disks can be mounted on stand-alone or LAN-linked microcomputer workstations and made available to end-users. Since ondisk products are especially relevant to end-users, they will be dealt with in more detail in the separate chapter on end-users; however, coordination with the total automated information retrieval environment is necessary. Decisions as to which ondisk products will be purchased should be based on statistical data gathered from the mediated and end-user online services showing which databases are accessed most frequently. The existence of an ondisk database in the library means that online use of the same database amounts to paying twice for the same information, which may require a policy change governing the use of the online database for discretionary or end-user use. The process of instructing end-users is the same whether they are using an online database or an ondisk database, and in fact end-users can transfer the skills learned for one to the other. Therefore, ondisk products enhance online services by making database access simpler and available for more hours, whereas online services make more databases available and permit the expert help of a search analyst for those who need it.

Ondisk products can be collected together in a searching lab with the mediated and end-user searching stations, or they can be distributed among branch libraries or service desks. (See Stewart et al. (1990) for many options in various libraries.) Consolidating them simplifies user instruction, noise abatement, security for expensive equipment, and the maintenance tasks of troubleshooting equipment failures and keeping printers supplied with paper and ink. Distributing them brings them closer to the collections they index and to the librarians with subject expertise relevant to the database content. Both options can be utilized in one library; for example, general reference tools can be consolidated, with a newspaper index on compact disk placed with the microfilm collection.

Procedures. A patron asking for assistance at the reference desk is told that the index she needs is available as a compact disk searchable by computer, or if she prefers, she can use the two paper copy indexes, *Current Index to Journals in Education* and *Resources in Education*, which are sitting on the reference shelves. One look at the long line of well-thumbed volumes, and the patron elects to use the automated version. The decision may be affected by whether or not there is a charge for using the ondisk products. She is directed to the automated information retrieval lab where the ondisk and online workstations are located. In the lab, a staff member meets the patron and asks which database she needs, then directs her to the appropriate workstation where ERIC is mounted, or perhaps checks out the ERIC disk to the patron and mounts it on an available workstation. It may be necessary for the patron to get on a waiting list if there are other users ahead of her. Once she settles at the workstation she finds simple written instructions (produced by the library staff) beside the microcomputer, and the staff member is available to walk her through the first steps of a preliminary search until a list of citations to view or print is retrieved. While the patron examines and prints the citations, the staff member moves away to help another patron. Satisfied with her results, the patron asks the staff member for help in finding the articles listed on the printout. Slightly harried by having ten users already working on searches, three of whom are demanding help, and five more people on waiting lists, the staff member politely refers the patron back to the reference desk where she will be told how to locate journals in the library and where the microfiche collection of ERIC documents is kept.

Advantages and Disadvantages. Fairly simple search engines designed for end-users and no connect charges or citation charges are the major advantages of on-disk products over online products. Many databases are available already and more database producers are putting their products out on compact disk; some databases, including many from the federal government, are only available on compact disk. The format is relatively durable and the technology is tested and proven. Off-the-shelf equipment and adequate support services from the vendors mean that no programmers or other specialists need to be on the library staff. Since there are no connect times, citation charges, or telephone charges to record, an end-user service based on ondisk products cuts out the record-keeping necessary in an end-user online service. If there are no packet-switching networks in the local community, or if telephone lines are unreliable, ondisk products make the hassle of dealing with telephones unnecessary (Tenopir, 1988). An ondisk database is available to patrons during those hours when mediated or end-user online services are not.

Expense is the major disadvantage of ondisk products. The databases are expensive, and many of the database subscriptions are on a lease basis—the library does not own the product and must return it if the subscription lapses. The equipment is expensive and is subject to downtime as are all computers and peripherals, and therefore a computer specialist on the staff may be needed just to keep all the machines running. Since end-users print many more citations than they will use, supplies can become a major expense. The different search engines used by different vendors are very confusing to end-users, and an automated database of any sort requires more staff effort to instruct the user than does the print equivalent. End-users who become accustomed to using automated databases will refuse to use print sources even though print sources may be far better for their needs.

Setting and Equipment. The organization of the library will determine whether ondisk databases should be consolidated or distributed. The necessary equipment incudes a hard disk microcomputer, preferably at least a 386 machine for faster searches, a CD-ROM drive, and a printer. Some CD-ROM vendors have an online update function that allows the user to access the online version of the same database. If this option is made available, modems and telephone lines will be needed. Questions of security and noise abatement must be addressed. It is possible to mount several databases on one workstation, but some programming skills may be necessary to get different search engines from different vendors to reside together. In a consolidated unit, a local area network (LAN) that places the database disks in one tower of linked CD-ROM drives and allows access to them from any microcomputer in the LAN makes it possible for two or more searchers to access the same database at the same time, thus obviating the need for waiting lists or appointments. However, LAN equipment is expensive, and many of the database producers have a higher price for databases mounted on a network. Regardless of the configuration, whether consolidated or distributed, LAN or single-database workstations, staff must be available to assist the users.

Locally Loaded Databases

A locally loaded database is the machine-readable tape of a commercially produced database loaded with search software on a local mainframe, frequently in such a way that is accessible through the library's OPAC terminals (see *Locally Loaded Databases* (1989). It is usually available to users outside the library either through dial-up ports or by hardwired terminals in remote locations such as researchers' offices or dormitories, and can be available even when the library is closed. Users can access the database without appointments and in fact without dealing with the library staff in any way. This puts a locally loaded database beyond the purview of the typical automated information retrieval service. Usually the same unit that manages the online catalog, such as the automation or systems office or in some cases the cataloging department, manages the locally loaded commercial database. However, a locally loaded database impacts on an automated information retrieval service a great deal.

For one thing, it is incumbent on the automated information retrieval service to instruct all users on the limitations of the locally loaded database. Because locally loaded databases are expensive to lease and consume a great deal of mainframe storage and computing capacity, it is virtually impossible for libraries to load enough databases to provide something like comprehensive coverage of relevant literatures, and yet most users will assume as usual that the computer is covering everything and finding everything. All public service staff will be engaged in a continuous battle against this assumption, a continuous defense of print tools and the hundreds of online and ondisk databases not loaded locally, especially in an academic library where the population essentially turns over every four years. One immediate impact on the automated information retrieval service is a decline in mediated searches and increased demand for more end-user products.

An automated information retrieval service already accustomed to instructing end-users may find itself called upon to provide instruction and expert assistance with the locally loaded database, especially if Boolean operators and keyword searching are incorporated in the search engine loaded with the database. Even more than usual, it will be necessary for the service manager to keep the library staff informed of other databases and other service options so that the staff can in turn refer users to sources more appropriate to their needs.

THE IMPACTS OF AUTOMATED INFORMATION RETRIEVAL

In the scenario that opened this chapter, Professor Smith never set foot inside the library. He examined indexes and the library's holdings from a remote computer in his office, sent queries and received messages from the library staff via computer, and eventually received a downloaded copy of the article he needed the same way. Some libraries are now experimenting with fax boards installed in networked microcomputers, whereby the text of printed materials in the library's collection can be scanned in the library and the resulting digitized text sent by E-mail to remote terminals. This leads to the concept of a "library without walls," or at least a library building where patrons are infrequent visitors. It may happen in the future, but for now the services offered by automated information retrieval are integrated with the traditional library services and are still seen as an expensive supplement to such services, something new that must prove itself and defend itself in times of budget cuts. Nevertheless, a library already using one or more of the automated information retrieval options would find it very difficult to discard that service regardless of how deeply the budget is cut, because automated information retrieval quickly becomes an irreplaceable part of library service that impacts on the staff, the budget, the collections, and the users of the library.

Staff

Unfortunately, automated information retrieval options are frequently seen as a burden, an extra duty for reference librarians drafted as mediated searchers. Certainly, in most libraries additional staff is not hired when a mediated search service is instituted, and traditionally it is the reference staff that must attend training sessions and set aside a few extra hours each day to meet the appointments and handle the paperwork. End-user online and ondisk services that claim to be user-friendly are not so friendly in the long run. Just as with the print tools, users need instruction, and in fact teaching a novice to use ERIC ondisk takes much longer than teaching the same person to use the print versions. Not only must the arrangement of the index be explained, but also search protocols, Boolean logic, and even keyboarding and using the printer. Libraries with multiple ondisk installations have found that full-time attendance by a staff member is necessary, and the ondisk or end-user online installation becomes another service point that must be staffed. The library staff not only resents the added demands on their time and skills, they can also resent the usurpation of office space to provide room for the additional services.

Bibliographic instruction staff are greatly affected by the presence of end-user services, because they find that they must become expert searchers themselves in order to teach users how the products work (Dreifuss, 1982; Shill, 1987; Steffen, 1986). Database searching provides an ideal environment for teaching library skills, in that it requires users to articulate their questions logically and offers immediate feedback to demonstrate whether or not the search strategy is effective, but the burden on the BI staff is immense. Different search engines, a knowledge of different databases and which ones are available in what format, and wrestling with balky equipment are new skills the BI staff must master. And yet, ignoring the automated information retrieval options available in a library is a serious disservice to the users, not only during their career in the academic library but also in the future outside the library in a world where online and ondisk services and products are becoming an increasing part of the work environment.

There will always be those librarians who resent the intrusion of computers in libraries because they are not comfortable using them, due to fear of breaking the computer or a lack of skills or a reluctance to perform and possibly make a silly mistake while a patron is watching, or any combination of these, and some librarians fear that the computer is taking over their jobs. For many, training and frequent reinforcement of the training can overcome the fears and lack of skills, but at some expense of the time of the trainee and of the trainer, and possibly of connect time as well. For others, no amount of training can vanquish the reluctance to choose an automated option, and these people are likely to resent those who are comfortable with automation and prefer it to the manual solution. Any library that deliberately elects a dichotomy of trained staff who are allowed to choose an automated solution as opposed to those untrained staff who have no choice is building a body of resentment between the haves and the have-nots. Certainly all public service librarians should receive training, whether they use it or not, if only so that they may know when to refer a patron to an automated solution.

Naturally, a powerful tool such as automated information retrieval produces positive impacts on the staff. Those who are comfortable with searching recognize immediately that their ability to serve the public with quick, accurate answers has been greatly enhanced, and their access to the world of knowledge outside the library walls is increased. Search analysts working in a mediated search environment enjoy the close and extended interaction with patrons during the private consultation lasting up to an hour, which is a far cry from the anonymous and often harried exchanges at a busy reference desk. The librarian's self-esteem is increased. The public's perception of the library and of librarians is improved by the use of automated information retrieval. They are gratified by the extensive individual attention they receive during a mediated search, and by the quick answer produced by a ready-reference search. End-users invariably prefer an online or ondisk search to the manual manipulation of a printed index. The provision of automated tools demonstrates to the public that the library is a high-tech place and the librarians are skilled professionals, not at all like the traditional image of libraries and librarians.

Budget and Collections

Automated information retrieval has both positive and negative impacts on the library's budget. Obviously, paying for equipment, supplies, training, and connect time can be seen as the gilding on the lily for a library that can scarcely afford daisies. When it comes to a choice between adding another search station or buying books and serials for the equivalent $3,000–$4,000, a library cannot be blamed for dithering over the decision. Automated information retrieval is undoubtedly expensive and unfortunately the expense is very visible in a way that traditional library services are not. Online vendors send monthly bills that clearly show how much each search costs, and those searches added nothing tangible to the library's collections since most likely one search represents the answer to one question for one individual, and there is no way to make that one answer accessible to all users of the library without performing and paying for the same search again. The impact of automated information retrieval on the budget is closely linked to its impact on collections, especially if the library is committed to free access to the automated resources (Lancaster and Goldhor, 1981; Rice, 1985; Wall et al. 1990).

Declining library budgets and increasing prices for library materials have made it obvious that no library can collect all the materials its users may need. The "80/20" rule is cited more and more frequently—80 percent of the demands made of a library are answered by 20 percent of the library's collections. Recognizing that it is not possible to satisfy all the users all the time, libraries may be turning to a commitment to identify, purchase, and maintain the critical 20 percent of the collection that serves the majority of users, and serving the remaining 20 percent of users by providing access to, rather than ownership of the materials they require.

Access is the stronghold, the very backbone, of automated information retrieval. A contract with an online vendor greatly increases the number of reference tools available to the librarians. Rather than purchasing an expensive index that may not be used very often, the reference staff accesses the tool online and on demand, and if their judgment that the tool will be little used is correct they have saved money. As more and more full-text sources become available online or ondisk, the same decision to prefer on-demand access rather than ownership becomes more relevant to more applications. Librarians can foresee many economies: not only is the cost of purchasing the printed material saved, but the costs of processing, housing, and maintaining the material are saved. Many library materials are purchased in the expectation that they will be used, but the 80/20 rule indicates that the probability of their being used are against it. On-demand access looks like an economical alternative.

In the early days of automated information retrieval, several authorities predicted that there would be a migration from printed tools to their automated versions; libraries would cancel their subscriptions to the paper copies of indexes in favor of online access. This has not happened to any great extent so far, but the likelihood is becoming greater with the advent of CD-ROM. An end-user searching an ondisk database housed in the library is so similar to an end-user searching the printed version of the same tool that the migration from print to ondisk does not seem as great and risky a leap as the migration from print to online. Furthermore, libraries that have added an ondisk version of an existing print index have actually seen the migration occur: users will line up and wait to use the ondisk version while the printed version sits ignored and gathering dust. In such an atmosphere, maintaining subscriptions to both seems a waste of money. Even more likely is the migration from online to ondisk (Anders and Jackson, 1988; Tenopir, 1991). It is a waste of money to subsidize access to the online version of an index when the ondisk version is available and provides the same automated information retrieval advantages and enhanced access, so some libraries have disabled or forbidden online access to databases that are available locally ondisk or as locally loaded databases.

Overall, it appears that libraries are not migrating from print as much as they are deciding not to purchase the print format in the first place when online or ondisk versions are available. This complicates collection development considerably because, in addition to deciding to purchase a tool, one must now decide which format, online, ondisk, or print, is appropriate for the population to be served (Tenopir, 1988).

Access increases demand for ownership, especially when access is through locally loaded databases that are available through the same terminals and the same search protocols as the online public access catalog, in which case they look like the OPAC and therefore appear to be part of the local library collection. Automated access produces citations in seconds; interlibrary loan takes an average of sixteen days to get a requested item into the hands of the requester. This produces a conflict of expectations in the user, and the burden falls entirely on the interlibrary loan office. The effect of online access on interlibrary loan services was noticed and studied early, and this research continues (Connolly and LaGuardia, 1986; Griffin, 1985; Martin, 1978).

One automated search can produce hundreds of citations instantly, and the patron is overwhelmed. "How can I deal with this?" he or she cries, and probably descends on the interlibrary loan office with printout in hand. Interlibrary loan staff are beginning to believe that more effort should be devoted to ownership rather than access, and this will become more critical as more libraries concentrate on building that 20 percent of their collections that serves 80 percent of their users, and depend on a nebulous network of interlibrary loan agreements to supply the rest. Unfortunately, a good portion of that magical 20 percent is largely the same material for many libraries. By looking inward and developing only those basic collections used by the local population, libraries may be inadvertently drying up the pool of resources traditionally accessed by interlibrary loan. The burden on interlibrary loan thus becomes even greater. A mediated search service can alleviate some of the burden by providing abstracts so that patrons can make more informed decisions, or by eliminating from the printout those items the patron will not use such as non-English publications or older items, and by printing CODENs—the standard alphanumeric abbreviation for the journal title—or at least full journal titles so that interlibrary loan staff can identify the items needed. But end-users who perform their own searches are not nearly as selective, either in producing the printout or in choosing relevant items from the printout. The migration from mediated to end-user services means trouble for interlibrary loan.

The Users

Library users like the results of automation. Most prefer an OPAC to a physical card catalog, most prefer an ondisk database to the printed version of the same index, and most prefer an immediate ready-reference answer to their questions rather than a lengthy search through printed tools. Most feel that, given access to the right resources, they can perform their own end-user searches as well as or better than a librarian can do it for them; thus there is a definite migratory trend from mediated search services to end-user searching. A library that offers a large variety of end-user resources will experience a decline in the demand for mediated searching.

Users do have unrealistic expectations of automated information retrieval which can only be dispelled by increased bibliographic instruction activities and a strong commitment from the reference staff to explain all the options available to library patrons. Younger patrons feel quite comfortable with computers (perhaps more comfortable than the library staff) and they feel confident in their ability to master the computer. Mastery of the computer does not translate into mastery of library use techniques, and yet users who are accustomed to getting their answers from a computer are not likely to approach the human beings at a reference desk for help, especially when they do not realize that they need help. This is the greatest drawback of automation—the fact that users expect the computer to know everything and tell everything, and a nonanswer from the computer is interpreted as the final answer beyond which there is no recourse, certainly not recourse to a fallible human librarian.

Patrons are more receptive to explanations of computerized databases than they are to explanations of print tools, so it is possible for library staff to dispel misconceptions once they have been approached for help. It does take longer to explain an ondisk database rather than the printed tool, and it is difficult to explain to patrons why there are different search engines for different tools such as the OPAC and Knowledge Index and SilverPlatter's ERIC database. Different search engines make it difficult for patrons to transfer skills from one database to another; the learning curve for automated information retrieval is steeper than for printed sources. It appears that users perceive these drawbacks as minor barriers, since the majority of them will prefer an automated solution to a print tool. The computers and terminals in libraries do not gather dust from lack of use.

REFERENCES

Anders, Vicki and Kathy Jackson. "Online vs CD-ROM: the impact of CD-ROM databases upon a large online searching program." *Online* 12 (November, 1988): 24–32. Statistics from a mediated service and an end-user online service show decreased use of databases made available to end-users on CD-ROM only a few months after the ondisk products were purchased.

Association of Research Libraries, Systems and Procedures Exchange Center. *Online Bibliographic Search Services*. SPEC Kit 76. Washington, D.C.: ARL Office of Management Studies, 1981.

Armstrong, C. J. and A. J. Large, eds. *Manual of Online Search Strategies*. Boston: G. K. Hall, 1988. "Intended for searchers who already have some knowledge of online searching . . . to provide the kind of inside information needed to carry out effective online searches in unfamiliar subject areas or databases." A hefty volume with lots of examples.

Auster, Ethel ed. *Managing Online Reference Services*. New York: Neal-Schuman, 1986. A collection of previously published papers detailing planning, operations, and management of traditional mediated search services.

Beaubien, Ann K., ed. *Fee-Based Services: Issues and Answers*. Proceedings of the Second Conference on Fee-Based Research in College and University Libraries, Ann Arbor, May 10–12, 1987. Ann Arbor: Information Transfer Source, University of Michigan Libraries, 1987. A collection of papers addressing fee-based services aimed at nonaffiliated businesses and other clientele.

Belanger, Sandra E. and Nancy J. Emmick. "Use of ready reference searching in business reference." *Journal of Academic Librarianship* 12 (November, 1986): 298–303. A study examining business-related ready-reference searches in an academic library found the procedure cost effective for the right questions. The catch is figuring out which are the right questions.

Bellardo, Trudi and Judy Stephenson. "The use of online numeric databases in academic libraries: a report of a survey." *Journal of Academic Librarianship* 12 (July, 1986): 152–157. Numeric databases available from major vendors are those most frequently searched in academic libraries, usually by search analysts.

Bonta, Bruce. "Online searching in the reference room." *Library Trends* 31 (Winter, 1983): 495–510. Discusses the importance of interpersonal relations as a necessary part of the information transfer process.

Brownmiller, Sara, A. Craig Hawbaker, Douglas E. Jones and Robert Mitchell. "Online ready reference searching in an academic library." *RQ* 24 (Spring, 1985): 320–326. A description of a careful plan for implementing ready-reference searching, in this case performed exclusively by trained search analysts.

Brownrigg, Edwin, Clifford Lynch and Mary Engle. "Technical services in the age of electronic publishing." *Library Resources and Technical Services* 28 (January/March, 1984): 59–67. Predicting a "long twilight" as libraries and publishers rearranged themselves in an electronic publishing evolution, the authors examine the overall nature of technical services in such an environment. The authors predict that the online catalog will become an online shopping guide.

Champlin, Peggy. "The online search: some perils and pitfalls." *RQ* 25 (Winter, 1985): 213–217. The author argues that some patrons have been neglected because of the elite treatment given to online patrons, and even those patrons requesting searches may be deprived of the information they need because of the restrictive nature of the online search.

Chang, Amy. "Developing an electronic information service in an academic library." *College and Research Libraries News* 52 (April, 1991): 237–239. An example of a campus E-mail system offering access to library options including interlibrary loan.

Chen, Ching-chih and Peter Herndon, eds. *Numeric Databases*. Norwood, N.J.: Ablex, 1984. A collection of contributed articles providing background information on the types and use of numeric databases, and case studies from a few academic and research libraries.

Cleverdon, Cyril. "Optimizing convenient online access to bibliographic databases." *Information Services and Use* 4 (April, 1984): 37–47. A fascinating paper arguing against the large, comprehensive databases and standard Boolean logic because they are user-hostile. Citing the 80/20 rule, the author argues that a less comprehensive, broad-coverage database using "quorum function" searching is ideal for end-users.

Connolly, Bruce and Cheryl M. LaGuardia. "The impact of database searching on interlibrary loan—eliminating the negative." *Online Review* 10 (June, 1986): 185-189. An interesting twist: rather than discussing what ILL offices can do to meet increased demand, this article details procedures the search service can undertake to "modify patron behavior in such a way as to encourage efficient individual research" (p. 186) and thus reduce the demand.

Dreifuss, Richard A. "Library instruction in the database searching context." *RQ* 21 (Spring, 1982): 233-238. While limiting himself to mediated searches, the author explains how online searching can be used to teach basic library research concepts.

Gilreath, Charles L. *Computerized Literature Searching: Research Strategies and Databases*. Boulder, Colo.: Westview Press, 1984. Examples are drawn from various databases and disciplines. Although the search engine examples are dated, this is a good study guide for carefully planned search strategies.

Griffin, Mary Ann. "Collection development to information access: the role of public services librarians." *RQ* 24 (Spring, 1985): 285-289. A philosophic discussion of the access vs. ownership question and the public services librarian's role in resolving it.

Hitchingham, Eileen, Elizabeth Titus and Richard Pettengill. "A survey of database use at the reference desk." *Online* 8 (March, 1984): 44-50. The results of surveys conducted in 1981 and 1982 of mainly academic, government, and hospital or medical libraries having some form of computer-assisted ready-reference available.

Hoover, Ryan E. "Computer aided reference services in the academic library: experiences in organizing and operating an online reference service." *Online* 3 (October, 1979): 28-40. Describes the beginning of an online service in a university library, including the management decisions made along the way and the organization of the service.

Josephine, Helen B. and Maxine H. Reneker. "In defense of FIRST and freedom of access to information." *College and Research Libraries News* 50 (May, 1989): 377-379. The legality of a fee-based service in an Arizona library was challenged by a local information broker.

Kibirige, Harry, M. "Computer-assisted reference services: what the computer will not do." *RQ* (Spring, 1988): 377-383. The author emphasizes that computer searching provides patrons with citations, not materials, and the local collection or interlibrary loan are inadequate to meet the patrons' expectations once the citations are in hand.

Knapp, Sara D. "Reference interview in the computer-based setting." *RQ* 17 (Summer, 1978): 320-324. The author emphasizes the importance of requiring the user to be present during a mediated search in order to interact with the database and refine the search in progress.

Kroll, Rebecca. "The ripple effect: the impact of online on library operations." In *Dollars and Sense*, edited by Bernard F. Pasqualini. 38-50. Chicago: American Library Association, 1987. This article touches upon many of the library functions affected by online, such as reference operations, end-user training, collection development, and funding.

Lamb, Connie. "Searching in academia—nearly 50 libraries tell what they're doing." *Online* 5 (April, 1981): 78-81. They are all doing pretty much the same thing, namely standard mediated search services with searching performed by search analysts and by appointment.

Lancaster, F. W. and Herbert Goldhor. "The impact of online services on subscriptions to printed publications." *Online Review* 5 (August, 1981): 301–311. The article reports on surveys conducted to see if the anticipated migration from print to online was actually occurring.

Li, Tze-chung. *An Introduction to Online Searching*. Westport, Conn.: Greenwood Press, 1985. A general introduction to the searching process. There are separate chapters for *DIALOG*, BRS, and ORBIT search protocols.

Locally Loaded Databases in Online Library Systems. A special issue of *Information Technology and Libraries* 8 (June, 1989): 99–185. Case studies detailing the experiences of Georgia Institute of Technology, Carnegie Mellon Library, Vanderbilt University, Dartmouth College, and Arizona State.

McKinney, Gayle and Anne Page Mosby. "Online in academia: a survey of online searching in U.S. colleges and universities." *Online Review* 10 (April, 1986): 107–124. Reports on the results of a survey conducted in 1984 to describe the extent of online searching in academic libraries.

Martin, Jean K. "Computer-based literature searching: impact on interlibrary loan service." *Special Libraries* 69 (January, 1978): 1–6. One of the earliest studies, showing a 50 percent increase in ILL activity due to online searching activities.

Neufeld, M. Lynne and Martha Cornog. "Database history: from dinosaurs to compact discs." *Journal of the American Society for Information Science* 37 (July, 1986): 183–190. Provides an overview and chronology of automated information retrieval.

Piternick, Anne B. "Decision factors favoring the use of online sources for providing information." *RQ* 29 (Summer, 1990): 534–544. Focusing on the characteristics of online sources that distinguish them from printed sources, the author presents a list of seven factors that affect the choice of online over printed sources for answering requests for information.

Reese, Carol. "Manual indexes versus computer-aided indexes: comparing the *Readers' Guide to Periodical Literature* to InfoTrac II." *RQ* 28 (Spring, 1988): 384–389. Details some of the common misconceptions and mistakes of end-users.

Rice, Barbara A. "Evaluation of online databases and their uses in collection evaluation." *Library Trends* 33 (Winter, 1985): 297–325. Discusses evaluation of vendors and databases for possible inclusion in a search service, and also how database access can be used to evaluate the print collection.

Sieburth, Janice F. *Online Search Services in the Academic Library: Planning, Management, and Operation*. Chicago: American Library Association, 1988. A detailed and valuable handbook, concentrating on the operations of a mediated search service.

Shill, Harold B. "Bibliographic instruction: planning for the electronic information environment." *College and Research Libraries* 48 (Springs, 1987): 433–453. The article is "intended to convey the importance of strategic thinking and planning for developing bibliographic instruction programs that will provide information-retrieval skills . . . and to demonstrate to administrators the importance of including patron instruction programs in libraries' long-range planning activities" (p. 435).

Steffen, Susan Swords. "College faculty goes online: training faculty and end-users." *Journal of Academic Librarianship* 12 (July, 1986: 147–151. A description of a well-designed training program for end-users, the problems experienced by end-users, and the problems librarians experience with end-users.

Stewart, Linda, Katherine S. Chiang and Bill Coons, eds. *Public Access CD-ROMS in Libraries: Case Studies*. Westport, Conn.: Meckler Corporation, 1990. Case study examples of how CD-ROM installations have been handled in several different types of libraries.

Tenopir, Carol. "Decision making by reference librarians." *Library Journal* 113 (October 1, 1988): 66-67. Comparing online, ondisk, and print products, Tenopir offers guidelines for answering the question of which is the appropriate technology for a particular reference tool.

Tenopir, Carol. "The impact of CD-ROM on online." *Library Journal* 116 (February 1, 1991). Examines the migration possibilities from online to CD-ROM.

Thesing, Jane I. "Online searching in perspective: advantages and limitations." In *Online Searching: Technique and Management*, edited by James J. Maloney. 16-21. Chicago: American Library Association, 1983. A useful introduction to the question of when to go online.

Tobin, Carol M. "Initial considerations for an online search." In *Online Searching: Technique and Management*, edited by James J. Maloney. 22-25. Chicago: American Library Association, 1983. Lists and discusses, with examples, seven factors in deciding if a question is suitable for an online answer.

Video to Online: Reference Services and the New Technology. New York: Haworth Press, 1983. A special issue of *Reference Librarian*, no. 5/6, the Fall/Winter, 1983 issue, devoted to library applications of technology including online searching.

Vigil, Peter J. *Online Retrieval: Analysis and Strategy*. New York: Wiley, 1988. The author's emphasis is on understanding computers and the human/computer interface to teach effective searching of commercial online databases.

Wall, Celia, Roger Haney and John Griffin. "Hard copy versus online services: results of a survey." *College and Research Libraries* 51 (May 1990): 267-276. The authors report on the rate of migration from printed abstracting and indexing sources due to online availability, in smaller liberal arts colleges.

Watson, Peter G. "Library organizational patterns in online retrieval services." In *Online Searching: Technique and Management*, edited by James J. Maloney. 75-82. Chicago: American Library Association, 1983. Discusses the options of placing an automated information retrieval service in the institutional organization chart and the advantages and disadvantages of each option.

Williams, Martha E. "Data bases—a history of developments and trends from 1966 through 1975." *Journal of the American Society for Information Science* 28 (March, 1977): 71-78. See also the Neufeld article to bring this history up to date.

2

Operations of an Automated Information Retrieval Service

Operating and managing an automated information retrieval service is not a one-time, set-it-and-forget-it procedure. The equipment, techniques, and products of automated information retrieval are continually changing, and the service must evolve to incorporate these changes. Such an evolution need not be a "survival of the fittest" type of challenge, although survival sometimes seems to be the most one can hope for. Instead, a well-managed service should have the policies, procedures, and staff in place that allow the flexibility to meet—and welcome—change.

A typical transaction in which a patron makes an appointment with a search analyst for an online search, or an end-user walks up to a CD-ROM station to perform his or her own search, assumes that equipment is in place and operating, that contracts with vendors have been negotiated, that search analysts have been scheduled for the service and are competent, and that procedures are in place to record the search and draw up an invoice if there is a charge for the service. This chapter provides a look behind the assumptions, a look at the underpinnings of the management of an automated information retrieval service.

The manager of the service deals, on a day-to-day basis, with the environment in which the service operates, with the paperwork generated by the service, and with evaluating every aspect of the service to be sure that everything works smoothly when a patron calls for an appointment or an end-user approaches a searching station. The environment includes the facilities and equipment, of course, but also refers to the policies, budgets, and personnel that must be in place before the service can function. Paperwork ranges from record-keeping and statistics to promotion and advertising. Individual searches should certainly be evaluated, and so should the search analysts, the service itself, and the manager of the service. This chapter examines these issues from the point of view of the manager of the service. It should be noted that certain issues such as budgeting and financing the service, staff, equipment, databases, and vendors, are covered in more detail in individual chapters and are merely mentioned here as items that come across the manager's desk in the day-to-day operations of the automated information retrieval service.

THE PERSON IN CHARGE

WANTED: ONLINE SERVICES MANAGER. ABC Library of Enormous State University is looking for a dynamic individual to manage its AIRS (Automated Information Retrieval Service) unit, which consists of a busy mediated online service, end-user online operations, a growing CD-ROM installation, and a reference assistance service on a campuswide LAN in the development stage. Budget: $100,000. Staff: three professionals (part-time), two clerks. Requirements: MLS degree from an ALA-accredited university, ten years experience, including five years in a supervisory capacity. Experience with DIALOG, ORBIT, BRS, SilverPlatter, WILSONLINE, NLM, etc. Proven competence in oral and written communication (send examples of published articles). Must be familiar with DBMS software, statistical software, and desktop publishing software. Must be able to troubleshoot microcomputers and peripherals necessary to services listed above. Desirable: experience with LANs, European languages, programming languages. This is a tenure-track position, and the successful applicant must be willing to meet the university's stringent requirements for promotion and tenure. Some night and weekend service on the reference desk required.

The paragon who meets these requirements probably will not be paid commensurate with the experience and skills needed, but certainly will have an interesting, busy, and varied job. Even the smallest operation needs managing, and the combination reference librarian/search analyst/service coordinator will need the skills listed above. He or she will find that a great deal of time is consumed by the details of keeping an automated information retrieval service running. There must be someone in charge; this is not an operation that will run itself once it is set in motion.

The primary responsibility of the manager is to see that the service meets its mission statement, that it performs what it has promised to do. This assumes that there is a mission statement or a policy in existence, and it is the manager's job to evaluate and reevaluate the service's mission constantly to insure that it is up to date, that it meets the requirements of the parent organization, and that all the day-to-day tasks performed facilitate the goal of accomplishing the mission. The manager monitors and controls when possible the environment in which the service operates, and is primarily responsible for the paperwork the service generates. Most important of all, the manager is the resource person to whom others refer questions on policy or procedures, questions from patrons on what databases are available and how to access them, questions from search analysts and end-users on strategies, and questions from upper management on how the service is performing and where it should be heading. This means that the manager must have an intimate, hands-on knowledge of all the details of the operation. Depending on the size and variety of the service, the manager may or may not be an active search analyst providing mediated searches or involved in instructing end-users, or possibly serving nights and weekends on the reference desk, but as with managers everywhere, he or she must be able to take on these duties when the need arises.

THE ENVIRONMENT

An automated information retrieval service operates within an established environment—its ecosystem, so to speak. The policy and procedures manual sets the rules of operation. The physical facilities, the contracts with vendors, and the budget are the raw materials in the environment, and the staff and users are the inhabitants. It is the interactions of the components in this environment that the manager must manage when possible and accommodate when they cannot be changed.

Policy and Procedures Manual

Unfortunately, policy is frequently determined on an ad hoc basis. A situation or a question arises, a decision is made on how to deal with it, and that decision becomes the tradition that loosely governs similar situations in the future. However, it cannot properly be called "policy" because it is not formalized, it does not have official sanction that will stand up to a challenge, and probably it is known to only a few people. Some type of policy may be available in fee schedules, staff meeting minutes, or in user guides that are written and somewhat formalized, but until they are compiled and rewritten into a formal document they may be contradictory and will certainly not be referred to by all the staff members of the library who should be working within the framework of the policy and interpreting that policy for the public. Especially for a service that can cost a great deal of money, and that may be recovering some or all of that money from the public, a policy manual is critical.

The policy manual should be a tool that helps the service achieve its objectives. It should be restrictive in that it sets the limits of the service and standardizes activities performed; it should be permissive in that it allows some leeway for exceptional circumstances and the freedom to interpret the policy as necessary; it should be flexible enough to accommodate change, and in fact a review mechanism for considering changes to the policy should be incorporated in the policy itself. The manual should be inclusive and detailed enough to serve as the operations manual for the automated information retrieval service; as such, it can serve as a training tool for new staff and as a job description that details for upper management the skills required of a service manager and the complexities of operating the service. To facilitate all these functions, it should be loose-leaf and organized in sections based on whether the information is intended for the public, for the service staff, or for library staff not actually involved with the service. Each page of a loose-leaf manual should be dated to insure that everyone is working with the latest version of the policy.

This brings up another very important point about the policy and procedures manual. To be effective and useful, the policy statements must be widely disseminated within the library. If librarians at the reference desk are telling patrons that anyone can have a mediated search performed when the policy manual states that the service is only available to library card holders, the policy manual is not fulfilling and cannot fulfill its purpose.

Services just starting up have the advantage of beginning with a formalized policy, whereas services that have been in existence for a time without a written policy must gather together all handouts and fee statements, as well as any oral traditions, in an attempt to glean existing policy statements from them. These should be compiled and rewritten into a formal statement, ideally by a committee headed by the service manager and including search analysts, other librarians impacted by the service such as reference librarians and interlibrary loan librarians, and the administrator to whom the service manager reports. This group can identify any weaknesses or gaps in the policy and insure that it is consistent with existing library policy. Finally, the policy should be sanctioned by the library administration.

The ideal policy manual contains a statement about why the service exists and identifies the goals and specific objectives toward those goals. It shows the service's position in the larger organization and defines the scope of the services available. It should formalize the modes of operation to provide a framework for day-to-day decisions and to insure that all patrons are treated equally. The rights and recourses of users should be spelled out. Depending on the size and complexity of the service, it can include all or some of the points listed below (Foreman, 1983; Katz and Clifford, 1982; Pensyl, 1982).

Mission, Goals, and Philosophy of the Service. This can be a very general statement such as "To support the research efforts of ABC University." This is the place to include definitions, or alternatively, to swear religiously that the document will be free of jargon. For the purposes of patrons and of staff, definitions of a search, a database, a vendor, citations/printouts, a user, an end-user, or any other terms that are likely to cause confusion or be subject to misinterpretation should be included. Any policies of the larger organization that apply to the automated information retrieval service can be restated here, perhaps with an indication of how the service enhances or improves or impinges upon the mission of the larger organization. Issues of copyright or database restrictions should be addressed, perhaps with a general statement on copyright and a referral to the published restrictions of individual database producers. It is important not to weigh the policy manual down with too many statements that are subject to change by individuals or organizations outside the control of the service manager. Certainly such database restrictions should be on file and readily available in the manager's office. Users frequently ask if they can download, upload, publish, or disseminate the product of a database search, and this question can be answered only by the published restrictions and policies of the database producers and vendors. Most vendors supply a list of database restrictions once a year.

Organization Chart. The position of the service in the organization chart of the library and the lines of supervision should be made clear. Also, the managerial organization of the service can be detailed, explaining who is in charge and what the duties of that person are, the proportion of time devoted to various duties, and how to report problems. This can be quite a detailed job description for the manager's position and may in fact be the only place where all the duties and responsibilities are written out down to the smallest detail; for example, the manual may be the only place where it is spelled out that, if a printer runs out of paper, the manager is responsible for ordering paper and replacing it. The duties and responsibilities of the search analysts and other staff can be explained, including the percentage of time they are expected to devote to the service, and how they are chosen and by whom. A statement about the continuing education responsibilities of the searching staff and how it is financed is appropriate here.

Scope of the Service. This can be a list of the databases or the vendors available for searching, but the most important point to cover in this section is the responsibility for deciding which databases or vendors are selected. Who decides which CD-ROM database will be purchased, and by what criteria? Who decides if an online search will be performed instead of a manual search? Under what conditions will an online search be performed? Is access to certain databases limited? For example, will searches of ERIC online be performed on demand even though the database is available to users on CD-ROM? Which system manuals or database manuals or thesauri will be purchased? Are SDIs and demonstrations available? Are all subjects searched from a single location, or are medical subject searches performed exclusively at the medical library? A statement absolving the library staff from responsibility for the contents of databases is appropriate here. Also, if special services are offered to a certain clientele—for example, graduate students get free searches—it is appropriate to include the definitions, criteria, or conditions that must be met to be included in the clientele group.

Who Will Be Served. A college or university library may limit service to faculty, staff, and students. A public library may limit service to registered card holders. It is also important to point out who will not be served. Priorities can be defined; for example, the policy can state that end-users have priority over library staff when using CD-ROM databases, or vice versa.

Modes of Operation. It is this section that becomes a procedures or operations manual for the service, and also insures that patrons receive equitable treatment. The hours of availability can be detailed, and also the options open to patrons when the office is closed—whether they can pick up printouts, for example, or drop off search requests. The policy should state whether or not appointments are required and if the patron must be present during the search, or whether telephone or mail-in searches are accepted. Will library staff search CD-ROM databases for patrons on demand, or are patrons expected to perform their own searches? The steps involved in conducting a mediated search can be detailed, such as handling initial inquiries, referring users to the online service, making the appointment, conducting the search interview, the preparation expected of the analyst such as consulting thesauri, conducting the search, delivering the printout, and following up with explanations of interlibrary loan or stack guides. This can be compiled in checklist form to serve as a training tool and to provide performance standards for search analysts. It is especially important to explain precisely the modes of operation expected of end-users of online or CD-ROM databases—time limits, waiting lists, and appointment procedures, for example—because the likelihood of conflict is greatest with end-users.

Performance Standards. Turnaround time is an example of a performance standard that can be included in the policy. How long should a patron wait for an appointment? How long should a patron wait for a printout? Are there certain minimum standards of legibility or appearance of the printout? Detailed procedures spelled out in the Modes of Operation section above can be used as performance standards for the search analysts, and in fact the entire policy and procedures manual can become the basis for reviewing the performance of the service manager.

Financial Considerations. If users are charged for the service, the goals for cost recovery should be spelled out here. Does the service expect to recover all direct costs? Direct costs plus a percentage? What happens to the service if the budget runs out? The fee schedule should be explained in great detail, even if it is subject to frequent change. The loose-leaf organization of the manual lends itself to easy updating, and this section can be extracted and reproduced for broad distribution if necessary. It should be clear who is responsible for setting the fees, and how fees are determined. The library administration may want to add a statement on the source of funds if searches are subsidized. The policy should detail payment procedures, where and how to pay, how bills are collected, and if any penalties accrue for delinquent accounts. The patron's liability should be explained. Does the patron pay regardless of results or is there some recourse for an unsatisfactory result? What procedures must a patron follow in questioning a charge?

Discretionary Use by Librarians. This section details the circumstances under which librarians or other staff may use the service for ready-reference, for practice, or for demonstrations to users. The budget or the method by which online searches are subsidized should be included.

Client Concerns. Questions of confidentiality can be addressed here. What kinds of records are kept and who has access to them? Also, the responsibilities of patrons should be explained. Are they required to make any advance preparation such as completing a search request form or getting the approval of a business office? Explain the procedures for making a complaint. This section should explain to patrons that the purpose of the policy is to assure consistency in contacts with clients. It can also protect the library if an action—or inaction—of a staff member is questioned.

Emergencies and Contingencies. This catchall section absolves the library from responsibility for power failures, equipment failures, or telephone outages. It should explain what recourse patrons have if a mechanical failure interrupts a search, and should detail any financial liability on either side. Does the library pay for an interrupted search or does the patron pay? Definitions are important here; the patron must not be allowed to claim a mechanical failure when the content or structure of a database causes a failure to retrieve what was expected. It should also detail actions the staff must take in an emergency. For example, if there is a power outage, all microcomputers should be turned off as soon as possible because they could be damaged by a power "spike" when the electricity comes back on. How should end-users be handled when the building must be evacuated due to a fire alarm or other emergency? Will they be allowed to resume the search once the building can be reoccupied?

Evaluation and Review. The policy and procedures manual should conclude with a statement requiring an annual review of the document. Managers may want to include a statement allowing the manager to review any public handouts, brochures, speeches, etc. regarding the service to be sure that they are consistent with the service's policy. Procedures for revising and amending it should be detailed.

The manual should include copies of all forms used in the service and examples of reports generated by the service. It is also helpful to include copies of handouts and brochures issued to the public, since these amount to interpretations of the policy and may be the only exposure the public has to the formal policy. Needless to say, any handout or brochure should be consistent with policy.

Finally, once the policy has been compiled in a final draft, it should be reread from the point of view of the patron. If the policy sounds like a barrier behind which the library staff faces off with the patrons, if it is a list of what the patron cannot do and a list of actions the staff takes to enforce the policy, start over. The policy and procedures manual should be an enabling document that allows the library to provide the services demanded by the users.

Facilities

The manager is ultimately responsible for the location of the automated information retrieval service, for the furniture, equipment, and supplies needed, and for the security of the facilities and control of access. Equipment—the microcomputers, printers, and such—is addressed in more detail in a separate chapter; the location of the service may be beyond the control of the manager and largely determined by the physical layout of the larger organization. However, the manager deals with questions of equipment and location on a day-to-day basis, and certain management issues will be dealt with here.

From the manager's point of view, the ideal location for an automated information retrieval service is a single and separate room in an accessible area, clearly marked by the service's professionally designed logo, with CD-ROM stations in one area and online stations in another, separated by a barrier that provides visual separation and a barrier to noise. During the day mediated searches can be performed on the online stations, and at night end-users will take over the area. Noisy printers will not be an issue since they are collected together in a single location and separated from other public use areas by a wall—a soundproof wall, one hopes. If a piece of equipment fails it is an easy matter to reconfigure or reroute traffic, since all the equipment is easily accessible and compatibility of equipment was planned in advance. Protecting the equipment is a simple matter; special wiring was installed with an eye toward adequate supply of electricity and surge protection, and the door can be securely locked when the service closes for the night. Naturally, the CD-ROM stations are connected by LANs, therefore patrons never handle the disks and thus security for the disks is not an issue. Lighting can be controlled to prevent glare on the screens. Staff can monitor the area easily and are readily available to help patrons. The room is clean and attractive, all the furniture matches; there is an air of intent and studious activity. In an adjoining room the lights are dimmed as a class assembles for a demonstration.

There probably is not such an ideal installation in existence. In reality, search stations are scattered throughout the building, none of the furniture matches and much of the equipment is incompatible, and if the printer on the ERIC CD-ROM station fails, ERIC searchers will do without until it is repaired. Branch libraries or separate divisions within the library may run their own services without any coordination. As much as possible, the manager should insure that equipment under his or her control is compatible and parts are interchangeable so that printers and modems and CD-ROM drives can be switched or shared among search stations. If funding allows, it is a good idea to have one of each of the components of one entire search station set aside as spares, so that parts are available when a piece of equipment fails on an active search station. In practice, it is very difficult to maintain a spare machine, since there is always some way it can be put to use. Designating one search station as a "demo" machine can be a method of keeping spare parts on hand, assuming that demonstrations and teaching can be postponed if it is necessary to cannibalize the station. A necessary piece of equipment is a simple tool kit containing the correct screwdrivers and wrenches needed to work on microcomputers and peripherals. The manager will have to decide how much troubleshooting and repairing of equipment he or she feels comfortable with, but inevitably some will be required. In academic libraries, it may be possible to hire a computer science student part-time to deal with the machinery.

A file containing the purchase orders or lease agreements, warranties, and repair records for each piece of equipment should be maintained. This file can also serve as the inventory of equipment if an annual accounting is necessary. Repair records can be maintained using a DBMS software package (Butkovich, 1988). If at all possible, equipment used for the automated information retrieval service should be designated as public access equipment and kept entirely separate from office machines.

The manager must insure that appropriate documentation—system manuals, thesauri, database manuals—are available to support searching activities. Standing orders with the vendors will supply much of it, and careful perusal of the literature crossing the desk will alert the manager to the availability of new or updated database manuals. Whether or not the documentation is catalogued and listed in the library's public catalog depends on local usage, but it should be housed apart from the regular library materials in an area readily convenient to search analysts. The service manager should have the final word on whether an item from the collection can be checked out or otherwise removed from the collection. Services that are scattered among branch libraries or CD-ROM stations in various locations will need either to share or duplicate some documentation; a statement in the policy and procedures manual may be needed to prevent or minimize conflict over who gets what documentation. It can get very expensive and should be accounted for in the service's budget. Much of the material is loose-leaf. The manager must institute a system for checking it in, filing it, keeping the collection in order, and assuring that the latest editions are available to the search analysts. It is in fact a small special collection and requires the same management techniques.

Paper and ribbons or ink cartridges for the searching stations are the supplies most in demand. End-users especially consume an inordinate amount of these supplies and are inclined to be especially frustrated and vocal if supplies run short. Care should be taken to insure an adequate supply on hand during weekends and vacation periods when access to stores may be curtailed. Other supplies needed by the service include the forms used (detailed below) and standard office supplies such as file folders, and the consumable supplies used for the maintenance of the equipment such as drive-head cleaners, screen wipes and cleaning solution, aerosol canisters for blasting dust and paper residue out of keyboards, and hand-cleaning pads for removing the inkstains when one changes a ribbon.

Security is a two-pronged issue. Expensive equipment must be protected, and unauthorized access to online systems must be prevented. If searching stations are contained in a lockable, secure room, security is an easy matter, but most often CD-ROM search stations are in public areas, and service desks with ready-reference terminals may not be secure. Several office furniture manufacturers offer computer workstations with locking rolltop doors, but the locks on these are of poor quality and the rolltops themselves will cave in if someone merely leans on them, so these workstations provide more of a visual barrier than an actual one. Microcomputers and peripherals can be cabled and locked down with commercially available security cables, but someone determined to steal the equipment can easily pry the cables loose with a screwdriver, and in fact the cables are more of a barrier to library staff who have a legitimate reason for moving the equipment. Conventional wisdom says that the determined thief can steal anything he or she wants to, therefore it seems best to stop worrying about absolute security and simply place as many barriers as possible between the equipment and the less-determined thief who is tempted to take something on a whim. Managers will want to look into insurance coverage for the equipment, but this is something controlled usually by the parent organization, and the manager may not be able to influence it.

On the other hand, preventing unauthorized access to online systems is something the manager can and should control, since a large bill could be run up by a curious patron who simply signs on to an expensive database and walks away without signing off, (most vendors have a "time-out" security system that automatically logs off after a stated number of minutes of inactivity), and an even larger bill can result from deliberate unauthorized use. Barriers to access already exist: one must know the telephone access number and the network identification code for the various vendors, and one must sign on with a vendor account number and a user password, both of which are "masked" by most vendors—in other words, these do not display on the screen or the printout as they are typed. However, as more people access networks and bulletin boards and systems from home computers, these conventions become known to a wider population who may be tempted to use this knowledge to break the library's code in order to gain unauthorized access. Most systems allow the user to assign an individual "user password" as a final step in signing on, and this password should be changed as soon as it is received and changed at varying intervals a few times a year; it should certainly be changed when someone who was authorized to use the password leaves the organization.

Passwords usually follow the same conventions as filenames used in word processing and other software and are limited to no more than eight characters. It is best to use only alpha and numeric characters, since punctuation or control characters may be reserved by the system for commands and could cause untoward results. Unfortunately, easily remembered passwords such as the name of the library are also easy for others to figure out, and it can be disastrous to use the same password on all systems. If communications software is used for automatic logon and the passwords are stored on the floppy or hard disk, then access to the disk must be controlled with a password. There are utility software packages that allow password assignment to control access.

Finally, managers should be sure that all authorized use of online systems is recorded, and these records of authorized use should be compared to vendor invoices to be sure that there has not been unauthorized use of a password. If such use is detected, the password must be changed. It is very time-consuming and tedious to check every invoice against recorded use, so the manager may decide to check at intervals or only if an invoice is suspiciously high. If unauthorized use is occurring on the library's machines at times when the area is not monitored or after closing hours, simply removing the modem or the power supply may be all that is necessary to stop it (Parker, 1985).

Relations with Vendors

Once a contract has been negotiated, most communication with a vendor is in the form of online news or the vendor's published material. The online services usually have a news bulletin that either displays automatically when a user logs on or must be requested to be seen. It is important to read these messages at least once a week, as they contain important information about price changes and system changes, databases that are temporarily down or that have been reloaded in such a way that techniques for searching them have changed, and information on special offers such as free or reduced price searching in particular databases. Published materials such as monthly newsletters, brochures, and database documentation should be routed to the searching staff at the least; if library staff perform searches to answer reference questions, a broader routing list may be needed.

When an offline printout is lost in the mail, or a communications glitch interrupts a search, it is necessary to contact the vendor directly. Most of them have toll-free telephone numbers for this purpose. Any communication pertaining to a particular search must be identified by the account number or password on which the search was done; therefore the manager must have a card file or "Rolodex" record for each account, which must be in a secure place to prevent unauthorized access to the passwords. It may be convenient to have multiple accounts with the same vendor if searching is performed in several places—at different service desks, for example—or separate accounts for different purposes such as an account for ready-reference searching and an account for mediated searching. Each account is billed separately by the vendor, and this makes it easier for the manager to determine how much is being spent for different uses or in different areas. Training and documentation can be billed to an account and will show up on the invoice along with any searching done in the same month. A service that has multiple accounts will find it convenient to have all nonsearching expenses such as these on one account and thus on one invoice where it is easier to extract them from other charges. Most services will not discuss passwords over the telephone for security reasons. If a password is lost or forgotten it can be retrieved by contacting the vendor, but this must be done in writing. Many vendors have fax numbers if a password must be retrieved in a hurry.

Communications with optical disk vendors usually consist of receiving updated disks and returning the old ones if necessary. Local library policy may require the disks to be received and checked in through the library's acquisitions or serials department, but it is faster and more certain to have them sent directly to the automated information retrieval service manager. In this case, the manager must maintain check-in records. On the same record the manager should indicate the date superseded disks are returned, the version of software being used, when software updates are received, and when a contract or subscription comes up for renewal. In those operations where end-users handle the disks, it is quite likely that a disk will be scratched or otherwise damaged and will need replacing. So far, vendors are quite willing to do this with no more authorization than a telephone call from the service manager, and usually the disk is sent by express mail.

Both online vendors and optical disk vendors have organized users' groups that meet at annual conferences or library conventions. The optical disk vendors especially seem willing to listen to users' suggestions and to incorporate changes in their software, making this avenue of communicating with vendors a particularly rewarding one. More information about vendors and databases will be found in Chapter 5.

The Budget

Budgeting and financing an automated information retrieval service are such critical parts of running the service that they are dealt with separately in Chapter 3. On a day-to-day basis, however, the manager must monitor expenses and deal with a large amount of paper generated by paying bills and possibly receiving funds if the library charges for searches. In some operations the manager receives a lump-sum budget and has the option of determining how it will be distributed for supplies, training, demonstrations, maintenance, etc. In other operations, every cost must be recovered, and in some rare operations no one particularly worries about funds. Regardless, at some point, someone will ask, "How much does it cost and how much do you need for next year?"

Invoices from vendors must be monitored and approved for payment by the manager, who looks at them to detect unauthorized use, to extract nonsearching expenses such as training or documentation, and to be sure that the amount invoiced is covered by the budget either through costs recovered from patrons or by library funds if searching is subsidized. This is best done on a monthly basis, either at a scheduled time or whenever the invoices are received, using a simple manual accounting system or a software package for accounting. Simple accounting software designed for small businesses is most suitable. In a large operation it can be quite time-consuming to check every search against every invoice, and the manager may prefer to spot-check each invoice, or thoroughly cross-check all invoices received every third or fourth month. Invoices or copies of them should be maintained in the manager's office. A great deal of statistical information can be gleaned from the invoices for annual report purposes. Files of invoices are best maintained by vendor and by date; if multiple accounts are established with a vendor the manager may prefer to file the invoices by account, possibly to separate mediated searches from end-user searches or reference searches.

If the service bills patrons for cost recovery, more files must be maintained for invoices and receipts and follow-up on delinquent accounts, if any. Again, an accounting software package for small businesses can help maintain records, and many of them can be used to print the bill handed to the patron. It may be possible to shuffle this responsibility to the library's budget office, thus saving the manager some filing room and trouble, but communications between the budget office and the manager must be frequent and good, especially if penalties are imposed for unpaid accounts. Otherwise, the search service can be conducting numerous and expensive searches for a patron who never pays his or her bills. If the service is authorized to receive cash payments, a cash register and a system for reconciling the daily tapes are necessary. Operations with end-user services must decide if billing for small amounts of money—ten cents for a page of prints, $1.50 for online time—is worth the effort; the clerical time involved in billing, filing, and record-keeping can easily be costing the library more money than is collected.

Personnel

Training, supervising, and reconciling schedules are day-to-day functions of the automated information retrieval service manager. It is most important to be sure that every search analyst and everyone who works in an end-user operation is thoroughly familiar with the policy and procedures manual to insure equitable treatment for all patrons. Scheduling can be a particularly touchy subject when personnel have other duties at the reference desk or in collection development. The job description should detail the percentage of time to be dedicated to each activity, and the percentages should be reviewed at the end of the year or at personnel evaluation time. It may be a good idea to detail in writing what is expected of a search analyst if they have no appointment during scheduled search time because a patron failed to show up. This can be done either in the policy and procedures manual or in the job description. These and other matters regarding personnel are addressed in more detail in Chapter 4.

The manager should be sure that there is at least one person among the search analysts who can keep the service running in the absence of the manager. A familiarity with the location, contents, and use of all files in the office, a working knowledge of how invoices are handled, and the ability to manipulate the record-keeping and statistical functions are the bare minimum skills needed. Large-scale operations may have a designated position for an assistant manager, whose day-to-day duties are the managing of some aspect of the operation such as a CD-ROM unit, and who is trained to take over when the manager is absent.

THE PAPERWORK

The pieces of paper generated by and received by the service manager every day are varied and numerous. The activities of an automated information retrieval service are amenable to counting, and in order to generate statistics, records must be kept. Furthermore, the service must be promoted or advertised, and instructional materials especially for end-user services must be written and kept up to date. Schedules for mediated searches and end-user searches, reports of activity to the parent organization, and evaluation of the service contribute to the paperwork the manager must manage. Instructional materials will be dealt with in the chapter on end-users; scheduling is explained in detail in the chapter on staff. This section details the promotion and advertising, forms, record-keeping, statistics, and reports the manager of an automated information retrieval service deals with on a day-to-day basis.

The many forms, reports, brochures, and handouts generated by the service will have more impact and be more useful if they are planned as a unified series of documents. Pieces of paper intended to be seen or used by the public need a logo or some other distinction that sets them apart from other library brochures. Well-designed logos are nice; they can be used not only on the paperwork but also on signage that marks the service's headquarters or location. However, they can be expensive to design if professional artists are employed, and it can be difficult to get a logo in enough sizes and styles to fit on every piece of paper the service generates. A distinctive type-style or even a particular color of paper can be enough to identify the service's brochures.

Promotion and Advertising

Advertising the automated information retrieval service is continually necessary because the offerings of the service are continually changing, and also because the clientele of most libraries is continually changing, especially academic libraries. Libraries, like doctors and lawyers, have been reluctant to get involved in promotion, but advertising activities have increased lately, as libraries realize that service is enhanced simply by explaining what is available to the public. Actually, libraries have been doing this for years, but only recently have the marketing techniques used by major advertising firms been applied to the products and services available in libraries.

The automated information retrieval service is a unique product that can and should be marketed, if only to reach those potential patrons who need information but are not willing to ask a librarian if such a service is available. The tendency of people not to ask for assistance is most evident in libraries, and advertising can get around this problem. Students are not learning about automated information retrieval from their textbooks or their professors (Clark, 1989; Schumacher, 1986 and 1989). Advertising can also overcome the misconceptions many people have about automated information retrieval—that it is always expensive, or that anyone can do it without instruction, or that it can only be done by trained professionals, or that libraries only have access to the same simplified databases as are available through home computers. Finally, advertising that increases use of the service contributes to the perpetuation of the service. The equipment, the online time, the subscriptions to CD-ROM databases, and in fact everything about automated information retrieval costs money, which probably will not be forthcoming in future years if the service is not used.

Some of the techniques used by expensive advertising firms can be borrowed and applied to promoting automated information retrieval services (Edinger, 1980; Norman, 1982; Sherman, 1980; Smith, 1980a and 1980b; Tuggle and Heller, 1987; Weingand, 1987; Wood, 1984). One of these marketing concepts requires a reorientation from looking inward at the raw materials that make up the service to looking outward toward the consumers' needs. In other words, one must sell the benefits of the product rather than the product itself. Most of the potential clientele of the service are not interested in the technical specifications of a database any more than they are interested in the philosophy behind the library's classification system; they simply want to know what the service will do for them. Any advertising should explain what makes the product unique and what aspects of the product best meet potential users' needs—speed of access, for example, or the availability of a printout rather than copying citations by hand.

Another useful technique is to identify the market. Who are the clientele currently using the service, why are they using the service, and are they likely to be repeat customers? Are there potential customers who could use the service if they knew it would be useful to them? The manager should define the target groups for the advertising campaign, and should be aware that their differing needs may require a different advertising approach. One all-purpose brochure may not be enough. If there are restrictions on who may use the service, it is equally important to define what groups should not be targeted.

It may be useful to identify the competition in order to identify ways to increase usage of the service. For example, a print index competes with a computerized index, and the advertising campaign can emphasize the advantages of speed and size of the database. If there is an information broker in the local community, advertising can emphasize the advantage of having the automated information retrieval service in the same building as the materials. It may be that the automated information retrieval service views end-users or individuals with their own contracts and passwords as competition, in which case the expertise of the search analysts can be emphasized. Conversely, the manager with more business than he or she can handle may wish to emphasize the convenience of end-user searching. Individuals with their own passwords can be attracted to the service with promises of expert advice on search strategies or database selection.

Promotion and advertising campaigns should have a stated goal that keeps the program unified and on track. If the goal is to increase usage of the service the promotional materials must be designed with an eye toward that goal. Unfortunately, most of the brochures and handouts used in libraries today merely describe the service and do not explain to potential customers how they will benefit from the service; therefore the brochure has the effect of "preaching to the choir," in that it tells people already knowledgeable about computerized searching that it is available and nothing more. Finally, it should be the goal of the campaign to avoid false advertising. Everything promised in the brochures and other materials must be available as advertised. If the goal of the publicity campaign is to increase demand, the manager must be sure the facilities are in place to meet the demand, otherwise poor public relations will result.

There are several methods a publicity campaign can use (Cochrane, 1983). The printed brochures and handouts with a unifying logo or type style have been mentioned several times. It is important that these be free from jargon, and they should have a "quality" look to them, as much as the budget will allow. Printed materials and exhibits should be displayed in an area used by a large public and not just in the office or locale of the automated information retrieval service where, once again, they will merely preach to the choir. Other printed media include regularly published newsletters such as the library's newsletter or a campus newspaper; in these media it is important to repeat the message frequently to insure that new readers are exposed.

Nonprint media—audio-visual campaigns—present a special problem. They are particularly expensive to produce and distribute and update, especially if professional talent is employed, and if library staff attempt to produce a video or slide-tape without professional help the product is most often amateurish with an unsophisticated "homemade" look that is either laughable or irritating to a public accustomed to slick music videos and million-dollar-an-episode television programs. There are microcomputer software packages for animation that can produce interesting and sophisticated on-screen demonstrations, but they are expensive, they consume a great deal of staff time to learn and to manipulate, the resulting programs are difficult to update, and if they are displayed in the library they require a microcomputer that probably could be put to better use—as a search station, for example. Computerized searching is a high-tech product, which perhaps could best be advertised through high-tech presentations, but managers will want to look closely at the advertising budget and decide whether an amateurish video is preferable to quality brochures.

In a closed and close-knit community such as an academic library or a special library, word-of-mouth advertising can be the best way to promote automated information retrieval. This assumes that there is a body of satisfied users, so extensive effort must be made to assure that users will have nice things to say about the service they received, since dissatisfaction and complaints will also be spread by word of mouth, probably much faster and more widely than the good things. Search analysts promote word-of-mouth advertising by demonstrating concern for the patrons' information needs and competence in operating the system. The manager promotes word-of-mouth advertising by assuring the smooth and seamless operation of the entire service, from making appointments to delivering the printout. Bad word-of-mouth advertising results from what the patron sees as barriers to using the service, such as inflexible policies regarding scheduling or appointments, poor service from a careless or uninterested search analyst, poor results that have to be paid for, and even poor ambience—a noisy and unattractive setting or an ugly printout on cheap paper with barely legible print. Word-of-mouth advertising can be stimulated by offering free searches for a day or in a particular database. This can be done cheaply if the manager coordinates the offering with the free or reduced cost promotions of vendors. Demonstration searches to key individuals or to meetings and workshops can also stimulate word-of-mouth promotion. A "canned" search—one that has been thought through and tested before being displayed in public—is the safest approach, but the demonstrator will probably be asked to try the audience's latest research topics once the canned search is complete. For this reason, a trained search analyst should perform the demonstration. A large-screen projection system provides a quality demonstration. If the purpose of the demo is to encourage word-of-mouth publicity, it will not be forthcoming if the audience has to hunker around and squint at the small-screen display of a portable microcomputer.

Another form of word-of-mouth advertising is that provided by the library staff. The manager must be sure that any staff member likely to deal with the public knows what is available and how to get service, otherwise potential patrons who have read the advertising material are likely to be turned away by staff who have not read it.

Forms

The amount and type of forms needed depend on several management decisions regarding the operations of the service: whether appointments are required, whether patrons will be billed, whether patrons will evaluate searches, etc. Packets of forms collected from various libraries are available on loan from the MARS (Machine-Assisted Reference Sector) office at the American Library Association headquarters in Chicago. Types of forms are detailed below. It is important to emphasize that forms should be planned as a unified series that shows a logical progression from start to finish, and that they should record the kind of information needed for the record-keeping and reporting functions the manager plans to undertake. Forms intended for distribution to the public should have the distinguishing "mark" the service has adopted, either a logo or type style as discussed above. The types of forms are:

SEARCH REQUEST FORM: a form filled out by the patron requesting a search (see Illustration 1). At a minimum it should include the patron's name and affiliation such as an academic department, the date and time of the appointment, an indication (name or initials) of the search analyst, and a brief statement of the search topic. It may also include the method of payment, if a fee is charged. A more detailed search request form can include space for the patron to write out the search topic, a paragraph describing the research question and expected results, a list of keywords, a statement of limitations such as dates or dollar amounts or number of citations needed, and a statement of where the patron has found information on the topic already. Requiring the patron to prepare in advance by writing out the search topic can be invaluable in organizing the patron's thoughts and helping the search analyst understand what the patron wants from the search (Daniels, 1978). Everyone who has worked at a reference desk has had the experience of helping a patron who cannot articulate what he or she wants and winds up asking for something else that is close to the subject but not precisely what is needed; as a result, the librarian spends time answering the wrong question. In a computerized literature search the librarian can spend money as well as time. If patrons are not present during the search, the written-out search topic is a necessity, and the patron may need assistance and directions from a search analyst while filling out the form.

SCHEDULING SHEET: For mediated searches, this indicates the day, time, search analyst, and patron. For end-user searches, day, time and patron are needed.

SEARCH STRATEGY WORKSHEET: To be filled out by the person who performs the search, either a search analyst or an end-user. End-user forms should be more detailed, perhaps with examples and instructions appended. The form should provide space for concept groups, logical operators, any limits placed on the search such as date or language, and the databases used.

SEARCH LOG: This records for each search the date, time, databases used, online time per database, and citations printed per database (see Illustration 2). This is the minimum needed for checking invoices to verify charges. The log may also include information from the Search Request Form such as patron name and affiliation, searcher, and brief topic to provide a more detailed log of searching activities. If the log is used primarily for checking

Illustration 1
Search Request Form

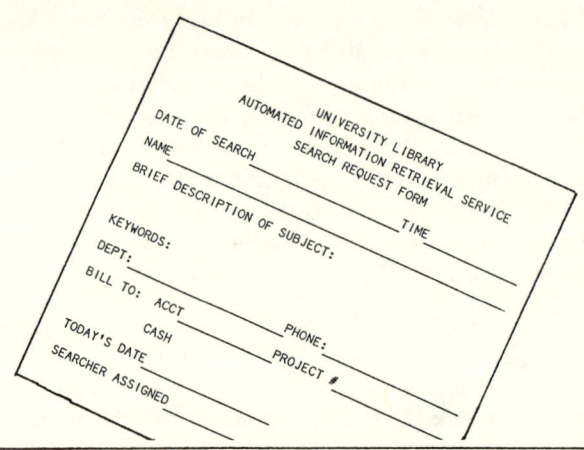

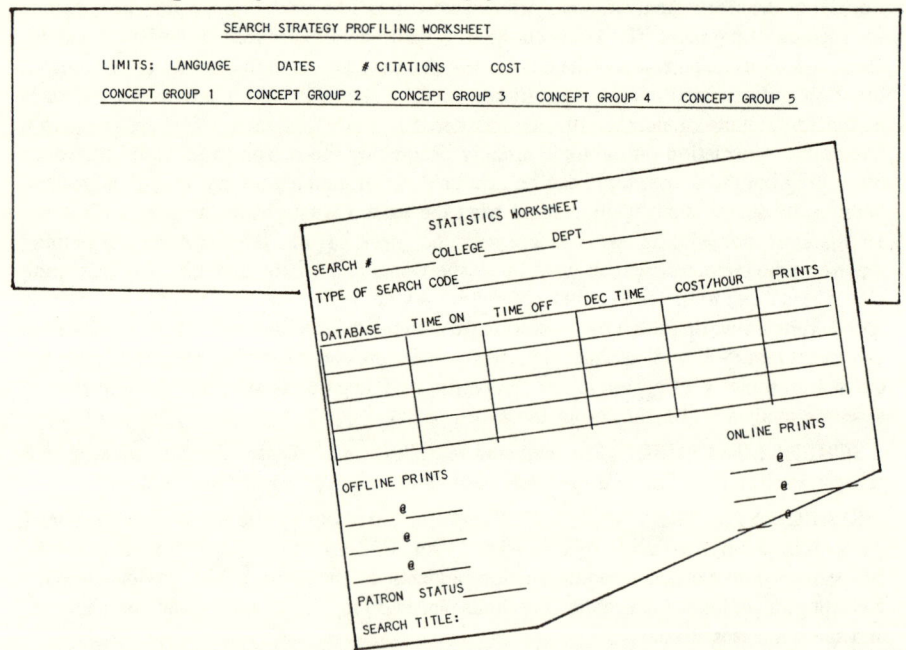

A folded legal size sheet provides the search request form on the front, the search analyst's worksheet on the inside, and a data collection form on the back that is filled in by the search analyst. The form is filed with other paperwork in a patron file.

**Illustration 2
Search Log**

DATE	SEARCH #	SEARCH TYPE	PATRON NAME
910115	1	free	carter, d
	2	for fee	black, i
910116	3	free	park, p
	4	demo	
910117	5	for fee	doe, j
	6	demo	
	7	free	cook, k
910122	8	free	walker, m
910125	9	for fee	yu, h
910128	10	for fee	lewis, d
910130	11	free	davis, j
	12	free	west, k
910131	13	for fee	parker, w
910205	14	free	cheng, x
	15	free	noble, h
910211	16	free	brown, w
910212	17	free	clark, s

A search log produced by the Database Management System records to provide a cross-index. The search number can be used to retrieve completed forms from the DBMS database; the patron name links searches to a paper-copy record in a filing cabinet. Different logs can be printed for checking against invoices.

invoices, the manager may prefer to have separate logs for each vendor and even separate logs for each password. Ready-reference searches need only a brief search log since search request forms and appointment sheets are irrelevant to the ready-reference routine, and busy reference staff should not be bothered with shuffling many pieces of paper (see Illustration 3). Invoice checking is greatly simplified if there is a separate password set aside for ready-reference searching.

CHARGE FORM/INVOICE: This should be a multipart form to provide a receipt for the patron and records for the business office and the search service.

EVALUATION FORM: Evaluating the individual searches and the service as a whole are dealt with in more detail in a later section of this chapter. Here it is important to emphasize that the evaluation form is the final step in this integrated series of forms and must be linked to the preceding forms by a search number or other identifying indicator.

It is possible to combine forms to cut down the individual pieces of paper that need to be filed or otherwise handled. For example, the search request form and search worksheet can be on the front and back of a single sheet of paper; space on the same sheet can be reserved for the information that makes up the search log and is transferred to the official search log later at a more convenient time

Illustration 3
Ready-Reference Log

VENDOR: _____

DATE	SEARCHER INITIALS	FILE NAME OR #	TIME ON	TIME OFF	CONNECT TIME	CITATIONS PRINTED
			: :	: :		
			: :	: :		
			: :	: :		
			: :	: :		
			: :	: :		
			: :	: :		

Certain searches such as ready-reference, demos, training and practice searches need not be recorded in great detail. This type of log sheet filled in by the searcher can be used instead of the more detailed search request form. To facilitate invoice checking, a separate sheet should be maintained for each vendor or system.

after the appointment is completed. An end-user scheduling sheet can be devised that can become the search log as appointment are completed. All the paperwork that relates to one search should be tied together by an identifier—a search number (Futas, 1984; McKinney, 1983).

Record-Keeping

A good record-keeping system allows the data gathered to be viewed in a variety of ways, to be shuffled and reshuffled depending on the analysis needed. A manager can manually go through the search logs to find out how many times a particular database was searched, and then flip through the logs again to determine an average number of citations printed per search or the average price of a search, but the best way to manipulate the data is to computerize it. Computers can store, sort, and do mathematical functions much more efficiently than humans (Fujitani and Williams, 1990; Kwan and Raeder, 1988; Speer, 1987; Titus, 1987). A database management system (DBMS) is the answer. It is preferable to choose a commercial software package rather than attempt to program a system especially designed for the service's records simply because someone else has a chance of understanding and using the commercial system if something happens to the person who programmed it. Commercially available software such as dBase or PFS Professional File are easy to use, widely available, flexible enough to meet the record-keeping and reporting needs of the service, and are designed to provide the shuffling and reshuffling needed to manipulate the data.

The database should be stored on the hard disk of an office microcomputer. The hard disk provides the storage space and speed of access needed for a large accumulation of data, and an office microcomputer is more readily available than a mainframe managed by the parent organization. Data should be entered every day, possibly as soon as it is created, and the manager should be able to access the data on demand. All these requirements point to the advantages of a microcomputer with a hard disk and commercially available DBMS software.

The task of collecting data should be simple, and transferring the data to the computerized DBMS system should be simple enough for clerical staff to perform routinely without supervision. Search analysts should not spend a lot of time collecting and manipulating records and statistics (see Illustration 4). Data that is difficult to collect or record may not get recorded by a busy search analyst. Clerical staff should not spend a lot of time figuring out how to enter data in the database, because it becomes too easy to enter mistakes. It is the manager's job to make data collection simple and straightforward, even if this means a few extra steps for the manager when manipulating the data to produce reports or statistics. Coding data can simplify its collection by reducing the number of characters that have to be recorded—BIOL substitutes for Biology Department, for example. However, coding can complicate matters if there are a lot of codes to remember and if they are applied haphazardly. There should be a comprehensive list of all codes used, and the manager must diligently enforce their use by anyone collecting or entering data. DBMS software cannot make allowances for improperly coded data.

The forms used by the service and the record-keeping database should be designed in conjunction with each other to facilitate the transfer of data from the forms to the database. Also, the manager should decide what pieces of data must be retrieved and what kinds of reports are needed before designing the database, since searchable fields must be identified to the DBMS software. It is important to investigate all the capabilities of the software: report-printing functions can be used to print the bill that is handed to the patron, data can be transferred to a graphics software package to produce pie charts or bar graphs, or the data can be uploaded to a spreadsheet package for planning purposes. Careful planning of the record-keeping database can mean much less manual handling of data on the part of the manager.

The database becomes a "filing cabinet" containing the raw data detailing searching activity. It is critical to make a back-up copy of the database at regular intervals; for example, a month's worth of data can be downloaded to a floppy disk at the end of each month. At the end of the fiscal year or calendar year, the entire database can be transferred to floppy disks or tape and a new file started. The paper forms should be filed as well. A logical method is to file the search request form and any other pieces of paper relating to that search alphabetically by the patron's name. It is a good idea to keep the paper copy of the actual search in this file as well, since it may be necessary at a later date to refer back to the search if the patron requests an update or wants to try the search again from a

Illustration 4
Automated Statistics and Records

```
DATE: 910117    SEARCH #: 5        SEARCH TYPE: for fee
DB LABELS: 5  51  44  112
NUMBER OF DBS USED:  4
```

DB	TIME ON	TIME OFF	DEC TIME	COST/HR		PRINTS
5	12:45:21		.159	100.00	15.90	39
51			.027	112.00	3.024	0
44			.019	106.00	2.014	31
112		12:58:39	.009	51.00	0.459	10

```
TOTAL PRINTS: 80
    OFFLINE PRINTS                              ONLINE PRINTS
        39 @  .68   = 26.52                         @        =
        31 @  .90   = 27.90                         @        =
        10 @  .15   =  1.50                         @        =
           @        =                                @        =
TOTAL DEC TIME: 0.214
TOTAL CONNECT COST: 21.397
TOTAL PRINTING COST: 55.92
TOTAL COST: 77.317
    PATRON NAME: doe, john
    STATUS: non-u      COLLEGE: 12          DEPT: non-u
    SUBJECT: Cryopreservation of fish
    SEARCHER: tr
```

DBMS software provides records, statistics, and billing from one form. In this example, the small type represents input by a clerk taking the information from a worksheet filled out by the search analyst. All calculations of connect costs and printing costs are performed by the DBMS software.

slightly different angle. If space in the filing cabinets allows, the paper copies of forms and searches should be kept for two years. The search log sheet ties the database file and the paper file together. If a disaster occurs and an errant keystroke erases some of the database, the database can be reconstructed by pulling the forms from the paper file and rekeying the data. This explains why the search log sheet should be updated daily and a back-up copy of the database should be made frequently.

The database, the paper forms arranged by patron name, the search logs, and the invoice files provide a record of the year's searching activity and would certainly seem to be adequate for any reporting purposes. However, there are some activities that are not recorded because they do not refer to a specific search, such as the addition of a new search analyst to the staff, the purchase of a new CD-ROM database, or the receipt of special funding that allows searching without charge to the user. These items will certainly affect statistics but are not themselves recorded as a statistic. Therefore, the manager should keep a calendar that records special events such as training sessions, demos, and new services added, to keep the staff informed and also to refresh the manager's memory at annual report time.

Statistics

Statistical reports assure the administration that the automated information retrieval service is performing as planned and also provide the data needed for future planning. Managers should try to anticipate the kinds of information the administration is likely to ask for and should be flexible enough to provide new types of data that were never requested before but are needed now. Obviously a record-keeping system set up on DBMS software and a thorough knowledge of how to manipulate the DBMS will answer most of the unanticipated questions, if (and *only* if) the data was recorded in the first place. There is a delicate balance between recording enough data to answer all the questions and recording too much unnecessary data that wastes time and storage space.

Typical statistical reports reduce a large volume of data to numbers or graphic representations of numbers (see Illustration 5). Not all services will need to record and analyze every countable activity, but the list below represents the kind of data included in typical annual reports or usually requested in questionnaires and surveys:

NUMBER OF SEARCHES: Before this statistic can be recorded the manager must define what constitutes a search (Hawkins and Brown, 1980). Is it any access to a single database? Is it the activity required to answer a patron's request, regardless of the number of databases searched? Most services have adopted the latter definition for statistical purposes. A problem may arise when two entirely different questions are asked by the same patron, both of which are answered in the same search session. Is an SDI run every month counted as one search or as twelve? How is a search interrupted by a power failure or a telephone glitch recorded? The issue of what constitutes a search should be addressed in the policy and procedures manual, and the manager should frequently remind the search analysts of the prevailing definition.

NUMBER OF DATABASES: Again, consistent definitions of what constitutes a database must be determined. A database such as CA Search that is fragmented into "packages" based on the span of years covered can be counted as one database or as several databases. Does one count searches of PSYCINFO in DIALOG, PSYCINFO in BRS, and PSYCLIT on CD-ROM as three different databases or as three searches in one database?

ONLINE SERVICE: Which online service or vendor was used and for how long is a piece of data frequently requested on questionnaires. This statistic can also be used as justification for dropping or adding a service. This can be recorded as the number of times the service is accessed or as the amount of time the service was used, in hours and minutes. If the latter figure is used it can be collected from vendor invoices and need not be yet another number collected and manipulated during record-keeping activities.

TIME: Usually seen as time online, the manager must determine if it is to be rounded off and if it is to be recorded in hours and minutes or as decimal time recorded in thousandths of an hour. It is far easier for both humans and computers to add decimal time. Time

**Illustration 5
Sample Statistics**

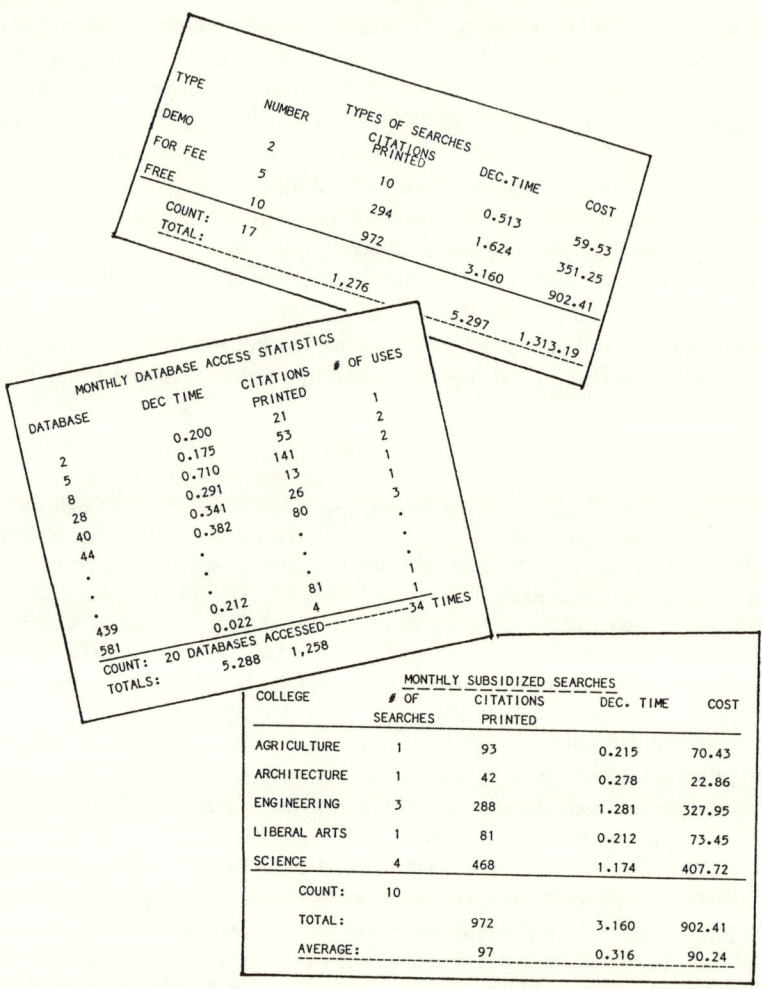

The DBMS software can be used to sort the data and provide totals and averages for various reports as in these examples. Data can be transferred to a graphics software package and presented as pie charts or bar graphs as well.

can also include the preparation time spent before going online to interview the patron and profile the search, and the time spent after the search, reviewing the printout or recording the search statistics. If these times are recorded they should be kept separate from online time, especially if online time from the search log is compared to invoices for checking purposes.

CITATIONS: These should be broken out by database. Managers may want to distinguish between online and offline citations, and the form of the citation such as browsing format, citation only, or citation plus abstract. Full-text databases may require counting by number of pages, and end-users certainly prefer to count the number of pages rather than the number of citations. The two types of counting cannot be mixed in a DBMS package; if both methods are used there should be separate fields for recording the number of citations and the number of pages.

SEARCH PURPOSE: This distinguishes ready-reference searches, demos, SDIs, mediated searches, practice time, and "housekeeping" functions such as reading the online news or updating price lists, etc.

REQUESTER DEMOGRAPHICS: Academic libraries especially need to know the status of the requester, such as undergraduate, graduate student, faculty, or staff, and the department affiliation. This data can be put to good use in determining the target audience for promotion and advertising activities.

COST: Some online services provide an estimated session cost at logoff, or a price list generated by the library may determine the cost, or the cost can be the invoiced cost. It may be important to break out online costs from printing costs. The policy and procedures manual should specify how costs are determined.

PAYMENT: If only partial costs are recovered, the payment will not be the same as the cost discussed above. A manager may also want to record the mode of payment, such as cash, interdepartmental transfer, or a charge to an account number.

SEARCHER: Recording the initials of the search analyst can generate some delightful and surprising statistics, such as who performs the fastest searches, the most expensive searches, or the most fruitful searches in terms of citations retrieved. Managers may use this field as a way to track where searches are performed if searching is taking place in branch libraries or at different service desks.

DATE/TIME OF DAY: These figures are useful for sorting data but may not actually be analyzed themselves unless the manager is looking at the effect of holidays and vacations on searching activity. They should be recorded for the search log since they are critical for matching and checking vendors' invoices.

SEARCH NUMBER: This is a unique number assigned to each search as defined above. Although it may not be analyzed itself, it provides a key for sorting and analyzing the other data and is the identifying item for keeping track of all the data and paper relating to one search.

Some search services will find other items that need tracking, such as the password, the telephone network used, or possibly a brief subject statement, and some services may decide that it is not necessary to record all information for all searches. The manager should devise a form and a record-keeping system that is flexible enough to allow for variables, especially if searching is performed in branch libraries or if different policies apply to different searches. For example, if a branch library uses only one vendor it would be a waste of time to require the branch to record the online vendor on each form. If all ready-reference searches are subsidized from the library budget it is not necessary to record the method of payment. It will probably be necessary to devise different record-keeping forms for mediated searches and end-user searches.

Online searches, whether mediated or end-user, leave a paper trail in the form of invoices from vendors that need to be checked and that can themselves be used as a source of statistical information. Optical disk searches are different. A large CD-ROM installation that serves a hundred or more users a day will be hard pressed to gather comprehensive statistics on each and every search, the users will resent the infringement on their time, and if it is important to keep users moving so that a search station is available for the next user, collecting statistics may be impossible. A CD-ROM installation that is located in a room with a discrete entrance can install an electronic counting device or a gate that provides at least a count of people coming and going. Some CD-ROM vendors are developing software that can be installed with the searching software and can keep track of usage (Alley, 1989), or a local programmer can develop such a program. Most LAN packages designed for use with CD-ROMs have statistical software built in. These cannot provide accurate counts of users in busy installations where one user follows immediately on the heels of another since they depend on a "time-out" feature or a system restart to distinguish one search from another. Another option is to make an intensive effort to gather comprehensive statistics only at intervals—for one busy week each semester, for example—and use them to provide an average for the year. This has the advantage of providing a fairly accurate count for a certain period without bothering the users or the staff unduly by requiring them to count and report each transaction for longer than a week at a time, but care must be taken to select representative times of the year for gathering the statistics.

Statistical data should be gathered, coded, and entered into the record-keeping system on a daily basis. Search analysts should be encouraged to complete the paperwork immediately after each search is performed rather than allowing their memories to grow so cold that it is impossible to reconstruct the details of the search or allowing the different pieces of paper relating to the search to get lost. Papers should be filed and data entered into the database daily and backed up daily, if only to prevent a disastrous loss of data should a power outage or power surge erase it from the computer's memory. And finally, the manager should check the data and manipulate it at regular intervals, preferably monthly at least. It is easy for a search analyst or a clerk entering the data to get into the habit of miscoding or making the same mistake over and over again, and if the data is not checked at frequent intervals the mistakes pile up. The manager should not have a lot of cleaning up and recoding to do at the end of the year when the annual report is due. Monthly reports may not be required by the library administration, but they help the service manager keep track of business, detect trends, keep the budget in control, and also detect any possible theft of service. Monthly reports make the compilation of an annual report much less time-consuming, and they allow for continuous evaluation of the service.

EVALUATION

Monitoring the automated information retrieval service—collecting the data and statistics—is the first and easiest step in evaluating the service. Evaluation is the process of analyzing the data collected to see if the goals of the service have been met, and to aid decisions regarding the management of the service to better meet the goals in the future. It sometimes seems that collecting the statistics is an end in itself, and it is certainly possible to spend hours and days collecting the statistics and arranging them into neat charts and graphs, but the time was wasted if they are not used to evaluate the service.

Just as gathering statistics can be a waste of time if they are not put to use, so can evaluation be a waste of time if it is not applied in a program designed to modify the service. It is useful to state clearly the goals of the evaluation process: why is evaluation being undertaken, what can be measured, and how will the results be applied? Such a statement of goals makes it easier for the manager to devise the forms and procedures for collecting and applying evaluation data. The policy and procedures manual should be examined with an eye toward measurable objectives such as performance standards, cost recovery goals, and clientele served. Methods can then be devised to measure attainment of these objectives, and procedures can be devised to modify any aspect of the service that does not measure up to the goals (Lancaster, 1972 and 1988; Penniman and Dominick, 1980).

Most services have a form that asks the patron of a mediated search to evaluate the search and perhaps the search analyst (Blood, 1981 and 1983). The form usually asks the patron to evaluate the following:

RECALL RATIO: the extent to which pertinent items were retrieved by the search. Unfortunately, most patrons have no way of knowing this figure and it is difficult and time-consuming for librarians to determine. The question asks, "Out of the total body of literature on this topic, what percentage was retrieved by the search?" In other words, if there are one hundred items pertinent to the topic and seventy-five were retrieved, the recall ratio is 75 percent. On evaluation forms the question is usually phrased something like this: "Are there pertinent items you already know about that were not retrieved by the search? If so, how many?" If the answer is "yes," it may simply mean that the items in question were not covered by the databases or the years searched, and therefore may be misleading; if the answer is "no," it may mean that the patron is bored with the questionnaire and cannot be bothered to count or otherwise assess the previously known items. Patrons are not the best judge of recall ratio. Librarians can get an estimate of recall ratio by performing parallel searches, either manual searches in the equivalent printed index if any, or by a second search analyst performing the same search independently. Obviously, this can get expensive in staff time and online fees, and it does require the patron to evaluate the second search to determine which items in it are pertinent. Furthermore, any two intermediaries will produce different results, sometimes *quite* different results, due to various searching styles and skill levels and the different interpretations each applies to the search question. Typically two search analysts working independently on the same question will duplicate only 40–50 percent of the items in the sets of resulting citations. It is an interesting exercise but it should not be undertaken for every search, due to the time and expense involved.

PRECISION RATIO: This question asks, "Of the items retrieved, what percentage are pertinent (relevant) to your topic?" The patron is the best judge of precision ratio, which gives an indication of how discriminating the search has been. Precision ratio is an especially important measure to patrons who are paying for the search, which leads to the next measure of evaluation.

COST PER PERTINENT ITEM: In a search costing $50 and retrieving one hundred items, ninety of which are pertinent, the cost per pertinent item is $.55. However, if in the same search only nine of the items are pertinent, each one costs $5.50. The point of the question is to determine if the search was worth the money the patron paid for it, and most questionnaires ask the same question in more general terms rather than requiring the patron to figure cost per item. It is instructive for search analysts to make this calculation on occasion, because it clearly shows that the better the search in terms of recall and precision, the lower the cost per pertinent item will be.

Recall ratio, precision ratio, and cost per pertinent item are the measurable evaluation points in a search, and of these only precision ratio is a question patrons can and should be expected to answer. Any other question on an evaluation form asks for a subjective judgment from the patron and is intended to form a broad picture of the patron's satisfaction—not necessarily with the particular search, but with the service. Other questions included on typical evaluation forms are listed below:

PATRON DEMOGRAPHICS: If this information was collected on the search request form or at the time the appointment was made, it should not be required on the evaluation form.

PURPOSE OF THE SEARCH: This information most certainly should have been gathered during the search interview process, but it may not have been recorded by the search analyst. The point of the question is to determine the patron's expectations: the user wants a comprehensive search, or the user wants to prove that nothing has been published on the subject, or the user wants a "jump start" and will be satisfied with a few pertinent items, or the user is trying to track down one or two known items. Obviously the patron's expectations impinge on the responses to other questions on the evaluation form. If the user is trying to prove that nothing has been written on the subject, the user hopes to find nothing and is willing to pay for nothing, therefore recall ratio and precision ratio are unmeasurable and cost per pertinent item is irrelevant.

NEW/UNKNOWN ITEMS: The user is asked what percentage of the pertinent items were already known to him or her, or what percentage were unknown. If the purpose of the search is to find information, patrons will be more pleased with a search that produces unknown items and therefore are likely to evaluate the overall search more highly when unknown items are found. On the other hand, the same patron requesting a comprehensive search may have already put a considerable amount of time into the research process and thus will retrieve a large number of known items, which may or may not cause the patron to be disappointed with the overall search. This is a tricky question to analyze since it depends so much on the expectations of the patron.

TIMELINESS: This can refer to the results of the search—the citations or other documents retrieved—in which case the question evaluates the database rather than the service received from the search analyst. It can refer to turnaround time for making appointments or for delivering printouts. If a patron wants immediate results but is only willing to pay for offline prints, a negative response to this question must be taken with a grain of salt.

SEARCH ANALYST: There is considerable debate on whether or not the patron should be asked to evaluate the search analyst. Some feel that users lack the expertise to evaluate the expertise of the search analyst, who can only be legitimately evaluated by his or her peers and supervisors. Others feel that general questions on the attitude and helpfulness of the search analyst are appropriate (Glunz and Wakiji, 1983).

REPEAT USER: There are two ways to ask this question: "Have you used this service before?" or "Will you use this service again?" The intention is to discover if the user finds, or has found, the experience valuable enough to repeat.

OVERALL SATISFACTION LEVEL: Some evaluation forms include this question as a check to previous responses, usually asking the patron to rate the service on a scale of one to ten and soliciting any comments the patron cares to make. The question itself can be worded, "How useful were the results of this search to you?"

An evaluation form, to be useful, must be completed by the patron, so it is imperative to make it as easy to fill out and return as possible. It should not have a daunting appearance that makes the recipient groan at the thought of completing it; this means it should not be long or have tiny print or be worded in such a way that the user has to read each question twice to be sure it is understood. Jargon should be avoided. The patron should not be asked to repeat information already collected such as name, affiliation, topic of search, etc. This information can be lifted from the search request form and typed on the evaluation form by clerical staff. Alternatively, the only identifying feature on the evaluation form can be the search number that links the form to the patron's file; this has the further advantage of adding an appearance of anonymity which may encourage frank responses from the patron. The purpose of the evaluation form should be stated in such a way that the patron feels he or she is contributing to the improvement of the service, and the patron should be assured responses and comments are strictly confidential. The easiest forms to complete are those that require the user to check yes or no or a multiple-choice list of options, or to circle a number or a percentage on a scale or range of choices. Comments can be invited after each question or requested as a general comment at the end of the form. Usually the most revealing information from an evaluation form comes in the comments users add, so the form should encourage comments by providing space for them and by assuring patrons that their comments are welcome and will be heeded.

Evaluation forms are handed to the patron with the search results; this means that the patron does not have to complete the form in order to satisfy his or her information need, and in fact many evaluation forms are tossed in the trash. The manager of the service will have to decide what rate of return is acceptable and how much follow-up to pursue in order to achieve that rate of return. The search analyst or manager can meet with the patron when the printout is picked up to discuss and retrieve the evaluation form at that time, if either one is available when the patron comes in. If prints were produced online the search analyst can ask the patron to complete the form immediately before the printout is delivered. Neither one of these methods allows the patron sufficient time to evaluate the results and figure the percentages required. Return of the forms can be encouraged by providing a self-addressed envelope at the least and return postage if the budget allows, and if the form is not returned within a certain period the manager can follow up by telephone, either soliciting return of the form or asking the evaluation questions over the phone. The detailed evaluation form described so far is not appropriate in some cases such as ready-reference searches, citation verification, known-item retrieval, and those searches intended to prove that nothing has been published on a topic. These searches either produce the desired results or they do not, and no numerical analysis can be applied to them; therefore these patrons should not be bothered with an evaluation form.

The evaluation form should be modified considerably for end-users, who are even less inclined to fill out detailed forms (Kleiner, 1987; Reese, 1988). A very busy service with a large number of users will probably want to sample selectively rather than try to get evaluations from all users. The form should be very short and require little more than check marks or brief responses, although space should be allowed for comments, which can be very gratifying and complimentary from end-users. Examples of evaluative information to gather from end-users include:

— Demographic information
— Reason for seeking information (term paper, speech, research, etc.)
— Number of citations/pages printed
— Sufficiency of retrieved information
— Assistance needed. Why? What sort?
— Time to complete the search
— Repeat user
— Overall satisfaction

The evaluation forms filled out by patrons have several shortcomings. They cannot be gathered for every search performed, the information they provide is difficult to interpret since it is impossible to get inside the head of the patron to understand why questions were answered in a particular way, they may evaluate the structure and function of the database rather than the search, and they exist in a vacuum—no other service or reference transaction is consistently evaluated in the same way. If patrons were required to fill out an evaluation form every time they received help from the service desk, there would be some context for comparing and ranking the product and service provided by automated information retrieval. There would also be some very irritated patrons driven mad by the number of forms thrust upon them. As it is, the form evaluates one search at a time, and only the individual search. The data collected from the evaluation forms should be used to identify inadequate searching and dissatisfied users and should be applied in a program of modifications designed to improve the service. This has value, but it is not enough. The service, as well as the searches, must be evaluated.

If the service has clearly stated goals, the statistics that have been gathered over the year can be used to determine if the goals have been achieved. Even without numeric goals, statistics can show the service's achievements and shortcomings. Statistics can point out nonusers of the service. If, for example, the statistics show that undergraduates seldom use online services, the manager may decide to increase promotion and advertising aimed at undergraduates or may try to find alternatives that undergraduates will use, such as CD-ROM. If a particular department was a major user in previous years but usage has decreased recently, the manager should try to find out why. Heavily used online databases are candidates for replacement by CD-ROM or locally loaded databases, and the statistics collected detailing use and costs provide justification for funding their purchase and management. Statistics can also justify the service's staffing and budget demands to upper management, or they can show where cutbacks can be implemented without damaging the level of service provided, or they can demonstrate the economy of replacing print tools with computerized access (Roose, 1985).

It is especially important for those services that charge for use to evaluate the quality of the product provided. Even a service involved in only partial or nominal cost recovery must meet the demands of the users who expect a product worth paying for. The characteristics of a quality product, such as accuracy and an absence of casual errors, timeliness, and appearance, are standards by which to judge the product delivered to the consumer, and the environmental factors such as quality equipment, procedures that work consistently, and trained staff can be evaluated based on whether they reliably turn out a quality product. In fact, a service that does not charge could benefit by applying some of the same quality control standards that fee-based services must use (Brill, 1981; Lunden, 1987).

The purpose of evaluation is to diagnose failures and to discover the modifications that need to be made in order to correct the failures. Evaluation is expensive in terms of both time and money, and it can be bothersome to the patrons; therefore it probably is not worth doing unless that final step—modifying the service—is incorporated into the evaluation process. A service with clearly stated goals is easier to evaluate, so one of the modifications a manager might make immediately is to identify some achievable goals and objectives such as:

— Recover X percent of operating costs
— Increase usage by ABC department
— Add X number of searching stations
— Send search analysts to ABC training sessions

Evaluation should cover far more than the evaluation forms for individual searches. It should also examine the environment and the paperwork involved in the service with the aim of identifying barriers to access and finding ways to eliminate the barriers. It should lead to an annual review of all aspects of the service including the policy and procedures manual. Finally, the manual itself serves as an evaluation tool of the manager to determine how well he or she has implemented the policy and directed the procedures involved in providing a quality service.

REFERENCES

Alley, Brian. "Bean counting on the cutting edge." *Technicalities* 9 (November, 1989): 1. A demand for CD-ROM vendors to install statistical reporting capabilities into the software. Alley states, "The right statistics can make a proposal bullet proof."

Blood, Richard W. "Evaluation of online searches." ERIC document ED227859. 1981. The more detailed (58 pages) precursor of the article below.

Blood, Richard W. "Evaluation of online searches." *RQ* 22 (Spring, 1983): 266-277. A presentation and explanation of the search evaluation form devised and recommended by MARS. Includes a forceful recommendation for establishing goals to be met by the evaluation form before actually devising one.

Brill, Faye. "A business perspective: or, what am I doing in the middle of this debate?" In *User Fees: a Practical Perspective*, edited by Miriam A. Drake. 117-120. Littleton, Colo.: Libraries Unlimited, 1981. A description of fee-based services in two different corporate libraries, one of which considered the library to be part of overhead, and the other a combination of overhead and charge-back.

Butkovich, Nancy J. "Computer maintenance in a medium-sized academic reference department." Poster session presented at the ALA Annual Conference, New Orleans, La. July 11, 1988.

Clark, Juleigh Muirhead and Susan Silverman. "What are students hearing about online searching? A survey of faculty." *RQ* 29 (Winter, 1989): 230-238. Based on the author's survey, the students are hearing misinformation if they hear anything at all.

Cochrane, Maryjane S. "Publicizing an online search service." In *Online Searching, The Basics, Settings, and Management*, edited by Joann H. Lee. 160-165. Littleton, Colo.: Libraries Unlimited, 1983. The emphasis is on publicizing a new service. Details different publicity methods such as handouts, demos, etc.

Daniels, Linda. "A matter of form." *Online* 2 (October 1978): 31-39. Includes examples of search service forms largely from academic libraries. Daniels advocates having patrons write a detailed search request form as the best method of organizing the patron's thoughts.

Edinger, Joyce A. "Marketing library services: strategy for survival." *College and Research Libraries* 41 (July, 1980): 328–332. A discussion of marketing for all library services, including the conditions within the library that must be changed in order to have a "marketing attitude" likely to succeed.

Foreman, Gertrude. "The policy manual for online reference services." In *Online Searching: The Basics, Settings and Management*, edited by Joann H. Lee. 103–106. Littleton, Colo.: Libraries Unlimited. 1983. A general review of why policy statements are needed and what they should include.

Fujitani, Sharon and Brian K. Williams. "Analysis of search statistics." In *National Online Meeting 1990*, edited by Martha G. Williams. 111–118. Medford, N.J.: Learned Information, 1990. The authors applied a spreadsheet program to track database access, number and types of searches, time, costs, and other data over a period of two years. The result is a valuable compilation of figures that can be used for planning.

Futas, Elizabeth. *The Library Forms Illustrated Handbook*. New York: Neal-Schuman, 1984.

Glunz, Diane and Eileen Wakiji. "Maximizing search quality through a program of peer review." *Online* 7 (September, 1983): 100–103. Describes a system of regularly scheduled meetings during which search strategies are critiqued by reviewers assigned from the search analyst staff on a rotating basis.

Hawkins, Donald T. and Carolyn P. Brown. "What is an online search?" *Online* 4 (January, 1980): 12–18. Many of the recommendations in this early paper defining a search for statistical and record-keeping purposes were incorporated in the MARS official definition.

Katz, Bill and Anne Clifford, eds. *Reference and Online Services Handbook: Guidelines, Policies, and Procedures for Libraries*. New York: Neal-Schuman, 1982. A collection of reference service policy statements from academic, public, and special libraries. A very useful browse to remind managers of all the points to cover in a policy statement.

Kershner, Lois M. *Forms for Automated Library Systems: An Illustrated Guide for Selection, Design and Use*. New York: Neal-Schuman, 1988. Acquisitions, circulation, and bibliographic processing forms are included, along with mediated and end-user searching forms. The loose-leaf format invites cut-and-paste photocopying to tailor the sample forms included to a library's particular needs.

Kleiner, Jane P. "InfoTrac: an evaluation of system use and potential in research libraries." *RQ* 27 (Winter, 1987): 252–263. An example of a thorough evaluation of an optical disk database system, in this case InfoTrac. The author concludes that such systems put appropriate or superior research tools in the hands of users.

Kwan, Julie and Aggi Raeder. "Tracking online search statistics in a multibranch library system: a dBase solution." *Database* 11 (December, 1988): 48–56. Discusses the type of data recorded and the mechanics of merging statistics from several branch libraries using a commercially available DBMS package. Also describes the types of reports generated from the statistics.

Lancaster, F. W. "Evaluation and testing of information retrieval systems." In *Encyclopedia of Library and Information Science*, vol. 9. New York: Marcel Dekker, Inc., 1972.

Lancaster, F. W. *If You Want to Evaluate Your Library* . . . . Champaign, Ill.: University of Illinois Graduate School of Library and Information Science, 1988. Chapter 11, entitled "Evaluation of Literature Searching Services," on pp. 127-137, is especially relevant. Lancaster has written several pieces on evaluation of automated information retrieval services. These two are among the most detailed and most recent.

Lunden, Elizabeth. "Quality control in fee-based library services: who cares?" In *User Fees: a Practical Perspective*, edited by Miriam A. Drake. 31-40. Littleton, Colo.: Libraries Unlimited, 1981. Describes a fee-based service in an academic library setting, aimed at users not affiliated with the university. The emphasis is on staff training and staff commitment to produce a quality product.

McKinney, Gayle. "Forms and record keeping for online searching." In *Online Searching: The Basics, Settings and Management*, edited by Joann H. Lee, 107-122. Littleton, Colo.: Libraries Unlimited, 1983. A detailed review of the types of public and internal forms needed. Especially useful for a manual system of record-keeping.

Norman, O. Gene. "Marketing libraries and information services: an annotated guide to the literature." *Reference Services Review* 10 (Spring, 1982): 69-80. A thorough bibliography covering the pros and cons and the techniques of marketing for library services, in the usual *RSR* format. This is dated now, but it covers the large body of literature that blossomed when marketing library services became fashionable.

Parker, M. D. "Password protection: some dos and don'ts." *Database* 8 (December, 1985): 107-110. Provides sound advice and solid examples for password security.

Penniman, W. D. and W. D. Dominick. "Monitoring and evaluation of online information system usage." *Information Processing and Management* 16, no. 1 (1980): 17-35. A survey of state-of-the-art monitoring of information systems, from the system or database producer's viewpoint. The author is affiliated with OCLC. Useful for a review of how professionals monitor human/computer interactions.

Pensyl, Mary E. "The online policy manual: a document that few have, but many can benefit from (especially librarians)." *Online* 6 (May, 1982): 46-49. A plea for the necessity of policy manuals and a thorough discussion of the types of information to be included.

Reese, Carol. "Manual indexes versus computer-aided indexes: comparing the *Readers' Guide to Periodical Literature* to *Infotrac* II." *RQ* 28 (Spring, 1988): 384-389. An example of preliminary evaluation based on a very small sample. The author concludes that users are very satisfied with the results of a computerized search even when, from the librarian's perspective, the search produced unsatisfactory results as compared with a manual search.

Roose, Tina. "Search records for decision making." *Library Journal* 110 (July, 1985): 42-43. From the author's "Public Libraries Online" column. An illustration of how statistics can be put to good use once they have been collected.

Schumacher, Mark. "Images of computer searching: depictions in educational research textbooks." *RQ* 26 (Winter, 1986): 200-205. (Note: the issue is mislabeled as volume 27.) The author examines college-level textbooks and discovers that automated information retrieval is misrepresented in most of them.

Schumacher, Mark. "Instructing the academic search service user: the faculty connection." *Research Strategies* 7 (Winter, 1989): 33-36. Fearing that potential student users of online databases were not receiving good information about online from teaching faculty, the author instituted a series of workshops for faculty to introduce them to the concepts and procedures.

Sherman, Steve. *ABC's of Library Promotion*. 2d ed. Metuchen, N.J.: Scarecrow Press, 1980. A standard reference on library promotion, perhaps of most use to public libraries.

Smith, Patricia K. "Marketing online services, part 1." *Online* 4 (January, 1980a): 60–62.

Smith, Patricia K. "Marketing online services, part 2." *Online* 4 (April, 1980b): 68–69. A two-part article discussing marketing strategy for online products. The author recommends defining online searching as a "specialty good," taps word-of-mouth as the most important publicity technique, and stresses good product design to encourage repeat business.

Speer, Susan C. "Managing online search statistics with dBase III Plus." *Information Technology and Libraries* 6 (September, 1987): 223–226. A practical, how-to article on using a commercially available software package to manage statistics, logs, and billing for an online operation.

Titus, Elizabeth A. "Toward better online reference statistics: getting computers to do the work." In *Dollars and Sense*, edited by Bernard F. Pasqualini. Chicago: American Library Association 1987. A description of one library's use of SPSS and PFS Graph to gather and analyze online searching statistics.

Tuggle, Ann Montgomery and Dawn Hansen Heller. *Grand Schemes and Nitty Gritty Details: Library PR that Works*. Littleton, Colo.: Libraries Unlimited, 1987. The authors examine the publicity campaigns of recent John Cotton Dana Award winners in part one of this text, and in part two offer practical tips for planning and designing effective programs.

Weingand, Darlene E. *Marketing/Planning Library and Information Services*. Littleton, Colo.: Libraries Unlimited, 1987. The marketing philosophies of today's business community transferred to the world of libraries. The author stresses the importance of planning—the selection of a planning team, mission statements, marketing audits, etc.—before beginning a marketing program.

Wood, Douglas. "Improving your image: how to promote a library or information service." *ASLIB Proceedings* 36 (October, 1984): 401–408. Written by the marketing manager of ASLIB, this article stresses the importance of personal contact and depicts some of the promotional methods librarians can use. Especially applicable to a special or company library.

3

Finance and Budget

There is no doubt that computerized literature searching is an expensive operation. A library contemplating initiating a searching service may consider the start-up costs alone to be overwhelming. An existing service faced with growing demands for more access groans at the thought of affording yet another searching station or adding another vendor whose search engine must be learned (Porter, 1987). The machinery is expensive. Online databases charging $100 or $200 an hour seem impossibly expensive, especially when compared to the wages paid for graduate student assistants or secretaries charged with going to the library and "looking a few things up," or when compared to the salaries of professional librarians.

And yet, libraries are finding ways to afford the expense. Ten years ago in the introduction to a collection of readings on user fees, the author complained about the financial plight of libraries, citing the rising costs of books and journals, inflation, and the static condition of library budgets expected to afford a growing range of goods and services (Drake, 1981). A decade has not ameliorated such complaints, and libraries are still trying to find ways to squeeze the last drop of blood from turnip-like budgets. Today the situation is made more difficult by more varied choices of access: mediated searches or end-user searches, CD-ROM or online, locally loaded databases as opposed to any of the above. Ten additional years of exposure to the benefits of computerized searching have increased the demand for more access. There are now library patrons who refuse to use the paper copies of indexes; even if the computer is out of order they prefer to come back at a later time rather than use the paper copies.

This chapter on the monetary aspects of automated information retrieval is divided into two parts: how much does it cost, and how to pay for it. The cost of a service depends very much on the volume of business expected, which affects the number of search stations needed. A service that expects to perform two or three mediated searches a day requires one search station; a service that provides mediated searches, end-user searches, and a dozen or so optical disk databases for a university population of thirty thousand needs far more search stations and preferably a local area network to link them. It is possible to use the same search station for multiple purposes, but scheduling may become a problem. A library that plans a centralized unit needs fewer search stations than one with stations distributed among various service points. The costs based on the different types of service offered are detailed below; the problem managers face is deciding how many multiples and which configurations are needed to make the service work effectively. Of course, another problem is finding the money to pay for the service, as detailed in the second part of the chapter. Sample budgets for an online service, an online end-user service, and a CD-ROM service follow the text, explaining the indirect and direct costs of each.

HOW MUCH DOES IT COST—ONLINE

Before the first search can be performed, furniture, equipment, and supplies must be purchased and staff must be trained. These are the indirect costs of online searching, which can be divided into acquisitions expenses, operating expenses, and overhead.

Indirect Costs—Acquisitions

Acquisitions covers all of the following, each of which is detailed below:

Equipment
   microcomputer/terminal
   modem
   telephone line
   printer
Supplies
   printer paper, ink or ribbon
   office supplies for record-keeping, billing if any
Documentation
   manuals
   thesauri
   subscriptions
   communications software
Contracts with vendors

Equipment. A library at the point of establishing an online service has the opportunity to decide whether to lease or purchase the equipment needed. Leasing has the advantage of providing a maintenance contract to keep the machinery or replacements in working order rather than requiring a member of the library staff to become a hardware expert who is expected to drop everything when the printer stops printing. Local policy at the library or the parent institution may prohibit leasing, however, and the local community may not have a reliable vendor. This is the time to ask if others have obtained good service from leased equipment and maintenance contracts. Leasing is a continuing expenditure and must be budgeted every year. Purchasing the equipment is a one-time expenditure and possibly a massive one as well; however, the machinery must be maintained, and if all of it was bought at the same time it will probably start to break down at the same time. Libraries that purchase equipment should examine local capabilities for repairing it and may want to consider designating a staff member charged with troubleshooting and simple repairs. Out of self-defense, anyone who works with the equipment every day will learn some simple troubleshooting techniques. It is not good public relations to shut down the online or ondisk service for two or three weeks while the computer is out for repairs.

Libraries that already have a microcomputer and printer in the office may incur no more expense than the purchase of a modem to enable the existing equipment to do online searching. If existing equipment can be freed from office duties for a few hours every day to allow it, a plain PC retired in favor of a fancier machine can serve nicely for most online searching.

Documentation. The documentation required for an online operation can be overwhelming. System manuals from each of the vendors must be purchased. The vendors dealing with multiple databases usually have sets of abbreviated instructions for each database—BlueSheets from DIALOG, AidPages from BRS, Quick Guides from ORBIT—and also longer, more detailed "database chapters" for each database. At the least, the abbreviated guides should be purchased and maintained from each of the vendors; a full set of database chapters from the vendor most often used may suffice. Many of the database suppliers write their own documentation explaining how to conduct searches using the search engines of different vendors, and also publish thesauri of controlled vocabulary terms. These supplier-produced manuals should be purchased from those databases that are used frequently or for those databases that are heavily coded and are searched most efficiently by using the codes. The PTS databases are one example of the latter.

Subscriptions to some of the professional journals that specialize in articles about online searching are useful for keeping informed about new databases, changes in old databases, and searching or cost-saving tips. A body of literature concerning cost-saving searching techniques has grown in recent years. Using "hedges" stored in the host computer, comparisons of costs among different vendors, saving search strategies, using off-peak hour services for mediated searches, using the smaller and more specialized databases rather than the huge ones, and substituting CD-ROM databases for online access are among the strategies covered. Such articles most frequently appear in journals largely devoted to searching, such as *Online* and *Database*, and also in the publications from the vendors, all of which should be made available to the searching staff. They can save hundreds of dollars in searching costs over the course of a year. Search analysts should have access to these journals; however, housing them in the searching area is not necessary and would soon consume shelf space better used by manuals and thesauri.

Communications software is required to connect the terminal with a host facility. Options abound, from shareware and freeware to very expensive packages with 300-page manuals and more bells and whistles than the average searcher will ever need. Any of them will work, but software designed for online searching that allows easy manipulation of printing, downloading and uploading, and storage of sign-on protocols and passwords are the best option. DIALOGLINK is an excellent example.

Contracts with Vendors. It is possible to dial in to some public access databases without first negotiating a contract, but the information in them is probably not what is needed. A password is required to access the multiple databases made available through the major vendors, and this means applying for a contract. Management must determine which vendor or vendors carry the databases most likely to be used and then must look at the contract options the vendors offer. It is possible to get a quantity discount from some vendors by paying in advance for a certain level of searching activity. Library networks such as AMIGOS or SOLINET have arranged group contracts with the vendors that combine the searching activity of the several library members of the networks and are able to pass on a functional discount to the members. Off-peak-hour contracts offer fantastic discounts in exchange for the inconvenience of searching only during nonbusiness hours. Some vendors offer academic discounts; a state-supported library may qualify for a government discount. If a library subscribes to the print equivalent of a database, it may qualify for a discount on access to the online database. All these options should be explored to get the cheapest rate for the type of service being offered. Some options require a considerable amount of up-front money; some require no more than a signature (Maloney, 1987, Anderson and Weston, 1987).

Indirect Costs—Operating Expenses

Operating expenses are another form of indirect expenses, consisting of the following:
Personnel
   Coordinator/manager
   Librarian/searcher(s)
   Support staff
Training
   Vendor training
   Database or subject-specific training
   In-house training
   Practice time
   Travel to training sessions, professional meetings
Promotion
   Printing and graphics
   Online demonstrations
   Complimentary searches

Personnel. The coordinator/manager and librarian/searcher may be one and the same person in a small operation, and indeed may be the reference librarian as well. The size of the operation determines the number of professionals. If there is enough searching activity to keep one person employed full-time, certainly there should be more than one person in the operation to allow for vacations, illness and other emergencies, and the sanity of the searcher. If the size of the library staff allows, it is convenient to have several people trained as searchers who specialize in particular subject areas—a business librarian who understands the vocabulary of business and the vagaries of the business databases, a medical searcher, a physical sciences searcher, etc.

The amount of clerical support required depends once again on the size of the operation and the functions performed: are appointments required, are statistics kept, are records filed, are bills issued and collected, are procedural questions about the service answered by the clerical staff or referred to the coordinator/manager?

Training. Training can be a very expensive proposition, possibly as much as $2,000 per librarian, involving travel to the various sessions and workshops constantly being offered in every region of the country, retraining for new databases or system enhancements, and practice time (Breen, 1987). The major vendors provide well-organized and thorough training sessions at frequent intervals in locations throughout the country. As an adjunct to these sessions, many will also provide a certain amount of free online time that the trainee can use in his or her home institution. Many offer both introductory sessions—covering the basics of Boolean logic and the command structure of the vendor's search engine—and advanced sessions covering special features offered by the vendor. Vendor training sessions are well worth the time and expense involved. If the online service deals with more than one vendor it is possible to send searchers to the introductory and advanced sessions of the primary vendor and to the advanced sessions of the other vendors in an effort to economize. In-house training by an experienced searcher on the staff can take the place of the vendor's introductory session to cover the basics of a system. In-house training is an economical method of training librarians who are not primarily searchers but are expected to use online systems to answer reference questions.

Online searching is very much a "use it or lose it" activity, and practice time is essential to keep skills honed. Some vendors have practice databases such as DIALOG's OnTap files; some periodically offer free or reduced cost access to certain files. It may be possible to negotiate for special training passwords such as BRS's Instructor program or DIALOG's Classmate program for in-house training. At other times there is no option but to access a full-cost "live" file in order to try out a search strategy or to see if the data needed is available in the file, and there should be funds budgeted to cover such practice searches. Otherwise, a searcher may simply ignore a file because he or she feels uncomfortable searching it, or a patron may end up paying for a searcher's mistakes caused by inexperience.

Promotion. Demonstrations of online searching promote the service and show potential users exactly what the system can do for them. The same low-cost options mentioned above can be used for demos. Complimentary searches fall into two categories: for demonstration purposes, and to cover horrible mistakes. It does happen; even the most experienced searcher makes mistakes such as typing the wrong file name or number, or ordering the wrong set of prints. Patrons should not be made to pay for mistakes, and searchers should not be so traumatized by the fear of making mistakes that they become timid and unimaginative and slow. Funds should be allocated for this purpose.

A logo for the automated information retrieval service is nice but not a necessity. It can be used on promotional handouts, appointment forms, and bills, if any, and it can be incorporated in signage that delineates the automated information retrieval office or area.

Indirect Costs—Overhead

Overhead costs include facility use and modification, furniture, and utilities.

One searching station requires a desk or other surface to accommodate the terminal, modem and printer, a chair for the searcher, and a chair for the patron. If security for expensive equipment is an issue, a computer workstation cabinet with a locking rolltop may be needed. Documentation needs to be close at hand in a bookcase. A single telephone line is needed for each searching station; if more than one searching station is operating at the same time, a line will be needed for each. A typical office phone with multiple lines that dial into a single instrument—a rotary arrangement—cannot be used for online searching because a modem cannot select a line for dialing out. Enough electrical outlets are needed for all the pieces of equipment to be plugged in—usually three outlets for the terminal-printer-modem configuration. A power strip can be used to supply enough outlets for a single station, but it does seem to be asking for trouble to put more than one station on a single power strip. Surge protection is cheap insurance for expensive equipment. All of this can mean extensive modification and rewiring if multiple search stations are envisioned—for an end-user service, for example—or if search stations are to be scattered among various service points. Local charges vary, but the single telephone lines for each of the online stations can in themselves add up to a considerable and continuing cost that must be accounted for every year.

Direct Costs

Direct costs are those expenses incurred as a result of producing a specific search. Direct costs are highly variable and consist of connect time, telecommunications, citation charges, and labor.

Connect time usually consists of two parts: the amount paid to the vendor, and the amount paid to the database producer. Most vendors do not specify in their documentation what percentage goes to the producer and what percentage to the vendor, but instead list a single rate, expressed as so many dollars per minute or so many dollars per hour. Telecommunications is billed on the vendor's invoice and is also listed as so many dollars per hour. Citation charges are likewise extremely variable depending on which database they come from and which format is printed—a simple citation, or a citation plus abstract, or a full-text document. As for the librarian's time, in a typical mediated search, one-half to two-thirds of the total time is spent interviewing the patron and negotiating the question. In other words, the searcher spends thirty minutes preparing and only fifteen minutes online. Online time is easy to track since most vendors calculate it and display the time when a searcher logs off, but the library that charges for personnel time will need to find a way to discreetly track the total time spent with a patron in a mediated search.

All of these variables make it very difficult to answer the question, "How much does a search cost?" Most vendors provide a fairly accurate estimate of total costs for a search session once the searcher enters the logoff command, but people usually want to know how much a product costs before they commit to buy it. This uncertainty puts online searches in the same category as car repairs or the plumber's bill, in that one can indeed wait in dread until the bottom line is totaled. Furthermore, the estimated session cost can be an embarrassment in those organizations that are billing patrons additional sums to recover some of the overhead and other indirect costs of providing a search service. (See Grimes (1983), Koch (1982), American Library Association (1987), Rouse (1981), and Drinan (1979) for summaries of direct and indirect online searching costs.)

HOW MUCH DOES IT COST—AN END-USER ONLINE SERVICE

An end-user online service incurs the same kinds of indirect and direct costs as the mediated online service, but in different proportions and at different rates. Once again the difficulty is in predicting how much use the service will get, but experience has shown that once the service is established and word gets around, the demand for it will increase.

Indirect Costs—Acquisitions

The equipment for a basic search station—terminal, model, and printer—remains the same, but the printer should be very reliable and very sturdy because all printing of citations will be online; most end-user services do not offer the option of ordering offline prints. It is possible to use the same equipment for end-user searching as is used for mediated searching, provided the equipment is in an area accessible to the public during nonbusiness hours. The volume of searching done by end-users is likely to be much greater than the volume of mediated searching, therefore more search stations may be required. Certainly more paper and ink or ribbons will be needed since all printing is done online.

The documentation needed for an online service is minimal. The system manuals provided by the vendors fit into one large notebook and usually include database-specific instructions similar to DIALOG's BlueSheets and BRS's AidPages. Database-specific manuals and thesauri can be purchased for those databases that are most frequently accessed, but probably they will be ignored by all but the most dedicated end-users. If they have been purchased for the mediated online service they can be made available to those end-users who want them.

The contracts with vendors are simple to negotiate since most were originally designed for individuals with home computers. Academic libraries may be able to negotiate for DIALOG's Classmate passwords, which are available at a lower rate than Knowledge Index passwords. Also, many academic libraries are eligible for CAS Academic contracts, supplying access to STN's Chemical Abstracts at approximately 10 percent of the daytime rate. A deposit account for a CAS Academic contract or for Wilsearch from H. W. Wilson further reduces the cost. If more than one search station is available, multiple passwords/contracts will be necessary so that two or more users can access the same service at the same time. BRS/After Dark charges a monthly minimum of $12 for each password. Front-end software packages allow business-hours access to the regular vendors at regular rates and can be purchased for $300–$400.

Indirect Costs—Operating Expenses

A good-sized end-user service can be operated by classified staff or student assistants. The occasional user who needs professional level help with a difficult search strategy is usually satisfied by instructions to seek help during regular business hours or to ask the librarian on duty at the reference desk. One staff member can comfortably supervise two end-users simultaneously. Taking appointments from end-users, record-keeping, and billing if necessary can consume considerable classified staff time for a large operation.

Most end-users do not want to read the lengthy documentation supplied by the vendors, so library staff time and supplies will be consumed by the production of simplified manuals and handouts designed for end-users. Other training options include computer assisted instruction (CAI) packages either produced in-house, supplied by the vendor, or purchased from some other library operating an end-user service, or librarians can conduct classes for end-users.

Indirect Costs—Overhead

These are the same as for the mediated online service, multiplied by the number of search stations made available to end-users. End-users are notoriously messy; they leave scraps of paper and crumpled printouts behind, so custodial time and costs may be a factor to consider.

Direct Costs

Connect time, telecommunications, and citation charges if any make up the direct costs of end-user searching. All of these are reflected on the monthly invoices received from the vendors; not all vendors provide an accurate search session total at the end of the online session. The charges for most non-business-hours services are based on dollars-per-minute rates or on the number and format of citations printed, just as the regular business-hours services are, but at such a reduced rate that it is surprising how many searches can be done and how many users can be satisfied by a non-business-hours online end-user service. If front-end software is used to access the regular vendors at regular rates, the service may need to limit access to a selected list of databases and certainly should limit each patron's connect time and prints to keep costs relatively predictable. If all direct costs are charged back to the patron such limits may not be necessary, but patrons should be warned of the costs they might incur.

HOW MUCH DOES IT COST—AN ONDISK SERVICE

Several management decisions must be made regarding the number of databases to be purchased, whether individual databases will be mounted on individual search stations, and whether multiple databases and search stations will be networked. Obviously there is a considerable difference in price if the decision is to serve three databases from one search station, or from three search stations.

Indirect Costs—Acquisitions

The minimum equipment needed for a CD-ROM search station is a microcomputer (640K RAM, 20MG hard disk), a CD-ROM drive, and a printer that is fast, reliable, and probably quiet. If end-users use the system, a great deal of paper and other supplies for the printer will be consumed. If end-users are limited in the amount of time they can access the system, some sort of timing device is certainly convenient and may be a necessity if demand for the system is great. An inexpensive kitchen timer is adequate.

An ondisk database differs from online databases in that one actually pays for the database once, either as a monograph (most of the full-text databases such as the *Electronic Encyclopedia*) or as a serial subscription renewable yearly (most of the indexing and abstracting databases such as ERIC or PSYCLIT). The documentation comes with the purchase or subscription, although most libraries will want to rewrite some instructions to be more suitable for end-users. It may be necessary to purchase thesauri; some ondisk vendors offer thesauri as part of the package.

Purchasing an ondisk database can be as simple as ordering a monograph; however, some database producers do require a signature on a contract that specifies the conditions of use, especially regarding networking, downloading, and uploading (transferring the entire contents of the disk to a mainframe computer). Some producers or vendors require prepayment. In some cases the library owns the product only as long as it maintains a subscription to it and must return all copies of the disks when the subscription lapses. Discounts may apply if multiple copies are purchased, or if the library maintains a subscription to the paper copy. This can be a consideration if the library plans to replace the paper copy with an ondisk version.

Indirect Costs—Operating Expenses

Personnel costs depend on the management decisions made regarding the disposition of the searching stations. If the ondisk stations are kept together in a unit it is possible to staff the area with classified staff or student assistants. Quite a large ondisk service can be handled this way. If the search stations are adjacent to a service desk, or scattered among the paper indexes in a reference collection, the staff at the desk can be expected to help users with the ondisk databases on demand, just as they help users with a paper index.

As with an online end-user service, most of the professional staff time will be consumed by writing manuals and handouts. Ondisk systems are supposed to be user-friendly; training can be accomplished with simple written instructions and the same kind of one-on-one, over-the-shoulder instruction librarians are accustomed to providing for print tools. Demonstrations for classes or other groups are useful for showing off the capabilities of the system, but the typical end-user will require one-on-one instruction once he or she approaches the keyboard.

Indirect Costs—Overhead

An installation of multiple search stations in one area may need to be rewired to supply all the outlets needed, and certainly surge protection is a good investment. Some ondisk products (DIALOG OnDisc, WilsonDisc) are configured to allow dial-up to the host online facility to update the data on the disks; therefore telephone lines and modems are needed for these search stations.

Direct Costs

As mentioned above, online connect time and telecommunications charges apply to those ondisk systems that permit dial-up; otherwise the only direct costs applicable to an ondisk operation for end-users are for printing supplies and possibly labor if staff is specifically assigned to supervise an ondisk installation.

PROJECTED COSTS FOR AUTOMATED SEARCHING SERVICES

The Annual Costs of a Mediated Online Service

The following is a list of likely costs to be incurred in setting up and operating a mediated search service for one year:

Microcomputer (640K RAM, 20MG hard disk, PC compatible)	$2,000
Modem (1200/2400 baud)	300
Printer (120/240 cps)	600
Printer supplies (paper, ribbons)	500
Documentation, including system manuals, brief guides, database chapters, selected thesauri	700
Communications software	200
Contract with vendor	500
Training	500
Facilities modification	100
Total Indirect & Start-up Costs	$4,900
Connect costs	$9,500
(625 searches x 15 minutes per search x $60 per hour)	
Telecommunications	1,700
(625 searches x 15 minutes per search x $11 per hour)	
Citation charges	8,000
(625 searches x 50 citations per search x $.25 per citation)	
Total Direct Costs	$19,200

This example illustrates the start-up and operating costs for a modest operation of a mediated search service for one year. It assumes that most overhead costs such as facilities rent, maintenance, and utilities will be absorbed in the library's budget, and it also assumes that furniture is scavenged from other areas of the library. Clerical support and a modest promotional campaign of letters and handouts can be covered by the library's budget as well. However, in this example, it was necessary to purchase the equipment for a search station. The library looked at the possibility of using an existing office microcomputer but felt that scheduling and sharing it with regular office tasks would be too much of an inconvenience for both staff and patrons. Although a 640K RAM, 20MG hard disk machine is not absolutely necessary for online searching, it is the minimum machine necessary for a CD-ROM station, and the library is planning for some future flexibility. Communications software was purchased for the microcomputer, and a new telephone line had to be installed.

The searcher/coordinator is a librarian already on the staff who has some experience with online searching and feels fairly comfortable doing basic, ready-reference type searches but needs advanced vendor training in order to provide competent mediated searches. The training session was held in a nearby city and required an overnight stay. Included in the training costs is $200 for online practice, which the library hopes will also cover searcher errors not charged against a patron's search. The library has a contract with one vendor that was obtained through a library network in order to get a quantity discount on rates. The network requires a $500 deposit for each password; searches will be charged against the deposit until it is depleted, and the deposit must be renewed each year.

Other start-up costs include the system manual for the single vendor and a full set of the brief guides supplied by the vendor for each database. After carefully surveying the databases offered and estimating the types of databases likely to be searched by the local clientele, full database chapters were purchased for only thirty of the databases and the more expensive thesauri were purchased for only ten databases. If usage shows that more are needed they can be purchased from the materials budget. After laying in a supply of paper and ribbons, the initial start-up costs total $4,900.

The search service is planned to be offered during business hours on weekdays only. Since the librarian/searcher has other duties, it is assumed that he or she will be able to handle only two or three searches a day, allowing an hour total to each patron, which would include approximately 15 minutes online and 45 minutes for explanations, question negotiation, and record-keeping. Allowing some 250 days on which searches could be offered and an average of 2.5 searches per day, the library estimates a maximum of 625 searches possible in a year. This assumes that the search service hits the ground running (which it won't) and allows no more than ten days for holidays, vacations, and emergencies such as a sick searcher or a sick machine. The library feels that it is better to plan for the maximum load rather than underestimate.

Looking at the prices of the databases most likely to be searched, the library estimates an average cost of $60 per hour. The local community has Sprintnet and Tymnet nodes, which are currently being billed at $11 per hour. The library estimates that the average search will produce fifty citations that will cost an average of $.25 each. Recognizing that these averages are very variable and based on educated guesswork, the library rounds up each figure to the nearest hundred dollars, once again feeling that it is better to be safe than sorry. Therefore the library estimates that the direct costs for one year of searching total a maximum of $19,200.

The Annual Costs of an End-User Online Service

The following outlines the projected start-up and operating costs for an end-user online service for a year:

Indirect Costs

Search station (micro, modem, printer)	$2,900
Supplies for printing	1,000
Contract (includes documentation)	50
Facility modification	100
Staff	???

Direct Costs

Connect rate total $20,000
   (250 days × 8 searches per day × 25 minutes per search × $24 per hour)

The same type of search station is needed for an end-user service as for an online service; in fact if mediated searches are offered during business hours only, the same station can be used for the end-user service at night and no additional equipment needs to be purchased. Printouts for end-users are all online. End-users tend to print a lot of citations, so they will consume more printing supplies than a mediated service. It is essential to have a reliable and fast printer.

The direct costs are based on Knowledge Index prices, simply because KI charges a flat rate for all the databases provided and does not charge for citations, making it much easier to calculate. The library has decided to make the service available from 6:00 p.m. to 10:00 p.m. Sunday through Thursday nights, and it has set a maximum of twenty-five minutes online per user, allowing a few minutes in between users for signing on, signing off, and record-keeping. Thus, it is likely that a maximum of eight users can be accommodated each evening.

After much debate, the library has decided to use existing staff at the reference desk to serve the end-users, while recognizing that the staff is likely to feel overburdened and harried by the additional responsibilities. However, if more than one search station is made available, additional staff will be required.

The Annual Costs of a CD-ROM Search Service

The start-up and annual operating costs for an end-user CD-ROM service would be as follows:

Indirect Costs

Microcomputer (640K RAM, 20 MG Hard Disk, 386 microprocessor)	$3,000
Printer	400
CD-ROM drive	1,000
Paper and ink cartridges	1,500
Subscriptions	3,000
Total Indirect Costs	$8,900

The library has chosen a slightly different configuration of equipment for its CD-ROM search station, by selecting a 386 machine that searches significantly faster than a less expensive machine, and a ThinkJet printer that is quiet but expensive to operate in that it consumes vast numbers of ink cartridges over a year's use. Acknowledging the fact that end-users print a lot of citations, the library has laid in a large supply of paper. The CD-ROM drive is a "stacked" drive, capable of loading two compact disks for the two CD-ROM databases the library has acquired. Both databases are from a single CD-ROM vendor using the same search engine and will be searched from the same machine. The library has chosen to service the CD-ROM installation from the reference desk and will not add staff at this time; however, the library plans to expand the service considerably in the near future as follows:

9 additional search stations consisting of microcomputer and printer ($3,400 each)	$30,600
13 additional database subscriptions plus network license fees	$20,000
Local area network linking search stations	25,000
Supplies of paper and ink cartridges for 10 stations	15,000
Facilities modification	1,500
Furniture	5,000
Staff	17,000
Total	$117,500

In other words, the library plans to mount fifteen databases and ten searching stations on a local area network, which will be a discrete service unit separated from the reference desk. Careful shopping for quantity discounts can allow purchase of the searching station hardware for less than this per-unit estimate. Considerable modification and rewiring will be required for the new unit, and new furniture for the ten search stations and the many users will be purchased. The library plans to staff the area using librarians and library assistants during business hours and student assistants for evenings and weekends, for a total of ninety hours per week. In addition, a half-time student assistant with microcomputer programming and troubleshooting experience will be hired. As there are no librarians on the staff with the expertise to install a LAN, the library will purchase one of the package deals from a CD-ROM vendor that includes not only the LAN equipment but also a technician to install and troubleshoot the initial operation.

HOW TO PAY FOR IT

As difficult as it is to estimate how much the direct costs of online searching may be, it can be even more difficult to determine how to pay for it, or rather *who* will pay for it. In the example above listing the costs for a mediated online service performing two or three searches a day, the maximum total direct and indirect costs were estimated at approximately $24,000. Where in a typical library budget can an extra $24,000 be found, or even an extra $5,000 to pay for the indirect costs if the library decides to charge back the direct costs to the user? The "fee or free" controversy has been raging for twenty years or more, since online searching was first offered in a publicly supported library. A recent (1986) policy statement from the American Library Association recognizes that many libraries charge fees in order to finance the operating costs of online searching, but goes on to say that such fees are "inherently discriminatory in publicly supported institutions, and may constitute for some individuals a significant barrier to access to the best available or most appropriate information technology" (*Freedom and Equality of Access*, 1986). Nonetheless, surveys of institutions offering online searching indicate that 80 to 90 percent of them charge users for some aspect of the service. (Surveys include Budd (1989), Curley (1986), DeWath (1981), Lynch (1982, 1982b, and 1988), Mowat and Cannel (1986), and Rouse (1981).)

In the early days of online searching it was easy to justify user fees because it was a new and unusual service, and because it was easy to see exactly how much it cost—the bills came in every month. Traditional library services, on the other hand, were more difficult to subject to cost analysis for cost comparison purposes, and publicly supported libraries had never charged patrons for an answer to a reference question or for adding a catalogued book to the collection. Now, many of those traditional library services—acquisitions, cataloging, circulation, online catalogs—are being performed or aided by computers, and a thoughtful library manager must question why patrons are charged for a literature search but are not charged to check out a book through the automated circulation system, especially since the automated circulation system is more expensive to develop and operate than the automated information retrieval service (Budd, 1989). Computerized literature searching is no longer new or unique; the surveys of publicly supported libraries indicate that it is available in the vast majority of them from small public libraries to large academic libraries, and in many of them has been offered for twenty-five years or so. Perhaps now it is time to say that online searching has become a traditional library service and to find ways to incorporate it into the library's budget, thus preserving the established values of the library profession (Govan, 1988). Nonetheless, there are practical arguments in favor of charging fees.

This section looks at the different ways to finance an automated information retrieval service, including charging fees, and provides a summary of the arguments for and against fees, and discusses incorporating the service in the library's budget by reallocating existing resources or existing funds, or by bringing in new money. (Examples of budgets and sources of funding can be found in American Library Association (1987), Drinan (1979), Evans (1983), Fortune (1984), and Matzek and Smith (1982).)

Charging Fees

The most telling argument in favor of charging fees is this: The service could not be offered if some of the costs were not recovered (Breen, 1987). Sometimes it simply is not possible to use library funds because the library's parent body or funding agency cannot be convinced to spend money on anything other than books and periodicals. It can be argued that fees are nothing new even in the "free" public library, since charges are traditionally assessed for photocopies or interlibrary loan—services that are seen as benefiting the individual requesting them rather than the public good. Computerized literature searches also are a "private good" rather than a public good, since one is produced to fit the needs of the individual and really is not relevant to any other user. Of course, any question negotiated between an individual and a librarian at a reference desk can be seen in the same light.

Other arguments in favor of user fees are summarized below:

— Fees force the public to recognize the value of information and the organizations and individuals who work with information.
— Fees discourage casual or trivial use of the service, which otherwise might drive demand beyond the capabilities of the staff and budget to meet it.
— Fees encourage efficient and cost-effective searching by forcing the search analysts to be accountable for their work.
— A fee-based service allows the library to serve individuals or corporations not affiliated with the library or its parent company, which is good public relations for the library (Warner, 1989).
— Fees collected can be plowed back into the service to maintain or improve it.
— Even in a "for-free" system, some patrons will demand such extensive searches that the library cannot absorb the costs and must either charge the patron or deny service.
— If libraries choose not to provide the service because it cannot be done without charging a fee, entrepreneurs will provide it, probably charging more than the libraries would have, and thus will supplant libraries in the information-providing business (White, et al. 1985).

The primary argument against fees centers around the concept of a free library supported by public funds—tax dollars or tuitions—wherein a charge assessed for any service amounts to double taxation. In fact, many databases were developed using public tax dollars, and charging for them is triple taxation (Roose, 1987). This argument goes on to say that charging a fee creates a class of elite information users based on their ability to pay and discriminates against those who cannot afford to pay. Second-class service results when a librarian tells a user, "If you can't pay for a computer search, you can use the paper copy." There is a fear that such a distinction between premium service and second-class service may spread to other areas of the library once a precedent for charging fees has been established (Nielsen, 1987). Other arguments in favor of a free service are:

- Far less record-keeping and paperwork is required, thereby saving staff time and overhead.
- Search analysts are freer to experiment with unfamiliar databases or unusual search arguments when they know they do not have to charge the patron for their experimentation.
- More searches are performed, therefore the proficiency of the searchers is maintained at a higher level.
- Under a for-fee system, totally inappropriate searches may be performed merely because the patron is willing to pay.
- The best a fee-based service can hope for is partial cost recovery. In a publicly supported library, a fee structure designed to create revenue is an "impossible dream" (Dubberly, 1986).

It must be recognized that any fee, even the most trivial one, is seen as a barrier (Meglio, 1987; Chessen, 1984; Roose, 1985). The patrons who have been conditioned to believe that the information in publicly supported libraries is free, the patrons who use online catalogs without paying for access or citations printed, the patrons who ask for assistance at a reference desk and never receive a bill for the service, will likely choose not to use services with fees attached. Libraries that have dropped fees share the common experience of watching demand for automated access leap skyward. It is a widely held belief that charging fees limits access to those users who are able to pay. This is only half of the truth. Charging fees limits access. Period. (For further discussions of the fee or free controversy see Giacoma (1989), Intner and Schement (1987), Kibirige (1983), National Commission for Libraries and Information Science (1985), and Smith (1989).)

Fee Structures

Management has determined that fees must be charged to patrons for use of the service. Once that question has been settled the question of the kind of fee comes up. Is the fee supposed to recover all costs of the search both direct and indirect, or just some of the costs, or is the fee supposed to make a profit for the library? Who decides how much the fee will be, and upon what basis (Jacob, 1988)?

The indirect costs include all acquisition of equipment and supplies, the operating expenses for personnel, training, and promotional material, and the overhead expenses. For a service that has been in operation for a while, obtaining accurate figures for all these expenses is troublesome but possible when it is clear that the costs were incurred only as a result of establishing the search service (Boyce, 1983). Recovering all costs brings with it some additional, hidden expenses, because a good deal of searcher and clerical time will be consumed by record-keeping, billing, and collecting. Special libraries in for-profit companies, the fee-based services in publicly supported libraries, and information brokers have the most experience with accounting for and recovering all costs, and their literature is worth examining for advice on the procedures. A library may want to consider establishing a fee-based service for clientele not affiliated with the library or its parent institution that provides document delivery and reference service in addition to computerized literature searches. Such services provide outreach to and good public relations with the local community and local businesses and do not overburden the library staff if they have been designed to pay for themselves. (For further information on fee-based services, see Brill (1981), *Fee Based Services* (1987), and Warner (1989).)

The most common procedure in publicly-supported libraries is to charge for the direct costs of the search, but even here there are variables. Does the direct cost include the searcher's time? This can add considerably to the cost (Koch, 1982). Is the direct cost the amount billed on the vendor's invoice? If so, is the patron expected to wait a month or so before the cost of the search is known? If the estimated session cost provided by the vendor at logoff is used, some patrons may be charged more or less than the actual billed cost of the search. In the long run these variations will even out for the library paying the bill, but this is no comfort to the individual patron who paid more than the library was actually billed for the search. A library cannot charge a patron for a mistake made by the searcher. Some provision must be made whereby searchers' mistakes can be charged to a library account.

Some libraries maintain their own locally compiled price lists that show for each database a total connect cost per hour that includes the connect cost charged by the vendor and telecommunications costs, and the unit price for each printing format both online and offline. These are useful for giving the patron an estimate of how much a search is likely to cost, and as soon as the search is finished the patron can be billed according to the prices on the list. However, price lists can be time-consuming to maintain since the price of one thing or another—a database royalty or a print format—changes every month. There are advantages to locally produced price lists: everyone knows before the search begins what rate is being charged, which allows the patron some rational way of keeping costs within his or her ability to pay, and the price list can be structured to reflect what the library wants to recover for the search service. For example, the actual billed price of a hypothetical database, including telecommunications, is $95 per hour, but the library's price list shows $100 per hour for the same database, because the library is attempting to recover some portion of its indirect costs or to provide a cushion to absorb costs of ready-reference searches or some other service. In this example, a fifteen minute search billed at the higher rate would bring in $1.25 above the actual recovery cost of the search. If the library is attempting to recover the costs of online printing supplies, the cushion could be added to the charge per citation.

Even if all direct costs are recovered, the library is already heavily subsidizing the search service by providing the equipment, space, furniture, utilities, and usually staff needed to perform the search (Breen, 1987). Recognizing this may make it easier for management to consider subsidizing some of the direct costs. For example, the library could charge a flat rate for searches. Experience has shown that expensive searches and cheap searches even out over time, and if necessary the library can adjust the rate so that it evens out in favor of the library, or in favor of the patrons, depending on the state of the library's budget. Flat rates have the major advantage of being simple to explain to the patron; the patron can easily decide if the product is worth the cost, whereas cost recovery based on connect time and citation charges is very difficult to estimate before the search begins. Furthermore, flat rates simplify bookkeeping and billing for the library staff. Another charging structure allows patron and library to share costs; the patron pays for the first ten minutes of connect time and the library pays for the second ten minutes, and so on; or, the library pays for the first ten citations and the patron pays for the rest; or, the library pays a flat rate of $25 per search and the patron pays the rest. Depending on how high the library portion is set, this can mean a free search for the majority of patrons, and rescues the library from responsibility for an excessively costly search. Many variations of cost sharing can be worked out based on how much the library can afford to subsidize the search service.

A library can choose to charge variable rates depending on the status of the patron requesting the search. For example, an academic library might recover all direct costs from faculty on the assumption that they have research grants and can afford to pay, support free or heavily subsidized searches to students, and charge full cost recovery plus a profit from patrons not affiliated with the university. Or, the library might subsidize an online end-user service while maintaining a mediated service based on direct cost recovery (Eaton and Crane, 1987). The greatly reduced cost of an off-peak hours service for end-users is a genuine option much preferable to the usual "use the paper copy or pay for a mediated search" choice libraries have offered in the past.

Another charging scheme that has been tried is voluntary recovery—the patron is told how much the service costs but is not denied service if he or she cannot pay. This has worked to recover the cost of printing supplies in ondisk units by placing a coin box near the printer and a sign asking patrons to contribute ten cents (or whatever) for each page printed. Different configurations of VendaCard-type technology can be attached to ondisk search stations if costs must be recovered.

Absorbing Costs in the Library Budget

There are only two sources of funds a library can call on: old money and new money. Old money is the library's budget, last year's budget, this year's budget, next year's budget, already much mulled over and thumbed through to find ways to pay for staff and materials and operating expenses. If the budget is already established and inviolate there are ways to reallocate existing resources to an automated information retrieval service. The salaries of librarians are already in the budget; one or more of those librarians can be designated as searchers rather than hiring additional staff for the search service. Amounts already budgeted for travel and professional memberships can be used to pay for training. Existing office automation equipment can be reallocated to the search service; with the addition of an inexpensive modem an old PC and printer can serve as an online search station, or an existing hard disk machine can become an optical disk search station if money can be found to purchase an optical disk drive.

When looking at next year's budget it may be possible to substitute some searching equipment in existing line items—purchasing a terminal instead of another plain PC or a fancy typewriter for the office, for example. The documentation could be purchased from the acquisitions budget. The start-up costs of a search service are the most overwhelming, but they are not annually repetitive. It may be necessary to ravage the equipment budget one year to pay for searching stations, but in subsequent years a much smaller amount is needed for maintenance and replacement.

The existing budget can be reallocated by canceling subscriptions to indexes and abstracts or other reference tools. This seems easiest to justify when a subscription to a CD-ROM database is substituted for its paper equivalent, and it can also be justified for very expensive and little-used paper indexes when online access to that index is subsidized by the funds saved. Libraries can decide not to purchase a new subscription to a paper equivalent when online access is available, and divert the funds to subsidizing the automated information retrieval unit (Chessen, 1984; Eaton and Crane, 1987; Hitchingham, 1984; Lancaster and Goldhor, 1981).

A complete upheaval of the existing budget can be an interesting and agonizing exercise, and it is necessary if searching is to be fully subsidized and money must be found to pay for the cost of access. It is justified by the fact that we live in the twentieth century and should be using twentieth century methods of storing and accessing data (Diodato, 1986; Dubberly, 1986; Johnston, 1989; Poole and St. Clair, 1986; Quint, 1987; St. Clair and Poole, 1989).

Here is an example. Professor Smith walks into the library and asks for an article published in the last two or three years in *Greenhouse Effect Report*. The good professor is not sure of the bibliographic details. The librarian directs Professor Smith to an index to find the full citation. The professor pores over several volumes of the index, then returns to the reference desk with the correct citation. The librarian shows the professor how to look up the call number for the journal and explains how to find it in the library. Professor Smith then goes upstairs into the stacks and luckily finds the correct volume on the shelf, then goes in search of a working photocopier. A pocketful of change and several minutes later, Professor Smith walks out the door with the article in hand. Now, here is the same scenario in a library that has chosen to divert funds from print-and-paper tools to computerized access. Professor Smith approaches the reference desk with the same request. The librarian searches a database for the correct citation, prints out the full text of the article and hands it to the professor who perhaps pays a nominal amount equal to photocopying charges to cover printing costs, perhaps not. Certainly the professor's time has been saved. The librarian's time has been used more efficiently; instead of lengthy and repetitive explanations about how to use an index, how to look up a call number, and how to find call numbers in the library's stack arrangement, the librarian has quickly delivered the product that was requested. Professor Smith did not want instructions on how to use an index, the professor wanted a copy of the article. It is quite likely that the library's money has been saved. Instead of buying, cataloging, processing, and giving shelf space to a journal that may or may not be used, the library has purchased access to data on demand. The product was requested, the product was delivered.

Examples such as this allow a critical look at the whole library budget and not just the acquisitions budget. Money was saved not only for the subscription price of the journal, but for technical processing time, for binding, for shelving, for the new building needed a few years down the road to house the accumulations of paper copies, and probably for interlibrary loan services in the event that the needed volume was lost or the article razored. The library knows that it has spent its money for a product that was needed rather than predicting that some articles in this journal may be needed at some time (Anderson, 1987; Diodato, 1986).

There are ways to ease into a reorganization of the budget to provide computerized access to, rather than ownership of, the data, to prove to the parent organization or funding agencies that it is feasible. Requests for new subscriptions can be monitored and checked to see if the text is available online. If so, the requester can be offered free access to the data on demand, and at the end of a year the online access costs can be compared to the costs of buying, processing, housing, and servicing the paper copy. Another method is to process interlibrary loan requests via online access to full-text databases rather than the usual means, and again compare the costs. One could include the cost of time lost while waiting for the material to arrive through the mail. Yet another method is to provide funds for ready-reference searching of online systems—searches performed by the reference desk staff when they deem that going online will provide the answer to a question faster, better, or exclusively (Droessler and Rholes, 1983; Hitchingham, 1984; Quint, 1988). A library that subscribes to a major vendor already has the bulk of its available reference tools online.

New Money

The experiments mentioned above can be undertaken to provide the data supporting a request for additional monies from parent organizations or potential donors, to bring in new money above and beyond the existing budget (Clark, 1986; Lee, 1984; Panas, 1984). Alternatively, local, state, and federal agencies or philanthropic organizations can be approached to provide seed money to undertake the experiments in the first place. In a university, there may be research funds available to subsidize such a project. Without spending its own limited resources, research funds obtained from a library's parent institution provide an excellent means for conducting pilot projects, allowing the library to decide which new products and services are best suited to become part of its basic services and included in its basic budget (Dodd and Anders, 1984; King and Kinyon, 1985). New money is especially valuable for providing the start-up funds needed to buy expensive equipment (Jackson et al., 1988). A plaque stating "DONATED BY THE FRIENDS OF THE LIBRARY" placed on an impressive-looking microcomputer may provide the continuing donor recognition needed to convince the "friends of the library" organization to buy it (Clark, 1990). It is more difficult to attach donor recognition to online access time, but it is possible; however, it can be dangerous to provide subsidized searches with money that is not guaranteed into the future because patrons will be disappointed when the subsidy is taken away. A CD-ROM database is a slightly safer investment of donated funds if there is some possibility that the library can assume the subscription cost in its budget if the donation is not renewed.

Managers are accustomed to finding money for online terminals in the equipment line of the library's budget, or to drafting reference librarians into the mediated search service rather than adding a new position. These are ways of "burying" the expense of automated information retrieval in the budget. Perhaps it is time to bring the costs out of hiding and to acknowledge that this is what libraries are or are becoming, and library budgets should be restructured so that the quickest and most efficient way of delivering information to patrons is funded in the same way as automated cataloging or automated circulation—not from the patrons' pockets but from the library's.

REFERENCES

American Library Association, Reference and Adult Services Division, Machine-Assisted Reference Section. "Online reference services: costs and budgets." In *Dollars and Sense: Implications of the New Online Technology for Managing the Library*, edited by Bernard F. Pasqualini. 105–116. Chicago: American Library Association, 1987. Presents a succinct review, with examples and bibliographies, of case studies on the costs and the possible funding sources involved in an online search service.

Anderson, Charles. "Budgeting for reference services in an on-line age." *The Reference Librarian* 19 (1987): 179–194. Budgetary considerations involved in integrating the use of online database searching as a ready reference tool are examined. Includes a methodology for analyzing relative costs of online and print sources, and concludes that online reference should be budgeted the same as traditional reference service.

Anderson, Charles and Ann Weston. "The costs of online searching." *Library Journal* 112 (April 1, 1987): 44–47. Within the environment of an Illinois public library reference desk, the author compares vendor costs for database access and the cost per search of experienced and inexperienced searchers, and in both cases finds the differences to be negligible.

Barker, Frances H. "Pricing of information products." *ASLIB Proceedings* 36 (July/August, 1984): 289-297. A review of the considerations and options in establishing the price of an online database, from the database producer's point of view.

Boyce, Bert R. "A cost accounting model for online computerized literature searching." *Journal of Library Administration* 4 (Summer, 1983): 43-49. Proposes standards of record-keeping that will allow libraries to keep track of the full direct and indirect costs of online searching to allow library managers to set policy from a knowledgeable position.

Breen, Margaret L. "Charging for online search services in academic libraries." *College & Research Libraries News* 7 (July, 1987): 400-402. Discusses current trends in fee structures and concludes that in the real world where bills must be paid, libraries have no choice but to charge patrons for some portion of the online search.

Brill, Faye. "A business perspective: or, what am I doing in the middle of this debate?" In *User Fees: A Practical Perspective*, edited by M. A. Drake, 117-120. Littleton, Colo.: Libraries Unlimited, 1981. A description of fee-based services in two different corporate libraries, one of which considered the service to be part of overhead costs, and the other a combination of overhead and charge-back.

Budd, John. "It's not the principle, it's the money of the thing." *Journal of Academic Librarianship* 15 (September, 1989): 218-222. By comparing the costs of online services to the total library budget, Budd argues that funding online services would consume a very small percentage of the total.

Chessen, James. "Economic outlook." In *Online Searching: The Basics, Settings, and Management*, edited by Joann H. Lee. Littleton, Colo.: 70-80. Libraries Unlimited, 1984. An excellent summary and explanation of different pricing structures analyzing the value of online searching and the transfer of this value from the library to the patron.

Clark, Charlene K. "Private support for public purposes: library fund raising." *Wilson Library Bulletin* 60 (February, 1986): 18-21. Summarizes the operations of an active development and promotion office in a university library.

Clark, Charlene K. "Going it alone: fundraising without a consultant." *The Bottom Line* 4 (Winter, 1990): 8-10. Discusses the importance of developing and implementing a fundraising plan that includes a "donor-literate" staff and effective donor recognition.

Cronin, Mary J. and Jay H. Kirk. "Bibliographic data base searching: the use and cost of a free service." In *Academic Libraries: Myths and Realities*, edited by Suzanne C. Dodson and Gary L. Menges. 352-356. Chicago: Association of College and Research Libraries, 1984. A description of the program at an academic library offering totally subsidized searches since 1978. Funding is drawn from the library budget.

Curley, Arthur, ed. "Fees for library service: current practice and future policy." *Collection Building* 8, no. 1 (1986). This special issue is devoted to fees. It presents a summary of the NCLIS (National Commission on Libraries and Information Science) study on the role of fees in academic and public libraries. Gives the results of a survey.

DeWath, Nancy van House. "Fees for online bibliographic search services in publicly supported libraries." *Library Research* 3 (June, 1981): 31. The results of a survey on fee structures in various libraries.

Diodato, Virgil. "Eliminating fees from online search services in a university library." *Online* 10 (November, 1986): 44-50. About 5 percent of the materials budget was transferred to the online budget in order to provide free searches to a university community. The author notes several results, including a quadrupling of requests for searches and a rise in the average cost per search.

Dodd, Jane and Vicki Anders. "Free online searches for undergraduates: a research project on use, costs, and projections." *Library Hi Tech* 2 (Spring, 1984): 43-50. An example of using university research funds to determine the costs of a proposed online service.

Drake, M. A., ed. *User Fees: A Practical Perspective*. Littleton, Colo.: Libraries Unlimited, 1981. A collection of readings on the fee or free controversy.

Drake, Miriam A. "Fees for service in libraries: who pays? who should pay?" In *User Fees: A Practical Perspective*, edited by M. A. Drake. 17-30. Littleton, Colo.: Libraries Unlimited, 1981. A good review of the issues—and the literature—in the fee or free controversy.

Drinan, Helen. "Financial management of online services: a how to guide." *Online* 3 (October, 1979): 14-21. Identifies direct and indirect costs and puts dollar figures to them based on experiences at a special library. Recommends recovering indirect costs because they amount to a significant sum.

Droessler, Judith M. and Julia M. Rholes. "Online services at the reference desk: Dialog, RLIN & OCLC." *Online* 7 (November, 1983): 79-86. A case study of providing no-charge ready-reference use of online in a large academic library. Cost figures are provided.

Dubberly, Ronald A. "Managing not to charge fees." *American Libraries* 17 (October, 1986): 670-676. Useful "how-to" information for public libraries interested in absorbing online costs in the library budget.

Eaton, Nancy L. and Nancy B. Crane. "Integrating electronic information systems into the reference services budget." *The Reference Librarian* 19 (1987): 161-177. A description of an automated reference center incorporating optical disk and online searching by end-users, showing costs and methods of funding.

Evans, John Edward. "Methods of funding." In *Online Searching: Technique and Management*, edited by James J. Maloney, 135-148. Chicago: American Library Association, 1983. A thorough review of the costs and sources of funds for online searching.

Fee-Based Services: Issues & Answers. Proceedings of the Second Conference on Fee-Based Research in College and University Libraries, Ann Arbor, 1987. Ann Arbor: Michigan Information Transfer Source, University of Michigan Libraries, 1987. A collection of papers addressing fee-based services aimed at nonaffiliated business or other clientele. Most of the papers are case study examples. M. A. Drake's firm negative to the question, "Should an academic library establish a fee-based service?" provides an interesting last word to the collection.

Fees for Services. SPEC Kit 74. Chicago: Association of Research Libraries, Systems and Procedures Exchange Center, 1981.

Fenichel, Carol H. and Thomas H. Hogan. *Online Searching, A Primer*. Medford, N.J.: Learned Information, 1984. The chapter "Costs and charging policies" on pages 77-93 is relevant. Provides a review of costs and a summary of fee structures.

Fortune, Joan. "Budgeting." In *Online Searching: The Basics, Settings, and Management*, edited by Joann H. Lee. 61-69. Littleton, Colo.: Libraries Unlimited, 1984. A brief chapter outlining three approaches to budgeting for online search services, and including a review of vendor and producer price policies and the need for accurate record-keeping.

Freedom and Equality of Access to Information: A Report to the American Library Association. Prepared by the Commission on Freedom and Equality of Access to Information. Chicago: American Library Association, 1986.

Giacoma, Pete. *The Fee or Free Decision: Legal, Economic, Political and Ethical Perspectives for Public Libraries*. New York: Neal-Schuman, 1989. An historical and political perspective on fee charging. An in-depth study, with many references and notes.

Govan, James F. "The creeping invisible hand: entrepreneurial librarianship." *Library Journal* 113 (January, 1988): 35–38. An argument against fee-based services and for the traditional (free) values of libraries.

Grimes, Nancy E. "Costs, budgets, and financial management." In *Online Searching: Technique and Management*, edited by James J. Maloney. 123–134. Chicago: American Library Association. Outlines the cost elements of establishing and running an online reference service, budget structures, and possible methods of funding.

Hersberger, Rodney M. "Financing and managing technology-based reference services in the undergraduate university library." *The Reference Librarian* 19 (1987): 209–223. A review of the different types of computerized databases and reference tools and how to integrate them into library service, especially at the small academic or undergraduate library level, with some practical suggestions for financing the high-tech tools.

Hitchingham, Eileen. "A survey of database use at the reference desk." *Online* 8 (March, 1984): 44–50. Results of a survey of online use to answer reference questions. Includes information on how various libraries have funded ready-reference searching, including cancellations and decisions to not purchase print sources.

Intner, Sheila S. and Jorge R. Schement. "The ethic of free service." *Library Journal* 112 (October 1, 1987): 50–52. A discussion of traditional fee or free issues but from a different perspective—OCLC's claim to copyright and ownership of its database.

Jackson, Katherine, Evelyn M. King and Jean Kellough. "How to organize an extensive laserdisk installation: the Texas A&M experience." *Online* 12 (March, 1988): 51–60. A generous donor made the installation of an ondisk unit possible. This article describes the process of working with the donor, selecting the equipment and databases, and setting up the unit.

Jacob, M. E. L. "Costing and pricing: the difference matters." *Bottom Line* 2 (1988): 12–14. A useful introduction to the concept of setting fees, which the author asserts is a complex process involving a high degree of subjective judgement that, unfortunately, most librarians do not apply when establishing fee structures.

Johnston, Wanda K. "Online search services in the community college." *College & Research Libraries News* 5 (May, 1989): 375–377. Reviews the status of online searching in community colleges and provides summary data from a survey. Concludes that the community college library is enhanced by providing free online access to users.

Kibirige, Harry M. *The Information Dilemma: A Critical Analysis of Information Pricing and the Fees Controversy*. Westport, Conn.: Greenwood Press, 1983. In addition to the fee or free controversy, discusses cost concepts, cost-based pricing, demand-based pricing, etc.

King, Evelyn M. and William R. Kinyon. "Information/reference." *Texas Library Journal* 61 (Winter, 1985): 126–127. Describes the use of university research funds as seed money to start and evaluate new online programs.

Knapp, Sara D. and James C. Schmidt. "Budgeting to provide computer-based reference service." *Journal of Academic Librarianship* 5 (March, 1979): 9–13. An early article on providing free searches with the cost of the service being paid from the library budget. It should be noted that the service accessed very limited numbers of databases through a local network, and the service eventually charged for printouts.

Koch, Jean E. "A review of the costs and cost-effectiveness of online bibliographic searching." *Reference Services Review* 10 (Spring, 1982): 59–64. A thorough review of the costs involved in establishing and maintaining an online search service, especially useful for pointing out the hidden costs overlooked in many cost comparison studies, assessing staff costs, etc.

Lancaster, F. W. and Herbert Goldhor. "The impact of online services on subscriptions to printed publications." *Online Review* 5 (August, 1981): 301–311. Reports the results of a survey among academic and special libraries. Notes some barriers to more widespread migration to online access; predicts greatly accelerated migration in the future.

Lee, Sul. *Library Fundraising: Vital Margin for Excellence*. Ann Arbor: Pierian Press, 1984.

Lynch, Mary Jo. *Financing Online Search Services in Publicly Supported Libraries: The Report of an ALA Survey*. Chicago: American Library Association, 1981. A comprehensive survey that shows that most libraries charge patrons for the direct costs of searching. The next two articles summarize the findings.

Lynch, Mary Jo. "Financing online services." *RQ* 21 (Spring, 1982a): 223–226.

Lynch, Mary Jo. "Libraries embrace online search fees." *American Libraries* 13 (March, 1982b): 174.

Lynch, Mary Jo. *Non Tax Sources of Revenue for Public Libraries*. Chicago: American Library Association, 1988.

Maloney, James J. "Contract options for lowering the cost of online searching." In *Dollars and Sense: Implications of the New Online Technology for Managing the Library*, edited by Bernard F. Pasqualini. 22–28. Chicago: American Library Association. A *Consumer Reports*-type checklist and explanation of the discounts and contract options offered by vendors, with an eye toward reducing libraries' costs for online services.

Matzek, Dick and Scott Smith. "Online searching in the small college library—the economics and the results." *Online* 6 (March, 1982): 21–29. A case study.

Meglio, Delores. "Full text online delivery: economic realities." In *Dollars and Sense: Implications of the New Online Technology for Managing the Library*, edited by Bernard F. Pasqualini. 88–96. Chicago: American Library Association, 1987. Written by an insider in the full-text online industry, this interesting article admits that any fee for information is a barrier but makes the point that most libraries have not done a cost accounting study of a manual print-source search, and would probably be appalled if they did.

Mowat, Ian R. M. and Sheila E. Cannel. "Charges for online searches in university libraries: follow-up to the 1981 survey." *Journal of Librarianship* 18 (July, 1986): 193–211. See the Lynch survey above.

Finance and Budget

National Commission for Libraries and Information Science. *The Role of Fees in Supporting Library and Information Services in Public and Academic Libraries.* April, 1985. ERIC Document ED 258 584. Presents selected summaries of recent studies on the use of fees, the rationale for setting fees, and the types of services for which libraries are charging fees.

Nielsen, Brian. "Do user fees affect searcher behavior?" In *Dollars and Sense: Implications of the New Online Technology for Managing the Library*, edited by Bernard F. Pasqualini. 29-37. Chicago: American Library Association, 1987. An interesting variation on the fee or free controversy that questions the librarian/searcher's response to the patron based on whether or not a fee is charged. The author concludes that fee-charging involves the staff in clerical activities that are not responsive to the needs of the library's patrons.

Panas, Jerold. *Mega Gifts.* Chicago: Pluribus Press, 1984. A guide to fund raising written by the "dean of fund raisers."

Poole, Jay Martin and Gloriana St. Clair. "Funding online services from the materials budget." *College & Research Libraries* 47 (May, 1986): 225-237. Argues that access provided by online searching is as legitimate a use of funds as that provided by processing materials, therefore online services should be funded from the acquisitions budget. The article is followed by responses.

Porter, G. Margaret. "Expanding the online search service: common sense and cost considerations." In *Dollars and Sense: Implications of the New Online Technology for Managing the Library*, edited by Bernard F. Pasqualini. 9-13. Chicago: American Library Association, 1987. Provides a checklist of items to take into consideration when planning an expansion of online services. As the author states, "Limited resources make it important to avoid a haphazard approach to expansion."

Porter, G. Margaret. "What does electronic access to bibliographic information cost?" *College and Research Libraries News* 52 (February, 1991): 90-92. Locally loaded database tapes, networked CD-ROMs, and gateway access costs are compared in this article. Actual costs are given when available, although the author warns that variable costs based on the size of the potential user population can make a big difference.

Quint, Barbara E. "Setting our priorities." In *Dollars and Sense: Implications of the New Online Technology for Managing the Library*, edited by Bernard F. Pasqualini. 1-8. Chicago: American Library Association, 1987. An impassioned plea from a passionate proponent of online access for redistributing library funds in order to avoid charging library users.

Quint, Barbara E. "How much a librarian would cost." *Wilson Library Bulletin* 62 (April, 1988): 60-62. From her "Connect Time" column. Compares the cost of subscribing, housing, and servicing print materials to accessing online information.

Rice, James. "Fees for online searches; a review of the issue and a discussion of alternatives." *Journal of Library Administration* 3 (Spring, 1982): 25-34. An even-handed look at the issues in charging for online services.

Rochell, Carlton. "The knowledge business: economic issues of access to bibliographic information." *College and Research Libraries* 46 (January, 1985): 5-12. A well-reasoned argument against charging fees for online services, with some practical suggestions on where the money should come from if not from the user.

Roose, Tina. "Online search costs in public libraries." *Library Journal* 110 (May 1, 1985): 36–37. From her column "Public Libraries Online." Compares per-search costs and draws the conclusion that those libraries not charging for online searches have lower per-search costs. (See Diodata, 1986, for a different result.)

Roose, Tina. "Free versus fee reexamined." *Library Journal* 112 (January, 1987): 64–65. Another one of Roose's columns that makes a pleas for free searches but unfortunately provides no concrete method of funding them.

Rouse, S. H. "Charging policies for online services in the Big Ten universities." In *User Fees: A Practical Perspective*, edited by M. A. Drake. 97–107. Littleton, Colo.: Libraries Unlimited, 1981. A seminal article describing the practices for providing online searches at major university libraries. This article is often cited in support of charging user fees.

Saffady, William. "The availability and cost of online search services." *Library Technology Reports* 24 (May/June, 1988): 291–502. This, and the 1979 and 1985 LTR articles of the same title, are useful for tracking the costs of online access.

St. Clair, Gloriana and Jay Martin Poole. "Bread not butter: funding online searching in hard times." *Acquisitions Librarian* 2 (1989): 189–204. Advocates funding online searching form the print materials budget and makes the point that online searches allow resource-deficient institutions to meet the demands of users.

Smith, Barbara. "A strategic approach to online user fees in public libraries." *Library Journal* 114 (February, 1989): 33–36. Discusses different fee structures.

Sweetland, James H. "What does it all mean?" In *Dollars and Sense: Implications of the New Online Technology for Managing the Library*, edited by Bernard F. Pasqualini. 97–103. Chicago: American Library Association 1987. Reviews historical issues in the fee or free controversy.

Warner, Alice Sizer. *Making Money: Fees for Library Services*. New York: Neal-Schuman, 1989. Based on information from questionnaires sent to Fortune 100 libraries and public libraries with fee-based services. Provides a basic introduction to fee-based services.

Waters, Richard L. and Victor Frank Kralisz. "Financing the electronic library: models and options." *Drexel Library Quarterly* 17 (Fall, 1981): 107–120. The publication date means that many of the electronic options used in the 1990s were unknown when the article was written, but many of the suggested options are still valid.

White, Herbert S., ed., et al. "Academic libraries, online searching, and turf: a symposium." *Journal of Academic Librarianship* 11 (November, 1985): 268–274. A symposium in print with several authors responding to the premise posed by White: Charging for online searches when many users have access to the option of doing it for themselves is a ceding of library turf.

Wilkinson, J. B. "Economics of information: criteria for counting the cost and benefit." *ASLIB Proceedings* 32 (January, 1980): 1–9. Especially relevant to company and special libraries, this article poses criteria by which to assess the costs and benefits of information.

4

Staff

For a service that uses computers to achieve results, effective automated information retrieval depends primarily on people. Search analysts and ready-reference searchers must negotiate questions with patrons; staff helping end-users must negotiate questions and teach. This chapter details the "people" aspects of automated information retrieval, including the skills needed by an effective search analyst and the factors affecting the searching process that an analyst must deal with during the search. Once search analysts have been selected and become part of the automated information retrieval staff, there are special concerns such as scheduling and evaluating the analysts and conducting staff meetings that the service manager must handle as the supervisor of the staff. Ultimately it is the service manager's responsibility to see that all searchers, and indeed all library staff and end-users, have the training in automated information retrieval that they need to accomplish their jobs. Most of this training will be through in-house programs designed and conducted by the service manager.

WHO SHOULD SEARCH: ATTRIBUTES OF A GOOD SEARCH ANALYST

Searching Skills

In the mediated search process, a patron poses a question he or she feels can be answered by an automated information retrieval search, or perhaps a librarian recommends a search to answer the question. The patron makes an appointment and meets with the search analyst. They discuss the topic. Perhaps the analysts asks, "What is your research about?" to get the conversation started. It may be necessary for the analyst to explain the procedures of automated information retrieval if the patron is not familiar with it, and explain costs if there are any. Shortly into the discussion of the topic, the analyst suggests a few databases that might have information on the subject and explains the content of the databases, how they might overlap in coverage, and names their print equivalents to see if the patron is familiar with them and agrees that they are suitable to the topic. Once the databases to be searched have been agreed upon. the analyst decides which vendor system or systems will be used to search them, and then begins profiling in earnest, dividing the topic into concept groups, checking relevant thesauri, suggesting synonyms, and applying the relevant search engine codes to the terms selected.

The analyst signs on and begins keyboarding, all the while explaining to the patron what is happening and what the numbers mean, and eventually prints a few citations in browsing format so the patron can sample the kind of information being retrieved. Perhaps the patron sees something that sparks a change or addition to the search strategy, which the analyst types in and combines with the previously created sets. The search is refined until the patron is satisfied with the results, and the results are printed out. After signing off, the analyst explains the codes and information on the printout, and if necessary tells the patron how to find the materials in the library or how to use interlibrary loan. It may be necessary for the analyst to figure a bill for the search.

When the patron is gone, the analyst records some figures for statistical and record-keeping purposes and probably drops the paperwork on the secretary's desk for data entry and filing. The search is done, unless the patron comes back with more questions, or needs an update, or the search strategy is pulled for review at the searchers' meeting, or there is a problem on the vendor's invoice. The search analyst can hope that it's done.

In this transaction, the search analyst applied several skills, attitudes, and aptitudes, from the reliability needed to meet an appointment on time to the general reference skills required to tell the patron how to use the final printout to find material in the library. Deciding whether the question is appropriate for a search—that it is not too broad, suitable databases are available, and alternative solutions are unlikely to get better results—requires all the skills of a good reference librarian plus a capacious memory. Within the private consultation format of the mediated search, the analyst must apply interpersonal and communication skills and project an attitude of confidence to reassure the patron. Perhaps the analyst has some background in the subject to be searched so that he or she can speak the same subject-specific language as the patron.

In profiling the search topic, the analyst applies analytical skills to break out the concept groups. A logical mind is needed, as is a quick, reliable memory for the commands and codes of different search engines. While searching, obviously some typing skills are necessary, and the faster one types the less online time and money is consumed by the mechanics of keyboarding. The analyst should appear confident, even courageous, rather than timid and uncertain, and should be able to make quick, decisive choices as information scrolls up the screen. The analyst must be able to talk to the patron and answer questions while at the same time concentrating on search input and output. Once again, a good memory is a must, and here two types of memory are at work. Long-term or background memory holds the system protocols, Boolean operators, and the mechanics of searching ready to be applied when needed, while short-term or working memory works on the problem at hand, and remembers the terminology and set numbers applied in this particular search. A few hours after the search is over, the analyst will not be able to remember that set 2 contained "cats or dogs or pigs" but will be able to remember the system protocol that requires set 2 to be referred to as "S2". An inexperienced analyst who must keep everything in working memory will be slow and confused.

The prodigious memory comes into play again when the search is over and the analyst explains what to do with the printout. Frequently the search analyst must turn into a reference librarian to tell the inexperienced patron how to use the library. Perhaps an hour has passed since the analyst first greeted the patron, and in that time the analyst has worked closely with the patron and with the computer, communicating with both in the language of each.

Now look at the transaction from another angle. This time the patron is an end-user approaching an ondisk database. Many months ago the search analyst wrote a simple, two-page handout explaining the mechanics of searching this particular database; the automated information retrieval service has in fact produced several handouts explaining the entire search process for end-users as well as system-specific handouts that concentrate on the protocols of a particular search engine. The patron has read all of the handouts, or perhaps the patron has read none of them; it does not matter if this is the patron's first encounter with the database. As soon as he or she sits down at the microcomputer, the patron will ask, "Now what do I do?" In addition to the written communication skills needed to produce the handouts, and all the skills required in a mediated search setting, the search analyst now becomes a teacher who, with infinite patience, tells the patron which keys to press and why to press them and explains what happens once the key is pressed. Eventually a printout is produced, and the search analyst explains how to use it to find materials in the library.

Factors Affecting the Search Process

Any interaction between a human and an automated database, whether it is a mediated search or an end-user search during which the user is instructed on how to use the database, has at least four variables that affect the success or failure of the search: the question, the patron or the person who asks the question, the setting and equipment used to answer the question, and the analyst or the person who ultimately poses the question to the automated database (Fidel and Soergel 1983).

The Question. As discussed in Chapter 1, some questions are not suitable for automated information retrieval; they are too broad, or so specific that the answer can be easily found in a print tool, or they require judgments that the computer cannot make, such as "find ten good articles on solar energy," or the patron would be better served by the serendipity inherent in browsing a printed list. It is possible for a search analyst to break down and rephrase a question so that it fits the thesaurus terms or the logic of an automated search but is no longer recognizable as the question the patron asked. On the other hand, the nature of the question can make the answer difficult to recognize. For example, the answer to the question "What is the net profit of XYZ Company?" is easy to find and not subject to too much interpretation, but if the question is phrased, "Should I invest in XYZ?" the answer might be extracted from a list of citations and data printed out, but it may take some time for the patron to discover the answer, and the search analyst may never know whether the search was successful unless the patron comes back with a hot tip to invest. The automated database is not a Ouija board that can answer the second question, but the application of a reasoned search strategy can supply the data from which an answer can be formulated. In the same manner as the librarian negotiating a question across the reference desk, an analyst must look beyond and around the question as it was asked to see if a judicious rephrasing of the question makes it suitable for an automated answer. Also, there may be unstated aspects of the question related to the expectations of the patron that the search analyst must infer. For example, a graduate student just starting a research project has different information needs from the researcher looking for one or two articles to confirm his or her findings. The analyst must determine what quantity and quality of information the user needs.

The Patron. The patron who is new to the notion of automated information retrieval needs an explanation of the process so that he or she can understand the purpose of the questions the analyst asks and understand the information displayed as the search progresses. The confused patron can be indecisive, and this is especially unfortunate during an online search when time is money. The inexperienced patron probably has not done any advance preparation such as thinking of keywords and synonyms or the type of literature needed to answer the question so that the analyst has some idea which databases might be suitable. When asked to discuss the topic, the inexperienced patron is quite likely to give a rambling dissertation from which it is difficult to extract concept groups. The expectations of the inexperienced patron may be unreasonable. Basically, such a patron needs a great deal of time and explanation and direction before the question is posed to the computer, and may take up more time during the search itself for explanations and repetitions and reminders. Patience is required of the search analyst, and the analyst must have the confidence and courage to advise and even direct the patron to the correct decisions. The experienced patron on the other hand may be too assertive. A little knowledge is a dangerous thing, and the patron with a little knowledge of automated information retrieval may try to insist that the analyst perform a search in a certain way that the analyst is pretty sure will not work, the patron may doubt the results of the search, and the patron may resent being charged for a search he feels he could have done better than the search analyst.

In between these two extremes are other patrons, the ones who are uncomfortable in the private consultation format or are worried about confidentiality and therefore communicate less than is desired, and those who love their subject and love to talk about it. Even when instructing an end-user who will do the actual searching, the analyst must get the patron to communicate something about the subject so that correct choices of databases and terminology and strategy can be made. Essentially, it is the patron's willingness to communicate and skill at communicating that can skew the results of the search.

The Equipment and Setting. The searcher who is worried about noisy telephone lines or battling a vicious glare on the display screen is not concentrating fully on the task in hand. Even baud rate, whether a plodding 300 baud that tries the searcher's patience or a speedy 2400 baud that increases the display rate to the point where the performance of simultaneous tasks is degraded, can affect the success of the search (Turner et al., 1990). The availability of appropriate documentation is essential. Obviously the electronic tools to perform the search must be in place and working and the environment must be comfortable, but there is one other environmental factor that is not so obvious: the cost of an online search. When the patron is charged for the search, accessing an expensive database makes both the patron and the analyst nervous. A timid and nervous searcher is not a good searcher. The patron's expectations are higher when there is a charge for the service, but the charge is not related to the results of the search; instead it is related to the means of producing the results. One pays for the privilege of accessing a database, not for the product. A service that charges patrons should expend considerable time and effort in explaining what the charge is for, and usually this is the search analyst's time and effort that is spent. In fact, charging for searches means that quite a bit of the analyst's time will be consumed by the explanations and clerical tasks involved with charging, and this is time that is not spent satisfying the information needs of the patrons.

There is a tendency for search analysts to provide a higher level of service to patrons who are charged for a search. Analysts are aware of the costs, and they will channel some effort into providing a cost-effective and thorough search, whereas searches not charged to patrons are less likely to be cost-effective and therefore are a detriment to the library's budget. Analysts and patrons work together to get satisfactory results when there is a bill to be paid. No-charge searches and searches performed on an ondisk database have an opposite effect. There is a tendency to shrug off poor results with the excuse, "It's worth what you paid for it." Or, time-wasting experimentation at the terminal takes the place of an effective search strategy planned ahead of time (Evans, 1983). Costs have both positive and negative effects. The search analyst should have the option of reducing a charge if there is a mistake that was not the fault of the patron; this will make the analyst much less nervous during the search.

The Analyst. The search analyst's communication and interpersonal skills are factors in determining the success of a search. If there is poor question negotiation, the analyst will not understand the question thoroughly and will produce a faulty search strategy. A poor interview technique, such as pacing that rushes through a checklist of milestones in order to get through the search rather than allowing the patron to think of and volunteer information, or asking closed "yes or no'' questions rather than the open "who, what, when, where, how" questions that allow the patron to expand the discussion, limits the exchange of information between analyst and patron (Auster and Lawton, 1984; Dommer and McCaghy, 1982; Somerville, 1982). Undoubtedly, the analyst should be in charge of the process—asking questions, leading the patron through the steps of profiling a search strategy, and executing the search—but the analyst should not be a dictator who tells the patron what he or she needs. Neither should the analyst be so timid that the patron is left floundering without direction while the analyst slavishly attempts to execute every suggestion. It is a delicate balance, a partnership in which each partner has skills and knowledge the other needs to accomplish the task.

The training and experience of the search analyst greatly affect the outcome of the search (Hock, 1983; Moureau, 1987; Roose, 1985). Obviously the analyst must know the search engines, and the more search engines there are, the more difficult it becomes to keep them separate and remember which protocol applies to which vendor. Experience is the best teacher. The experienced searcher has the techniques and mechanics of searching stored in long-term memory so that their application is automatic, almost unthinking. The experienced searcher is adept at scanning and picking out relevant information from a display whereas a neophyte starts with the accession number and reads through the entire citation, then reads it again to pick out keywords from titles and descriptors. The inexperienced searcher is timid and unsure, and this means slow.

The subject expertise of the search analyst is perhaps the most controversial factor (Girard and Moureau, 1981; Hock, 1983). Certainly subject expertise is useful for talking about a subject with the patron and for knowing and selecting appropriate databases to be searched. Sharing a common language with the patron reassures the patron, and the "instant thesaurus" carried in the analyst's memory can mean less recourse to the published thesauri, which are time-consuming and sometimes frustrating to use. Certain generally agreed-upon subjects do require some background, either formal training or extensive experience in searching them. These are chemistry, biomedicine, patents, law, and possibly some of the financial databases. A knowledge of the specialized vocabularies and codes of these subjects and others is undoubtedly useful, but it is not absolutely necessary. The limitless access points made available by free-text indexing mean that a search of just about any term will produce results as long as the term is spelled correctly, and sometimes even when it is misspelled. Subject expertise affects the recall ratio of a search—how many of the relevant items in the database are retrieved—rather than the precision ratio—how many of the items retrieved are relevant. Free-text terms properly manipulated assure bull's-eye precision. An experienced searcher, with well-honed interviewing skills and the ability to apply a variety of searching techniques, can produce at least acceptable results regardless of the subject.

Attributes of a Good Search Analyst

What should one look for to determine if a librarian will be a good search analyst? In most academic libraries search analysts are drawn from the reference staff, and there is a common belief that any good reference librarian can be a good search analyst. Certainly a search analyst uses reference skills in dealing with patrons and with databases, so being a reference librarian is a good start, but there are certain personal traits and backgrounds that distinguish the good search analyst. (Sources listing and expounding upon the attributes of a good search analyst include Bellardo (1985), Dolan (1979), Hammer (1982), Hock (1983), Somerville (1982), and Van Camp (1979).)

Communication skills are among the most critical of the personal traits needed by the search analyst, who must be capable of listening carefully and discussing objectively. A good question negotiation technique observed at the reference desk will be useful in a mediated search or while helping end-users. Working with a patron to negotiate a search strategy and explain the techniques and mechanics of searching takes longer than the average reference question transaction, and the private consultation of a mediated search typically takes an hour; therefore the search analyst should be people oriented, and should enjoy the close and extended contact with patrons. An ability to empathize with a patron's research problems is helpful.

Self-confidence, one might almost say courage, is a necessary attribute to reassure the patron that the search analyst knows what he or she is doing. A search analyst cannot be intimidated by the technology nor by an overbearing patron who insists on an inappropriate search or strategy in an expensive online system. Nonetheless, the good search analyst has the confidence to try new things, and to alter a search strategy in midstream if an alternative looks promising. The confident analyst is not so concerned about making mistakes that he or she worries and becomes timid, and when a mistake is made the analyst has the courage to admit it instead of allowing the patron to think that the database or the system itself produced a faulty result. Good analysts are not so overconfident that they believe they cannot make mistakes.

Search analysts must have a logical, analytical mind able to separate questions into concept groups and ignore the irrelevant concepts. Analysts must be skilled at problem solving. One needs a flexible mind capable of looking at a question from different perspectives and capable of formulating alternatives rather than being trapped into a particular search style that dictates that any question can be broken into three concept groups, no more and no less. The good search analyst is resourceful.

In common with reference librarians, search analysts need a capacious memory for reference tools, indexes and databases, the style of indexing or organization they use, and the types of materials they index. The analyst must also remember vendor systems, which databases are loaded with which vendors, the search protocols to use, passwords, telephone numbers, and even the varying layouts of keyboards. Also stored in the capacious memory are terminology, controlled vocabulary structures, synonyms, and spelling variants. The efficient search analyst remembers set numbers created during an individual search session. Both long-term and short-term memory must be in good working order.

There are certain attitudes shared by good search analysts. Enthusiasm for automated information retrieval communicates to the patrons and promotes continued use of the service. A "teacherly" attitude that promotes the sharing of knowledge about automated information retrieval insures a better understanding of the procedures involved and reassures end-users who may have been reluctant to approach librarians for help. Patience and persistence are needed when dealing with patrons and with computerized databases; both can sometimes seem to be withholding vital information. An economic attitude that balances costs with results is useful in online systems.

A search analyst must have the ability to work under pressure. There are time pressures and money pressures that require quick decisions, frequently with a patron anxiously hanging over the analyst's shoulder, watching and questioning every move the analyst makes.

Finally, the search analyst must be interested in continuing education. Computerized searching is a continual learning and relearning process as new databases are added, search engines are enhanced by the vendors, and new technologies become available. The search analyst must go beyond the formal training received and learn from experiences both good and bad. The analyst must be willing to take the time to study and prepare when called upon to search a new database or a different system.

The personal traits listed above must be combined with a preparatory background to produce a search analyst. Obviously, training in the mechanics and techniques of searching is necessary, but self-confidence, resourcefulness, and the ability to perform under pressure come with experience. Practice is essential, and if there are not enough patron-generated searches to provide the experience some provision must be made for hands-on practice time. Since many of the skills used by reference librarians are also used by search analysts, a background in reference work is useful. A search analyst who has done research at the graduate or professional level can empathize with the research problems of patrons. At least a rudimentary level of typing skill is needed, but patrons will have more confidence in a speedy, sure-handed touch-typist. Some subject expertise in the search analyst's background will provide a ready-made familiarity with databases and print tools, and insures that the analyst can speak the language of patrons working in the same subject.

Selecting Search Analysts

Self-confident, enthusiastic, logical, with a photographic memory and able to work under pressure, yet kind and patient and people-oriented, this combination of Star Trek's Mr. Spock and a saint is hard to find. There are those who say that any good reference librarian can be a good search analyst, and there are those who say that a good search analyst possesses a certain method of thinking or cognitive style that no amount of training can develop. In other words, search analysts are born, not made. Anyone can learn and memorize search protocols, but the ability to analyze the components of a query may be inherent (Dolan, 1979; Rholes and Droessler, 1984).

If search analysts are chosen from the reference staff, the automated information retrieval service manager has the opportunity to observe a librarian's interpersonal and communications skills in that person's transactions with patrons at the reference desk. It is unwise to judge interpersonal skills based on a person's interactions with fellow staff, because the person may behave very differently with strangers. Another trait that can be determined by close observation is something called "locus of control." A person can deem that events are controlled internally by his or her own behavior, or externally by fate or forces beyond control. The librarian with internal locus of control is more likely to pursue a question until an answer is found and to develop on his own a variety of skills to help in the pursuit. The person with external locus of control is more likely to believe in the value of luck rather than skill; this person is also more likely to be afraid of technology and develops a finger-freezing phobia when confronted by a terminal or microcomputer. Luck is nice; every librarian has experienced stumbling across an answer by pure luck, but a search analyst cannot count on it (Jackson, 1982).

The service manager can devise a simple test to screen out those who do not have the analytical ability to break a query into components by conducting a search strategy exercise. Most search analysts say that their reference ability has been enhanced by the experience of devising search strategies, so such an exercise is a useful training tool for all librarians. The exercise consists of a few typical questions that must be broken down into concept groups with synonyms or controlled vocabulary terms, and for which the appropriate reference tool, index, or database must be identified. The individuals who apply logic, imagination, and flexibility to the problem are potential search analysts.

Another way to select individuals who may be valuable additions to the search analyst staff is to look for those who like to search, the ones who always include an automated solution in the list of options they consider for answering a question. If the library permits ready-reference searching, a look at the log book to see who are the most frequent searchers is in order. Enthusiasm for automated information retrieval is one of the main attributes of a good search analyst.

THE AUTOMATED INFORMATION RETRIEVAL SERVICE STAFF

The staff of a search service may consist of one person who does everything and also works at the reference desk, or it may consist of several people, depending on the number of searches demanded and the number of options the service offers. Typically, there is a service manager or coordinator, one or more search analysts whose primary duty is to provide mediated searches, and clerical support staff who take appointments and provide typing and record-keeping support. If the service offers end-user online services there may be a portion of the staff designated to work nights and weekends when certain services are available. If there is a centralized ondisk service it must be staffed as well, perhaps by the search analysts who are experienced in search strategy development and interacting with databases, but more frequently by other library staff, simply because there are not enough search analysts to cover all the hours the ondisk databases are available (Pilachowski et al., 1985).

In most academic libraries, the search analysts are selected from the reference staff; they are part-time searchers for whom searching is one aspect of their daily routines and not a career (Chatterton and Pemberton, 1985). Searching must be juggled with reference desk assignments, collection development, and the research and publishing required of academic librarians. In other words, they have concerns not related to searching that the service manager must take into account when dealing with the search analyst staff (Grossman, 1984). Frequently the service manager is not the sole supervisor of the search analysts; instead they must keep two or even more bosses happy and look after their own happiness as well. Particularly in academic libraries, their tenure in a search analyst position may be transitory as they look ahead to advancement and promotion to other jobs in which the specialized training of a search analyst plays no direct part.

Staff can look at the matter of combined reference desk/search analyst duties in two ways. One is the elitist attitude in which the analyst thinks, "I have special skills and special responsibilities other librarians don't have." Indeed, most search analysts enjoy the mediated search format of a private consultation with a patron. They feel that their status is enhanced when they are consulted for their special skills, and they feel that they have given better service in the hour-long consultation than they can deliver in the quick and anonymous give-and-take at a reference desk. They are flattered when their special skills provide an answer that could not otherwise be found. On the other hand, they may feel overworked and pressured by too many responsibilities, with too much to do and too little time to do it. The provision of mediated searches carries with it extra, hidden duties beyond the interaction of the private consultation. If the analyst is unfamiliar with the topic or database or system to be searched, advance preparation before the appointment is necessary; afterwards there is the paperwork of record-keeping and billing to complete, and there are always new things to learn about old familiar systems and databases. It is not uncommon for the patron of a mediated search to adopt the search analyst as his or her personal librarian, the only librarian the patron knows by name, who must be sought and consulted on every matter related to the library whether it deals with searching or not. These add up to more time and more pressures than the apparent hour consumed by a mediated search.

For the comfort of the search analysts and the service manager, it is most important to have clear, written job descriptions, preferably detailing the percentage of time the search analyst is expected to devote to various duties. There should be some provision for adjusting or revising the job description if necessary, and it should recognize that a search analyst cannot spend all of the allotted time searching. For example, an experienced searcher probably needs one extra hour for preparation, paperwork, and study for each three hours of mediated search appointments provided. A new searcher just learning the business may need one hour of preparation for every hour of searching. Especially if there are more than two or three search engines in use, insufficient practice time to keep up skills in all the search engines is a major concern of search analysts because they will be slow and indecisive and they will make mistakes on the patron's time and money, with the patron watching. An enthusiastic and dedicated search analyst is concerned about improving his or her skills and should not be made to feel that there is no time and no money available for practice. If clerical staff is shared between the automated information retrieval service and the reference department, the same detailed job description is necessary, because handling the appointments and record-keeping of a busy search service can expand to consume a great deal of staff time. It is incumbent upon the service manager to make the record-keeping and other paperwork as simple and quick as possible for both the search analysts and the clerical staff.

The scheduling of mediated searches to be performed by search analysts who have other reference duties is perhaps the most sensitive issue the service manager deals with. The two most common ways of scheduling are: *On demand*, that is, when a patron requests a search he or she is linked with a search analyst and they negotiate a time for the appointment between the two of them; and *Scheduled hours*, when each search analyst is assigned to particular hours. When a patron requests a search he chooses the hour most convenient for him, and the searcher assigned to that hour provides the search.

There are advantages and disadvantages to both methods. In the on-demand system, the patron can be linked with a search analyst who has some subject expertise in the patron's area or is most experienced in searching the systems and databases the patron is likely to need. However, it does take longer to make the appointment, since the person who answered the telephone or met the patron in the first place must track down the appropriate search analyst, and the patron must repeat his information needs to the search analyst. Furthermore, the patron is at the mercy of the search analyst's schedule. Depending on how many non-searching duties the analyst staff handles, it may be impossible to accommodate drop-in patrons with immediate information needs. There can be a tendency for one search analyst, with a flexible schedule or appropriate subject expertise, to get most of the appointments. Search analysts can come to view appointments as impositions on their unscheduled time, something that must be fitted in between desk hours and collection development and all the other responsibilities they have.

In the scheduled-hour system, the patron can select any unfilled appointment that is most convenient, and drop-ins are more likely to be accommodated. Clerical staff can take the appointments without referring patrons to an analyst; therefore the act of taking an appointment does not require that attention or time of a professional. However, the search analyst with a background in medieval history is likely to get a few chemistry or physics searches. It is possible to steer the patron to an hour covered by an analyst with some subject expertise, but this once again puts the patron at the mercy of the search analyst's schedule. With assigned hours, the search analyst knows what is expected of him or her and does not feel that searching is something that must be squeezed in; the problem comes when the appointed hour goes unfilled, and the nonsearching staff of the department wonders with envy what the analyst is doing with the "free" time. One of the major advantages of this system is the variety of searching experience the analysts get rather than being pigeon-holed in a particular subject or database.

Flexibility must be built in to either system. Search analysts must be team players willing to fill in and cover for each other when necessary. The service manager should foster this attitude. The manager also needs to be firm enough to enforce an even distribution of searching responsibilities and to insure that each searcher has adequate experience to maintain skills. The manager should monitor the number of appointments each analyst handles and try to resolve inequities, either by adding more analysts, or training existing analysts to handle more subjects or databases, or by reducing the staff if there are not enough appointments to maintain the expertise of each. If an analyst is averaging five or fewer searches per week—less than one a day—probably that analyst is not getting enough experience to maintain proficiencies.

Even if the search analyst staff is happy with the workload, having enough searches to maintain skills but not so many that they feel overburdened, there are other concerns that the manager must deal with in order to have a moderately content staff. Charging for searches makes some librarians uncomfortable (Moureau, 1987; Nielsen, 1987; Roose, 1985). Older librarians especially, who were indoctrinated with the concept of free libraries before automated information retrieval brought in the practice of charging for information products, worry that the product they are providing must be worth the amount the patron is paying. This does not seem to be as great a concern with recent library school graduates, but all should be concerned with the concept of "information malpractice"—the idea of being held responsible, even liable, for the results of a search for which the patron paid (Mintz, 1984). Library schools constantly emphasize that librarians should not give legal advice or medical advice. A patent search, a search of WESTLAW or LEXIS, or a search of a medical database for which the patron pays looks very much like an authoritative answer. The use of a computer, the existence of a computer-produced printout, and the charging of a fee create expectations in the minds of users. Although the analyst is placing the printout in the hands of the patron and saying, "Here is the information. You interpret it," just as a reference librarian puts a law reference book in the hands of a patron with the same warning, the patron sees something quite different. The policy and procedures manual should have statements covering this situation, and the library may want the added insurance of a disclaimer form that patrons are required to read and sign before a search will be undertaken. Certainly the search analysts should be trained to instruct patrons in the proper use and applications of the information they receive in printouts. However, the service manager should emphasize to the search analysts that policy statements and disclaimer forms are not a license for providing sloppy, imprecise, and incomplete searches that the patron is nonetheless expected to pay for.

Deprofessionalization is another concern, not only of search analysts but of all librarians (Nelson, 1980). Information management is an esoteric skill that until recently was largely the province of librarians, then the information explosion made it a concern for nearly everyone. Search analysts believe that their professional status is enhanced by the use of computers in their own eyes and in the eyes of the patrons who consult them, and the mediated search format is a more professional and more formalized encounter than the one at the reference desk where the patron probably does not know and does not care whether his question is answered by a professional librarian or a clerk as long as it is answered. But now computers are putting the skills of information management in the hands of everyone. Search analysts feel that they are losing their jobs to end-users, and they may be right. Anyone can punch a button on a computer keyboard, and although it is the librarian who selects, installs, and maintains an end-user system, and teaches end-users how to operate it, the end-user sees himself and not the librarian as the information manager. The librarian is in the background rather than being the focus of the information management picture. The more end-user access a library makes available, the less demand there will be for mediated searches and for search analysts.

Evaluation is another concern of the search analyst staff (Glunz, 1983 and 1984). A good analyst will continually evaluate his or her own skill; an enthusiastic search analyst will always try to find ways to do it better next time. However, evaluation needs to be more formalized since individuals frequently do not perceive their own failings, and neither will the service manager unless there are procedures in place. As mentioned above, the automated information retrieval service manager may not be the sole supervisor of the search analyst staff and therefore will have only partial impact on the search analyst's total personnel evaluation and only partial influence in changing any undesirable behavior observed in the search analyst. Since a person with multiple duties may be able to slight one of those duties and still get good personnel evaluation marks for the others, it may be that the only real influence the manager has is in deciding whether to retain or dismiss a person from the search analyst staff.

The service manager has several options for evaluating the search analyst staff. A mediated search probably uses a patron evaluation form that is designed to get the patron's impression of the overall process, including the recall and precision ratios of the resulting printout. There is some controversy regarding whether or not the patron is capable or informed enough to evaluate the expertise of the search analyst; nevertheless, many evaluation forms ask the patron to rate the analyst's attitude and general helpfulness without asking for a judgment of the analyst's knowledge. Unfortunately, innocuous questions such as "Did the search analyst adequately explain the searching process to you?" or "Was the search analyst helpful?" do not elicit enough information for the basis of an evaluation of the search analyst unless the responses are consistently negative. Especially if the evaluation form is structured to allow the patron to answer the above questions like this:

YES _____ NO _____ If no, why not? _____

most patrons will check "yes" rather than going to the trouble of explaining themselves in the "why not" section. Any evaluative comment relative to the search analyst can be skewed by the patron's satisfaction with the results of the search; an unsatisfactory result may not be the fault of the search analyst but rather the fault of the question.

Patron evaluations should not be relied upon to provide a total picture of the search analyst's progress. The service manager should exercise some general oversight functions such as making sure that the analyst is on time for appointments, completes the paperwork adequately, and exhibits enthusiasm for searching, but this does not address the skill of the search analyst. Two ways to evaluate skills are by observation of the mediated search process, and reproduction of the search strategy.

By sitting in on a mediated search, the service manager can observe how a search analyst interacts with patrons and solves their information needs. If observation is a regular routine of the evaluation process, the manager should have a form or checklist to follow so that all analysts are judged by the same criteria rather than by general impressions (Beck, 1991). The checklist should cover each aspect of the mediated search process and may include such items as:

— Greeting patron
   Introduction
   Handshake
— Interview
   Explained process adequately
   Asked open questions
   Interrupted patron
   Suggested choices to patron
   Dictated choices to patron
   Used thesaurus
— Searching
   Database selection
   Appropriate use of search protocols
   Able to make explanations while searching
   Appropriate use of browsing formats
— Follow up
   Reviewed printout adequately
   Explained interlibrary loan

Certainly the analysts must be trained to apply the behaviors and procedures the service manager thinks are appropriate—every patron must be greeted with a handshake, for example—before they can be evaluated on them, and it is useful to review the checklist periodically and obtain from the search analysts at least some general agreement that the required behaviors and procedures are important. The policy and procedures manual should already spell out the steps an analyst is expected to complete in a mediated search. Observing allows the service manager to view and evaluate all aspects of an analyst's skills, from interpersonal skills to search strategy construction skills, and the checklist insures that the analysts know what is expected of them. The problem with the observation technique is that it violates the confidentiality of the private consultation between analyst and patron. The service manager sitting by and making ticks on a checklist can make the analyst and perhaps the patron very nervous. The manager must decide whether a regular schedule or a "pop quiz" format is more desirable, how often to observe, whether inexperienced searchers will be observed more frequently or on the same schedule as experienced searchers, how the results of the observation will be discussed with the search analyst, and many other variables. Whatever format is used, the service manager can be sure that evaluation by observation takes a great deal of his or her time.

A reproduction of the search strategy cannot evaluate the interpersonal skills of a search analyst directly, but this evaluation technique is noninvasive in that it does not interfere with the interaction between analyst and patron. After the mediated search is complete, the service manager or another search analyst takes the search question and does it again from the beginning including database selection, profiling the strategy, performing the search, and printing the citations. The two searches are checked against each other and the resulting printouts are compared, preferably by the patron who requested the search who can best judge the precision and recall ratios achieved by each. This does require some cooperation and expenditure of time on the part of the patron. Furthermore it can be expensive since the searching and printing must be done twice, and the library's budget must bear the expense of the second search and of the second searcher's time. To be effective, it should be done at random so that the analyst does not know which search will be reproduced. This technique does have some drawbacks; during the discussion of the results it becomes very clear that there is no one way to do a search correctly, and the presence of the patron responding to the searching process and making suggestions as the search goes on makes a big difference in how the patron's question will be interpreted.

Peer evaluation is a most valuable tool for the instruction and improvement of the search analysts' techniques, but it should be kept separate from the personnel evaluation the service manager performs. The reproduced search described above should be presented in a staff meeting where all the analysts can discuss the merits of the two searches and learn from them, and the original searcher can defend or explain the choices made. The review becomes a mini-workshop on searching. If peer review is used as an evaluation technique, the manager must take care to insure that meetings are not seen as an opportunity to "roast" one's colleagues and that the responsibility for reviewing searches and being reviewed rotates among all the searchers equally.

Staff meetings on a regular basis, especially for distributed services where search analysts work in different libraries or at different service desks, are invaluable for maintaining currency and quality. Peer review sessions in which an attitude of give-and-take or even intellectual fencing is fostered can make lively meetings. Calling attention to errors helps others avoid the same mistakes and if handled properly promotes a feeling of community among the searchers. If formal peer review seems too likely to lead to quarrels and hurt feelings, the manager can invite the searchers to present their own mistakes during a regular "show-and-tell" portion of the meeting; example of innovative solutions as well as examples of mistakes can also be included. The staff meetings should be a vehicle for reviewing and revising if necessary the policies and procedures of the automated information retrieval service, reporting new developments such as revised search engines or new databases or new equipment recently installed, and finding solutions to the problems searchers have in common. They are essential for instilling in the staff the integrity and sense of duty needed to provide a quality information product. Mini-workshops can be scheduled in which a searcher with particular expertise shares his or her knowledge or reports on a formal training session recently attended. The formal or informal atmosphere of the parent library will probably dictate whether the search analysts' staff meeting has a written agenda each time, but the meetings should have a regular structure familiar to the attendees, otherwise people will show up for the meeting and have nothing to say to each other.

TRAINING

Training is so large a portion of the automated information retrieval service manager's job that it practically becomes an unconscious routine. Training opportunities abound; library schools, vendors, and database producers offer classes and workshops, and the proliferation of ondisk databases allows the opportunity for self-training and experimentation. But the in-house training programs produced by the service manager should be the most in-depth and relevant programs for the staff, designed to cover all the automated information retrieval options available in a particular library (Online Training, 1981).

Library schools very early began to offer at least one class covering the techniques of automated information retrieval (Harter and Fenichel, 1982). Typically the classes include paper exercises on search strategy profiling and the protocols of one or more search engines. Students are given questions that they are required to break into concept groups with appropriate synonyms, either free-text or selected from thesauri, and apply the coding and logical operators of a particular search engine. Unless the library school has access to ondisk databases, these exercises are done on paper. When a new graduate is asked, "How much online time have you practiced?'' the answer is usually under two hours and often enough under thirty minutes. Obviously the cost of online time for a class of library school students is the limiting factor here. Practicing with ondisk databases does not force students to devise economical search strategies nor does it provide the experience of making quick decisions when every second not only counts, but costs. If online systems are used, they are most often the inexpensive Classmate or Instructor systems, and students are told not to worry about the costs but to worry instead about learning the system. When they take a job they are told to worry about the cost, and when the patron is hanging over their shoulders waiting for the results of a ready-reference search they no longer have the luxury of a leisurely pencil and paper profiling exercise. Library schools are doing a good job of teaching the mechanics and techniques of searching, but a little more emphasis on economics and speedy decision making would be beneficial.

The vendor training programs offer the advantage of much more online time. Typically there are two levels of training: a beginning session and an advanced session. Some vendors offer the beginning session in the morning and the advanced session in the afternoon so that a person can complete both in one day, or day-long sessions are offered on consecutive days. Vendor sessions naturally concentrate on the one search engine the vendor uses, but beginning sessions also cover the basics of Boolean logic and profiling. During the session students are usually allowed at least an hour online, frequently with two students working together at one terminal, and after the session most vendors assign special passwords to the attendees so that they can practice at greater length in their own institutions. Advanced sessions go into more depth covering the uses of the vendor's search engine. Advanced sessions assume that the student already knows Boolean logic and profiling and concentrate instead on particular techniques such as limiting, using hedges, code searching, and so forth. Vendors also provide training sessions in particular subject areas, where attendees learn the tricks of searching a group of databases such as business databases or materials science databases. These are usually quite well done and provide a valuable body of knowledge to experienced searchers.

Vendor sessions are very useful but they are not particularly convenient. There is a fee for each session and, although they are held in cities all over the country, many libraries will most likely have to send staff to a nearby large city and pay for the travel and lodging expenses as well as the fee. Beginning and advanced sessions are offered frequently, the specialized subject sessions less frequently and at fewer locations. It is possible to arrange for the trainers to come to a host library to conduct a training session, and this may save the library travel and lodging money if there are several people to be trained. The host library will need to provide the appropriate facilities such as a classroom with online access and multiple terminals for practice. Announcements of upcoming training sessions are carried in the vendors' newsletters and frequently in their online news or announcements files, as well as in direct mail flyers sent to libraries. Some sessions fill up rapidly, so it is advisable to monitor the newsletters closely and sign up for a session well in advance. It is the responsibility of the individual search analysts to monitor what is available and initiate requests to attend workshops or training sessions. The service manager must approve requests based on his or her judgment of how the search analyst and the service will benefit and on the state of the budget if workshop fees and travel are involved. The vendors are accustomed to dealing with all kinds of libraries, businesses, and individuals, and therefore can accommodate almost any billing requirement. Libraries with existing contracts with a vendor can have training sessions billed to a password usually used for searching.

Another problem with vendor training sessions is the repetition. Beginning sessions always cover profiling and Boolean logic as well as the simpler commands of the vendor's search engine. An experienced DIALOG searcher who attends a BRS beginning-level training session will learn BRS commands but will be irritated by the time spent on things he or she already knows.

Database producers also sponsor training sessions that typically cover a database's beginning and advanced level searching techniques in the search engines of the major vendors carrying the database. These can be especially useful for the staff of a branch library who may need to search the database frequently. Unfortunately, the sessions are offered infrequently and at few locations, and the cost ranges from free to hundreds of dollars. Such sessions are frequently announced in the major vendors' newsletters, in library science journals—especially those aimed at search analysts—and by direct mail flyers.

An In-House Training Program

Not all librarians have taken automated information retrieval courses in library school, and not all libraries can afford to send the staff who need to know automated information retrieval to vendor-sponsored training sessions. Most of the library staff do not need the in-depth training offered by vendors. The solution is an in-house training program run by the service manager. In-house training is not limited to the search analyst staff. It offers many levels of training based on a library staff member's need to know, whether that staff member is involved in providing mediated searches or simply needs enough knowledge to make an informed referral when a patron can best be served by an automated information source. The in-house program should serve end-users as well as library staff.

The first step in developing an in-house training program is to identify all the groups of people who need to be trained. For example, in an academic library these groups could include all librarians or perhaps all staff, all public service librarians, all staff expected to provide ready-reference searches, all staff expected to provide help for end-users, the end-users themselves, and the search analysts. Next, the service manager needs to identify the level of training appropriate to each group and develop a training package for each level.

An overview of what is available and how patrons can make use of it, whether by appointment or otherwise, is appropriate for all librarians and indeed for practically all the staff who work in the library. The intention is not to teach people how to search but to demonstrate what happens during a search and the circumstances in which automated information retrieval should be applied so that the staff themselves can take advantage of the service if the need arises and so that they can refer patrons to the automated information retrieval service office when asked. With some slight modifications the overview program can be presented to the public at faculty meetings, for example, or to university administrators or to potential donors who may be asked to underwrite an online program or subscriptions to ondisk databases. To be effective the program should include a demonstration of a search, either online or ondisk, and this requires the appropriate equipment—a large screen projection system certainly, and ideally a portable microcomputer with an internal modem and CD-ROM drive.

The program designed for the public services staff of the library goes into more detail, with the intention of providing the staff with the background needed to refer patrons to an automated information solution when it is appropriate. The program demonstrates a typical search but provides more in-depth information on the vendors and databases available in the library and demonstrates the tools to consult when a librarian needs to know if a particular index or a subject is available through the automated information retrieval service. It reviews the types of questions best suited to an automated solution. It details the variety of options available such as mediated or ready-reference or end-user services, and explains how patrons can access the options, when they are available, and what the costs are, if any. Also, the relevant sections of the policy and procedures manual are reviewed. At the end of the session a staff member should be able to determine if a patron's question is eligible for an automated solution, whether or not a database is available to answer the question, and to which service option the patron should be referred.

Staff members expected to provide ready-reference searches constitute the next level of training, which includes simple profiling, Boolean logic, and the protocols of a particular search engine. If there are many people to train at the same time, the service manager may opt to invite a vendor to present its basic training session at the library, or many vendors produce programmed instruction manuals and training diskettes that can be used by individuals for self-instruction, or the manager may decide to construct his or her own basic training program. These programs are system-specific; that is, they teach only one search engine. If more than one vendor is made available for ready-reference searching, the manager will probably want to devise an in-house program that concentrates on the search engine and skips the repetition of profiling techniques and Boolean logic included, in the vendor-produced introductory programs. Whichever method is chosen, the manager will need to arrange a session in which the library's policies regarding ready-reference searches, and any record-keeping and reporting procedures the staff are expected to fulfill, are explained. Practice time in online files is an integral part of this training program and must be included in the library's budget.

Similar in nature are the programs devised for end-users and those staff members who work with end-users. If end-user online services are available, the program should concentrate on the search engine and provide printed lists of the databases and subjects covered by the service. Training sessions for ondisk products cover both the search engine and the database. End-user training is likely to be a major role for librarians and will be covered in more detail in the chapter on end-users (Friend, 1985; Hubbard and Wilson, 1986).

Finally, the manager must devise some training programs for the search analyst staff (Mader, 1984; Tenopir, 1982). Search analysts should attend the vendor-sponsored training sessions, but the manager may decide that it is not necessary for all the analysts to attend the beginning-level sessions of each vendor due to the repetition of material in the beginning-level sessions. Vendor-produced manuals or computer-assisted instruction (CAI) packages can take the place of introductory sessions, with the search analyst skipping those parts of the manual that discuss profiling and standard Boolean operators. Mentoring, the practice of pairing an experienced searcher with a novice searcher, is an excellent training method to use in this situation. It relieves the manager of yet another training task and provides the novice searcher with a point of view and a technique different from the manager's. Since there is no one, correct way to do any given search, exposure to several different techniques as practiced by different search analysts gives the novice a broader base to build his or her own technique upon. Furthermore, vendor sessions and workbooks do not teach interviewing skills, a vital component of the search process. Novice search analysts should sit in as observers while experienced search analysts conduct mediated searches, if the patron does not object on grounds of confidentiality. Once the novice is conducting mediated searches, the presence of an experienced mentor offering moral support and advice when needed eases the nervousness any novice is likely to feel.

The manager may decide to forego the vendor's training packages and produce an in-house program, which may be the best and certainly the least expensive option when searchers are experienced and simply need to learn a new search engine, or when a search engine is used so seldom that a searcher would need to review the manual anyway before feeling comfortable about accessing the system. Training for the search analysts is a continuous process. Practice time is a must; searchers should feel comfortable about going online to try out a search strategy before they are required to perform the search for a patron, especially in unknown databases or seldom-used search engines. Most vendors have practice databases or periodically make certain "live" databases available at reduced cost or even free—DIALOG's free file of the month, for example. The service manager should make sure that all the analysts have a chance to try out these databases. Analysts should be encouraged to read the professional journals, the vendors' newsletters, and other relevant literature by routing the items to them and by providing the time needed to read them. Also, the staff meeting should have a training component included, either mini-workshops assigned to the search analysts on a rotating basis, or show-and-tell sessions in which all the searchers bring good and bad examples and hash them out together.

All this training will take a good deal of the service manager's time and effort, especially since any and all of the sessions must be repeated frequently when new librarians join the staff in any capacity and thus require anything from an overview to ready-reference training, or when end-users must be trained, or when a new database or search engine is added to the search analysts' repertoire. Training sessions may be aimed at an individual or at groups. Whether interacting with a group of enthusiastic end-users or gently explaining the realities of automated information retrieval to an upper level administrator, the service manager must be flexible and—like any good Boy Scout—always prepared.

One way to build flexibility into a training program is to prepare a set of interchangeable or modular handouts that can be distributed on paper or used on an overhead projector. A handout on Boolean logic with the familiar overlapping circles, a set of handouts illustrating search strategies developed from questions in different subject areas, a handout for the search protocols of each search engine, and a set of handouts listing databases suitable for different subjects are examples of a few of the tools the manager can develop. When a training session is needed, the manager simply dips into the file, pulls the appropriate handouts and staples them together, or stuffs the appropriate transparencies into a briefcase. A unique logo or type style is useful for identifying the material, and certainly if they are to be distributed as stapled handouts or workbooks to the public they should look like a unified package rather than a bunch of individual handouts stapled together.

When demonstrating automated information retrieval products to groups, a certain setting and equipment are needed. As already mentioned, a large screen projection system with an overhead projector and a portable hard disk microcomputer with an internal modem and internal CD-ROM drive are needed. A communications software package loaded on the hard disk can store telephone numbers, passwords, and sign-on protocols in one directory, and the search software for the various CD products can be loaded in other directories. The assistance of a programmer may be needed to get all the software packages to reside together. The classroom needs rheostat-controlled lighting, a projection screen, and a chalkboard. If online systems are to be demonstrated, a telephone jack is needed in the room. It is possible to get by without the portable microcomputer, but hauling around the components of a standard desktop microcomputer and a separate CD-ROM drive and modem, and wiring all this equipment together for every training session, can become a daunting chore very soon and may inhibit the ability to put on a training session when one is needed, especially if equipment must be taken away from search analysts or end-users. Providing demonstrations in classrooms is virtually impossible without the portable microcomputer especially configured for the purpose. A professor may say that a computer is already set up in the classroom or lab, but one never knows until one tries to use it whether or not it has the correct wiring, boards, chips, memory, modems, drives, and so on needed to do the job. In fact, one can count on something being wrong.

Not only does a program of training sessions take time, it takes money. The equipment described above costs several thousands of dollars and it should be reserved for training purposes rather than having part-time duty as an end-user or ready-reference workstation. The bibliographic instruction staff and the automated information retrieval staff between them can keep the equipment busy enough to justify its purchase and use solely for training purposes. In addition to the equipment, the manager must budget the paper and supplies used for training handouts, although these costs can be kept down by using the system of modular handouts. Finally, the manager must have an adequate budget for online training and practice. The BRS Instructor system or DIALOG's Classmate system allow inexpensive access (at this writing, under $30 per hour as an average) to certain databases in a classroom setting, including demonstration by the trainer and practice by the participants in the class. DIALOG's Classmate system uses the protocols of Knowledge Index, the user-friendly version of DIALOG. DIALOG's OnTap files (Online Training And Practice) allow access using regular DIALOG protocols but the OnTap files cost more than Classmate access. BRS Instructor uses regular BRS protocols but can be configured to the user-friendly system by selecting MENU when prompted to select a database. For staff training, most of the other major vendors have a CAI-type program online that can be accessed inexpensively. If several people are to practice online at the same time, multiple passwords will be necessary. It is possible to negotiate training passwords with some of the vendors that allow access to some databases for a limited period of time. One must contact the individual vendors to see what is available and how much it will cost.

Search analysts and ready-reference searchers will need to practice in "live" files on occasion at the full cost of the file. Staff need the practice and experience so that they will not be flustered when required to perform a search in a public area with the patron watching, and they should not be so nervous about the cost of every minute online that they become ineffective. Studies have shown that it takes from eight to ten hours of online practice time using a variety of databases to reach a comfortable level of skill and experience (Lee, 1984). Some of this practice time can be accomplished using ondisk files at no cost, or inexpensive training files at very little cost, but at some point before they are turned loose on the public they need the sweaty-palmed experience of spending $1.50 or $2.00 per minute in a live file. It is not unusual to spend $500 on in-house training and practice to bring a novice ready-reference searcher up to a level of comfort. Once the comfort level is reached, exercising the ready-reference option will keep the searcher in practice, but each time a new search engine is added to the options available for ready-reference searching there will be some additional costs until searchers achieve a reasonable comfort level in the new system, probably after two to three hours of practice. Training a new search analyst can cost significantly more at the initial stage when the analyst is being sent to vendor-sponsored training sessions and is spending several hours practicing, but thereafter a good search analyst can pick up new databases and new systems without considerable expense.

It is money well spent. When several end-user options are made available, the end-users collectively will spend far more hours searching than the library staff, but it is unwise to allow end-users to become more knowledgeable searchers than the librarians.

REFERENCES

Auster, Ethel and Stephen B. Lawton. "Search interview techniques and information gain as antecedents of user satisfaction with online bibliographic retrieval." *Journal of the American Society for Information Science* 35 (March, 1984): 90–103. An example of a carefully reasoned and executed research project demonstrating the effect of search analyst behaviors on the satisfaction level of the user.

Beck, Susan J., ed. "Information specialists' use of machine-assisted reference tools: evaluation criteria." *RQ* 31 (Fall 1991): 35–38. A checklist of skills, knowledge, and responsibilities expected of search analysts, prepared by the Machine-Assisted Reference Section (MARS) of the American Library Association.

Bellardo, Trudi. "What do we really know about online searchers?" *Online Review* 9 (June, 1985): 223–229. A review of the literature on the personal and cognitive traits of search analysts, concluding that "research evidence thus far does not support the more extravagant claims" requiring analysts to be exceptionally intelligent and personable.

Chatterton, Fred and Jeff Pemberton. "The online professionals—who does what." *Online* 9 (July, 1985): 15–24. Based on a search of the "Marquis Who's Who Directory of Online Professionals," the tables in this article show who is searching, their professional memberships, average ages, occupational fields, what kinds of libraries they work in, and the equipment and databases they use.

Dolan, Donna R. "The quality control of search analysts." *Online* 3 (April, 1979): 8–16. Believing that the skills characterizing an exceptional search analyst are inherent rather than teachable, the author has developed a pre-test to weed out those lacking the inherent skill before investing a lengthy training program in them.

Dommer, Janet M. and M. Dawn McCaghy. "Techniques for conducting effective search interviews with thesis and dissertation candidates." *Online* 6 (March, 1982): 44–47. Details the steps a search analyst must take to satisfy the varying literature search needs of graduate students.

Evans, John Edward. "Methods of funding." In *Online Searching: Technique and Management*, edited by James J. Maloney. 135–148. Chicago: American Library Association, 1983. Provides some interesting insights into the effects of charging or not charging for mediated searches.

Fidel, Raya and Dagobert Soergel. "Factors affecting online bibliographic retrieval: a conceptual framework for research." *Journal of the American Society for Information Science* 34 (May, 1983); 163–180. A detailed list of variables or factors that occur in the automated information retrieval setting, organized in a table according to themes.

Friend, Linda. "Independence at the terminal: training student end-users to do online literature searching." *Journal of Academic Librarianship* 11 (July, 1985): 136–141. Details an end-user instruction program conducted by the searching staff at Penn State University. The author concludes that end-user instruction will become a major role for librarians.

Girard, Anne and Magdeleine Moureau. "An examination of the role of the intermediary in the online searching of chemical literature." *Online Review* 5 (June, 1981): 217-225. Using five sample questions as illustrations, the authors show that a good search analyst can perform an effective search without extensive knowledge of either the database or the subject area being searched. A firm knowledge of how to search is the key.

Glunz, Diane L. "Quality assurance in computer searching." *Reference Librarian* 11 (Fall/Winter, 1984): 277-292. "Assurance of quality depends on the search analyst," the author asserts, and goes on to suggest ways to evaluate the service provided.

Glunz, Diane and Eileen Wakiji. "Maximizing search quality through a program of peer review." *Online* 7 (September, 1983): 100-103. Describes a system of regularly scheduled meetings during which search strategies are critiqued by reviewers assigned from the search analyst staff on a rotating basis.

Grossman, David. "Personnel: the searchers." In *Online Searching: The Basics, Settings and Management*, edited by Joann H. Lee. 5-11. Littleton, Colo.: Libraries Unlimited, 1984. A brief review of the duties of search analysts and the settings in which they are found.

Hammer, Mary M. "Search analysts as successful reference librarians." *Behavioral and Social Sciences Librarian* 2 (Winter, 1981/Spring, 1982): 21-29. A description of the reference skills a good search analyst must have.

Harter, Stephen P. and Carol H. Fenichel. "Online searching in library education." *Journal of Education for Librarianship* 23 (Summer, 1982): 3-22. "A general, in-depth picture of the status of instruction in online searching in schools of library and information science." The results of a 1980 survey of ALA accredited library schools and selected other schools having library science curricula.

Hock, Randolph E. "Who should search? The attributes of a good searcher." In *Online Searching: Technique and Management*, edited by James J. Maloney. 83-88. Chicago: American Library Association, 1983. Written by a former librarian engaged in training prospective searchers. Lists and explains the attributes that predict whether one might be a good searcher.

Hubbard, Abigail and Barbara Wilson. "An integrated information management program: defining a new role for librarians in helping end-users." *Online* 10 (March, 1986): 15-23. The library staff of a medical school library not only teach end-user database searching but other information management skills such as gateway and communications software, downloading, organizing reprint files, etc.

Jackson, William J. "Staff selection and training for quality online searching." *RQ* 22 (Fall, 1982): 48-54. The author questions the assumption that any good reference librarian can be trained to be an online searcher, and suggests a combination of library school, vendor-sponsored, and in-house training as necessary for the preparation of effective searchers.

Lee, Joann H. "Training." In *Online Searching: The Basics, Settings and Management*, edited by Joann H. Lee. 18-25. Littleton, Colo.: Libraries Unlimited, 1984. Answers the questions, what should training cover, who does it, what are some of the teaching methods used, and how long does it take.

Mader, Sharon. "Personnel management." In *Online Searching: The Basics, Settings and Management*, edited by Joann H. Lee. 12-17. Littleton, Colo.: Libraries Unlimited, 1984. The author stresses the importance of a policy and procedures manual, regular meetings, and mentoring in personnel management.

Mintz, Anne P. "Information practice and malpractice . . . do we need malpractice insurance?" *Online* 8 (July, 1984): 20-26. Written from the perspective of information brokers, this article warns that any library charging a fee for service might be liable to a lawsuit for information malpractice.

Moureau, Magdeleine. "Cost and know-how: the Matthew effect in information retrieval." *Online Review* 11 (December, 1987): 355-360. "The more you have the more you will get" and "From him that hath not shall be taken away even that which he hath" is the Matthew effect according to St. Matthew, and according to Moureau it applies to the search analyst who becomes more proficient with each search and is asked to do more searches due to a reputation for proficiency.

Nelson, Brian. "Online bibliography searching and the deprofessionalization of librarianship." *Online Review* 4 (September, 1980): 215-224. Nelson looks at technological change as a cause of deprofessionalization—the loss of professional or special status—as technology makes the role of the information intermediary less necessary.

Nielsen, Brian. "Do user fees affect searcher behavior?" in *Dollars and Sense: Implications of the New Online Technology for Managing the Library*, edited by Bernard F. Pasqualini. 29-37. Chicago: American Library Association, 1987. An interesting variation on the fee or free controversy that questions the search analysts response to the patron based on whether or not a fee is charged. The author concludes that fee-charging involves the searcher in clerical activities that are not responsive to the needs of the patron.

"Online training sessions: suggested guidelines." *RQ* 20 (Summer, 1981): 353-357. Developed by the Education and Training of Search Analysts Committee of RASD MARS. Suggests the type of information to be covered, the setting and equipment required, and administrative considerations for several types and levels of training sessions.

Pilachowski, David M., R. Patricia Riesenman and Patricia Tegler. "Online search analyst and search-service manager tasks." *RQ* 24 (Summer, 1985): 403-410. Compiled from findings by RASD MARS. Lists the tasks and skills needed by analysts and managers and includes a selective annotated bibliography.

Rholes, Julia M. and Judith B. Droessler. "Online database searchers: cognitive style." In *National Online Meeting Proceedings 1984*. 305-311. Medford, N.J.: Learned Information, 1984. The authors applied the Myers-Briggs Type Indicator test in a 1983 mail survey to determine the cognitive style of search analysts. "Search analysts appear to be more perceptive and more flexible than reference librarians who are not search analysts," is one of the results reported in the article.

Roose, Tina. "Online search costs in public libraries." *Library Journal* 110 (May 1, 1985): 36-37. The author compares per search costs from several Illinois public libraries and concludes that those libraries not charging for online searches have lower per-search costs because the librarians have more experience and are more at ease performing searching. Those libraries that charge perform fewer searches.

Somerville, Arleen N. "The pre-search reference interview—a step by step guide." *Database* 5 (February, 1982): 32-38. A checklist of do's and don'ts concludes this article describing the process of conducting the presearch interview and some of the problems that creep into the interview process.

Tenopir, Carol. "An in-house training program for online searchers." *Online* 6 (May, 1982): 20-26. University of Hawaii librarians would have to travel far to attend vendor sponsored training, so in-house training is very much in order. Separate programs for different levels of instruction are described, with course descriptions and class outlines.

Turner, Philip M., Neal K. Kaske and Gayle S. Baker. "The effects of baud rate, performance anxiety, and experience on online bibliographic searches." *Information Technology and Libraries* 9 (March, 1990): 34–42. A well-designed research project testing the stated variables on search performance, with implications for training both search analysts and end-users.

Van Camp, Ann. "Effective search analysts." *Online* 3 (April, 1979): 18–20. An early and frequently cited list of those qualities a good search analyst needs.

5

End-User Services

THE END-USER

Although some libraries for many years have trained end-users or have made end-user searching on the major vendors' systems available to them, and others have made BRS/After Dark or Information Access Company's Search Helper or Knowledge Index available to end-users since 1982, IAC's InfoTrac on twelve-inch optical disk was for most libraries the first extensive experience with end-user searching. InfoTrac then was, for the most part, a printed index that could be searched by a computer, rather than an interactive database. The computer provided quick switching from a controlled-vocabulary subject index to article citations largely drawn from popular magazines and journals, and it printed out the citations for patrons. There was no keyword indexing, and no Boolean operations could be performed. There was no printed manual available, and IAC's publicity stated that manuals and training were not required. This was true, since end-users accessed data in much the same way they would in a printed index, by making a stab in the dark at what they thought might be a reasonable subject heading—second-guessing the indexer—and waiting for the results.

The end-users loved it. Using IAC's evaluation forms or forms devised by the libraries, end-users stated that they were very satisfied with the results, that they did not need help to use it, and that they felt they could get the same or better results than a librarian performing the search for them. They lined up to use it and waited in line rather than using printed indexes nearby. They loved the printouts of citations and printed everything in sight; the early version of InfoTrac had a "print page" command that printed every citation displayed on the screen, and end-users printed page after page rather than browsing through the citations displayed and printing only the relevant ones. A buddy system developed whereby end-users would ask each other for help, or one user who had mastered the system brought in friends and instructed them; librarians were asked for help with the hardware, replacing ink cartridges, for example, or rebooting the system when it crashed. Patrons left the building when InfoTrac crashed rather than use printed indexes to find the same or indeed better information. Many patrons were angry when they discovered that not all the magazines indexed by InfoTrac were held by the library; some were disappointed to find that academic or professional level journals were not covered, although a good many users never recognized this deficiency. A professional highway engineer wrote on an evaluation form, "This is great! I found everything I needed." Among themselves the librarians whispered, "No wonder our highways are in such bad shape."

Librarians recognized InfoTrac's limitations. There were errors and inaccuracies in the database that gave it the look of a product rushed to market, they questioned the choice of magazines and journals covered, and although IAC directed its marketing campaign at academic libraries there was very little in the database that would interest a researcher outside the field of business. Most disturbing was the observation that InfoTrac users did not have an alternative solution in mind if InfoTrac failed to solve their information needs. Instead, if they found nothing, they assumed that there was nothing to be found. But patrons loved InfoTrac. A good many libraries installed it on the one month free trial offer from IAC, and then were afraid that the students might stage a sit-in if they removed it. (Articles describing the InfoTrac experience include Beltran (1986 and 1987), Ernest and Monath (1986), Hall et al. (1987), Kleiner (1987), and Reese (1988).)

Since this early version of InfoTrac, librarians have had a good, hard look at end-users and how they approach the problem of searching many different kinds of databases for information. Naturally enough, end-users make mistakes, and in many cases these are the same kinds of mistakes they make in using the printed collections in libraries. To begin with, end-users have misconceptions about databases: they frankly do not know what they are looking at. They make preparation errors before they attempt to search and most believe that advance preparation is not needed, just as new freshmen believe they do not need library instruction because they already know how to look things up in a library. They make searching errors, many of them, largely because they do not understand what a database is and because they failed to prepare.

End-User Misconceptions About the Databases

The naive end-user approaching a database for the first time, especially a locally loaded or ondisk database, quite often assumes that the database was produced by the library. Therefore, they think it covers everything in the library, that anything in the database should be in the library, and, most distressing of all, that librarians can "fix" the database if something is wrong with it. "Why don't you put the call numbers in here?" is the most frequent vocalization of this misconception, even from end-users who have been told and have accepted the fact that the database in question was produced by a commercial indexing company. This misconception is easily dispelled, provided the end-user asks or is exposed to the information in a BI session. Much harder to get across is the concept of multiple, subject-oriented databases. Naive end-users believe that there is only one superdatabase that covers everything and all subjects. For example, faced with an array of CD-ROM workstations, the naive end-user will probably sit down at the first one available and begin searching, under the assumption that all the workstations are the same. If the end-user is met by a staff member who asks which database he or she wants to search, the end-user is stumped. If given a choice of databases either by the staff member or by prominent signs posted at the various workstations, at least half the time the end-user will choose an inappropriate database (Allen, 1990b). This is the same problem librarians have faced in guiding a patron to an appropriate index, and good question negotiation can point the patron in the right direction. But the problem with automated databases is that the patron can bypass the librarian, walk up to a workstation and start typing, and the "user-friendly" search engine is just friendly enough to convince the patron that he or she is getting results. Even when the result is zero hits, an end-user will accept this answer from a computer.

End-users have misconceptions about the content of databases. The expectation of finding call numbers has already been mentioned. Many people expect to find the full text of articles, and they certainly expect a computerized database to be up to the minute and able to index the journal article they read last week. An end-user accustomed to using a database containing abstracts expects to find abstracts in every other database. The differences among free-text, keywords, and controlled vocabulary are very hard to grasp. Users have similar misconceptions about printed tools, and librarians will struggle to resolve these misconceptions in similar ways. What makes a computerized database different and affects the success of accessing the database is the way each record is structured into searchable fields. Although a librarian trained in information management can conceptualize the way in which an automated database record is derived from the information in a printed index, the end-user does not have that training and probably does not have the exposure to the differing arrangements of printed tools, and therefore does not have a model to build on. For example, an end-user searching for an author's name may have enough of a model to try variations of last name first or first name last, with commas or without, but definitely will not try variations of "au=" without instruction. A patron may know to search the correct year of a printed index for a known item, but does not conceive of publication year as a searchable field in a database covering multiple years. A patron searching for "management by objectives" can find information easily in a printed index but is heading for deep trouble on an automated system where any of these variations could apply:

— management-by-objectives
— management objectives
— management(w) objectives
— management adj objectives

None of these variations is intuitive. No end-user is likely to stumble across the correct choice without instruction.

An end-user may know that the database he or she is using is derived from a printed index, but end-users almost invariably prefer automated to print. Naturally enough, they prefer the speed and ease of handling a computer keyboard as opposed to multiple and often heavy volumes of print, and they prefer the convenience of a printout to copying citations by hand. Unfortunately, they do not accept or recognize that browsing through the printed version may produce better results than the automated version for certain research topics. The basic misconception here is that a modern computer is by definition superior to old-fashioned printed indexes, and only a librarian experienced in using both knows that this is not necessarily true. End-users will either force the computer to meet their needs by printing out long browsing lists of citations, or they will revise their needs to match what the computer can give them.

Preparation Errors

Information Access Company promoted its InfoTrac database with the claim that no instruction in its use was needed, that the librarian could simply point the user to the machine and thus be freed from routine questions and explanations. Librarians themselves are guilty of directing patrons to automated sources with the explanation that they are "easier to use," which is frequently not the case. The phrase "user-friendly" is thrown about casually. The information industry and information professionals promote the idea that no advance preparation is needed to use certain automated information sources. Librarians accept the fact that search analysts need extensive training and experience using the search engines of various vendors, and that profiling the search—writing it out on a piece of paper—before going online is a necessary step, especially in expensive online systems. But end-users are not always instructed or encouraged to prepare in advance.

End-users are themselves to blame. Not reading the instructions is a common human failing. People who are computer literate assume that they can figure the system out, and there are always help screens available to get them out of difficulties, or library staff on call to answer questions. If they have no mental model of the complexities of an automated database they have no reason to question their ability to access it. User-friendly systems are designed to provide an answer. The end-user wanting information about "cats" walks up to a CD-ROM workstation and types in the word "cat". Almost any database, from MLA Bibliography to COMPENDEX will provide an answer, and the end-user who does not have the appropriate mental model of databases will assume that this is THE answer.

"If all else fails, read the instructions," the saying goes. End-users may not recognize a failure in the response a user-friendly system gives them, so the basic lack of desire to read the instructions is reinforced. End-users seldom read the help screens, but this is largely the fault of the help screens themselves, which are long and wordy and usually not context-sensitive. Most end-users are not aware of the existence of thesauri and probably would not apply them anyway since the users are keyword or natural-language oriented and do not have the librarian's knowledge, the librarian's mental model, of a controlled vocabulary. For most end-users, printed documentation is irrelevant in a computerized environment.

Naive end-users do not have an understanding of the complexities of Boolean logic; they are unaware of sophisticated searching techniques. Therefore they see no need to write out a search strategy in advance. As with printed index users, they may not realize the amount of literature and the partitions of the literature on their subject until they start looking for information, but unfortunately the automated index will not graphically illustrate the partitions of the subject while displaying screen after screen of citations. In a printed index the subject headings and their subdivisions are evident on the page; only a very sophisticated user will be able to compile a mental index extracted from the descriptor field of the records displayed on the computer screen

Searching Errors

Without a good understanding of Boolean operators, end-users perform very simple searches. There is a natural tendency to cut corners in an effort to find something quickly, and here the automated database magnifies the error by producing quick responses. The end-user keys in "CATTLE AND DISEASE" on the AGRICOLA database and receives a response. At this point the end-user will view scores of citations either onscreen or by printing out a browsing list which the end-user takes away and examines in much the same way he or she would have used a printed index, rather than refining the search by adding other concept groups or limiting the search. The end-user may eventually find what is needed but this is an inefficient way to search that wastes time and supplies, and leaves the end-user with a false model of what an automated database can do.

End-users frequently do not have alternative strategies. If a search produces zero results, a good many end-users will accept the answer as definitive; in other words, they will believe that there is no literature on the subject to be found. Others may realize that there is an error but will not be able to revise the search to get around the error. In addition to a tendency to underspecify as in the "CATTLE AND DISEASE" example above, some end-users will overspecify by trying to get every concept in one line of command, like so: "CATTLE AND DISEASE AND PREVENTION AND SANITATION AND BARNS". Citations retrieved with this strategy, if any, will not be the only ones in the database on the topic of disease prevention by keeping the barn clean; the end-user has sacrificed recall ratio in a misinformed attempt to get the most precise citations possible. Neither strategy shows an understanding of concept groups or the use of "OR" to include synonyms. If the searcher recognizes that there should be more citations in the database, his or her alternative is likely to be: "CATTLE AND DISEASE AND PREVENTION AND CLEANLINESS AND BARNS." In other words, the end-user has retyped the entire command line with the exception of one synonym. Even end-users who create conceptual sets of synonyms frequently do not reuse the set numbers in different combinations with other sets, but will instead type the sets over again to put them in new combinations.

End-users do not pick up clues from system responses. For example, they recognize that the search is picking up words mentioned in passing, in the abstract for example, but they do not know how to prioritize the words by limiting them to title or descriptor occurrences. Other clues, such as field name abbreviations, word or phrase indexing, or the formats used for author name or journal title, do not register as things of importance that can be used to refine the search strategy. End-users frequently do not notice the dates of the citations being retrieved, even when their stated objective is to find the most recent articles.

Naturally, end-users make mechanical mistakes such as using the wrong protocols, mixing Boolean operators in the same line of command without regard to the processing order of operators, and improper use of function keys or function commands, especially if multiple search engines are made available to endusers. Trained search analysts make these mistakes as well, but search analysts recognize the consequences when such mistakes are made and know the appropriate documentation to consult for correcting the mistakes. End-users recognize that a mistake has been made, but transaction logs of their searches indicate that they are most likely to enter the same command again, sometimes several times, apparently assuming that the command is correct and the system has made a mistake. Alternatively, they may end the current session and start the entire transaction over again from the beginning.

All these misconceptions and errors mean that end-users take longer to search than a trained search analyst would, and the results they achieve do not match the recall ratios and precision ratios that search analysts strive for. Yet, when asked on evaluation forms if they are satisfied with the results the answer is almost always positive. When asked if they would prefer to have a librarian do the search for them, the answer is usually "no." When asked if a librarian might have done a better search than they achieved, most end-users do not believe so. When asked if the system was easy to use, very few end-users rate it as difficult, and the majority rate is as moderately easy or very easy to use. The truth is that end-user systems are easy to use but difficult to master. (Some of the articles describing typical end-user errors include de Stricker (1990), Janke (1984), Puttapithakporn (1990), and Sullivan et al. (1990).)

The End-User's Mental Model

The mistakes that end-users make and the responses they write on evaluation forms give an idea of the mental model they have of automated information retrieval. The naive end-user believes that there is one database; the experienced end-user recognizes two or three or possibly several databases but does not clearly understand the relationships and overlaps among databases. Neither has a good idea of how small or how large the database is; the end-user who finds nothing is no more astonished than the end-user who finds hundreds of citations. The database records have a certain structure, but most end-users believe this structure is for the convenience of the database and is irrelevant to the end-user. They think that automated information retrieval systems are very easy to use because the computer does most of the work; the computer analyzes and interprets the question and then provides the best answer. In other words, end-users assume the computer knows that "sanitation" and "cleanliness" are synonymous; therefore there is no need to specify them to the computer. Furthermore, they assume the computer understands the priorities and needs of the user and does not supply irrelevant information or false hits. If the user wants ten "good" citations on the national debt, he or she counts on the computer to make the value judgment. End-users believe that there is no recourse if the answer is unsatisfactory because if the computer doesn't know the answer, no one does (de Stricker, 1990b).

Why do end-users have this model? End-users approach automated information retrieval in much the same way they approach libraries, with very little understanding of the size, complexity, and arrangement of the collections, and yet confident that the information they want is in the library and easy to find. If it were hard to find, librarians would not allow people to wander around the building looking for it for themselves.

Both librarians and end-user services promote the idea that end-user systems are easy to use, and the end-users quite naturally agree. An end-user database will provide an answer of sorts to almost any question. Once the answer is in hand there is little motivation to learn how to get a better answer. End-users are infrequent searchers; even the most dedicated end-user cannot have the constant exposure that librarians have to build a different mental model upon. Of those end-users who have expressed a desire to do their own searching and have invested the time in extensive training, less than half search frequently enough to maintain skills, to apply the training such that it will be remembered. End-users tend to limit their searches to one or two databases and are unaware of others; this is not enough exposure to allow them to internalize the structures of databases and become comfortable with using them. Librarians, database producers, and vendors tend to forget that nonlibrarians lack a basic understanding of information management. The concepts of multiple databases and databanks and vendors, of controlled vocabularies and index structures, are vital to building an accurate mental model of automated information retrieval as it exists today, but these are the concepts that librarians skim over when instructing end-users, being more intent on helping the end-user operate the computer and get a quick answer—this being what the end-user wants.

Another reason end-users fail to develop an accurate mental model is that help is hard to come by. The help screens designed by end-user systems are hopelessly unhelpful. The instructions are too long and are arranged in a linear fashion such that the user must page through screen after screen; this makes relationships between menus or help screens hard to see. Frequently there is no interactive or context-sensitive help; the user who has produced an answer set must know that the next step is either to view or print the citations before he or she can call up a help screen explaining how to view the citations or how to print them. Most end-users will escape out of the help screens long before all of them have been read because they would prefer to spend their time searching inefficiently rather than reading help screens, especially if there are online costs or time pressures while using the system (Puttapithakporn, 1990).

Printed documentation has drawbacks as well. Most of it is too long and frequently too technical. It answers questions the end-user would never dream of asking or applying, and it does not answer the question at the time it is asked; in other words, the user who wants to print a citation from ERIC is not well served by being referred to the SilverPlatter manual. Many librarians have tried to bypass the lengthy documentation provided by the vendors by producing simple two-page handouts explaining the function keys and commands of a particular system. These work only if they are read. Reading the instructions requires advance preparation, something end-users are reluctant to do.

Bibliographic instruction sessions and workshops offered by the library can help to build a correct mental model of automated information retrieval, but the end-user who has obtained some sort of result from a database search is not likely to recognize that instruction might teach a different or a better way to get better results. Furthermore, workshops are like documentation in that they are a form of advance preparation; they are not offered at the time help is needed. Students avoid yet another class they must sit through, and faculty avoid the appearance that they need instruction from librarians. For the librarians, a great deal of time and work in preparing and conducting the workshops often ends in the frustration of low attendance.

Personalized assistance available on demand provides help at the moment it is needed, and provides context-sensitive help; the end-user who asks "How do I print the citations?" gets an immediate, short answer rather than having to read several pages of documentation. No end-user system is so user-friendly that help is not required as the users are searching, so libraries have found that they must provide staff to assist users on an individual basis. This consumes staff time. In a busy operation with multiple searching stations, the staff probably can do no more than context-sensitive assistance; that is, brief and limited instruction on the mechanics of searching, which does very little to change the searcher's mental model of automated information retrieval. If the time and the help is available, librarians have found that end-users are quite willing to revise their mental models and become better searchers.

The Advantages of End-User Searching

Understanding all the problems end-users have, why would any library opt to install an end-user operation? Simply because end-users exist, and they are here to stay. The library that does not participate in the end-user phenomenon will be bypassed (Cuadra, 1987; Janke, 1984). In an attempt to expand their markets beyond libraries, the vendors are promoting their services to potential end-users in mass market business, computer, and consumer magazines. The storage capacity of compact disks has made them familiar in the business world, and there are compact disk products aimed at the home computer user. As libraries automate their card catalogs, patrons come to expect the same kind of automated access to the periodical literature. Automated information retrieval for end-users is an information management technique that libraries cannot afford to ignore.

Library patrons certainly prefer automated information retrieval to printed tools, and they prefer to do it themselves. End-user products give them independence, a feeling of being in control of their information needs. End-user products are usually more convenient than mediated search services because the patron does not have to make an appointment and does not have to explain topics and information requirements to a librarian. They get immediate results since citations are printed online or at the ondisk workstation, whereas mediated searches frequently opt for offline prints to save costs. Although the library may be spending quite a bit for CD-ROM database subscriptions and the total bill for online end-user services can be high, the individual end-user pays little or nothing for a search. This attracts more users to the library and makes automated information retrieval available to more users. Undergraduates especially are deterred by the high costs of mediated services, and they are likely to become the major users of ondisk databases.

The library benefits from the provision of end-user services. The image of the library is enhanced, changed from one of musty books and hard-to-use indexes to a high-tech environment where computers make information easy to find. The increased use of indexes means that the library's collections will receive more use. End-user searching takes demand and pressure off the mediated service and ready-reference searchers to provide the kinds of searches that end-users can do for themselves. Finally, the mechanics and techniques of searching provide the means for expanding the patrons' knowledge about information management, in that explanations about databases and their structures and search strategies are necessary in an automated information retrieval environment. End-users will apply this knowledge to other aspects of library use, including printed indexes, just as librarians discovered that their information management skills were enhanced by a knowledge of the structure of automated information retrieval.

THE END-USER SERVICE OPTIONS

Characteristics of a User-Friendly System

The antonym or user-friendly is user-hostile. One imagines an angry scowl, locked doors guarded by watchdogs, an unfamiliar and strange environment where perhaps a foreign language is spoken and where stiff penalties result for even an innocent mistake. This describes precisely the "native" or command mode of the major vendors such as DIALOG, BRS, or ORBIT, where passwords and complicated protocols are required just to enter the systems, the command language is not intuitive, and mistakes cost money.

On the other hand, a user-friendly system should invite use. The connection to the system is either not needed or easy to make. End-user online systems should not require passwords or sign-on protocols, and in fact the library will probably want to keep the passwords secret so that patrons cannot use them outside the library. Communications software needs to be programmed to conduct the sign-on procedures invisibly so that the user's first interaction with the system is at the point where the system asks the user to specify a database. Ondisk workstations should be powered up and ready, and can have the database's introductory screen displayed; however, the image will eventually burn into the monitor's screen after a time, therefore many libraries prefer a blank screen, either by manually turning down the monitor's intensity after each use or by installing a "screen blanker" program that automatically blanks the screen after so many minutes of disuse. A blank screen is not user-friendly; some patrons may assume that the hardware is turned off and will start flipping switches in an attempt to turn it on, and others will walk away assuming that the system is down. Preferable is a "screen saver" program that moves an image or a group of characters—perhaps stating "STRIKE ANY KEY TO START"—around the screen at random, thus preventing burn-in and demonstrating to patrons that the system is turned on. A user-friendly ondisk system either has a single database installed on the workstation or immediately presents the user with a menu of databases available. Once a database is selected, the introductory screen is displayed, describing the database very briefly and presenting the searcher with the option to ask for help or to start searching.

Once the user has connected to the database, the interaction between the user and a user-friendly system resembles a dialogue. Commands are in a human language; for example, the user types "FIND" rather than "SELECT," or "PRINT" rather than ". .P". Abbreviations are clear and logical. Messages from the system should be easy to read and easy to find using menus or directories or windows; context-sensitive help is preferable although this approaches artificial intelligence and is difficult to provide. A user-friendly system clearly prompts the user to take the next step. Error messages are nonthreatening and nonaccusatory and should offer a menu of alternatives that are context-sensitive. Warning messages, on the other hand, should clearly threaten consequences and offer a way out of the difficulty. For example, if pressing the F7 key is the instruction to erase all input and restart the system, the user should be warned of this when the key is pressed and should be offered a choice of canceling the command or continuing with it. Experienced users tend to resent frequent warnings or systems that ask for confirmation of every command, and naive users may ignore or misinterpret the warnings, but they are necessary.

System defaults should be based on a logical analysis of the typical user's expectations. For example, if a user types "CAT FOOD" the user expects the system to find the word CAT immediately followed by the word FOOD. The default in this case assumes that a space between words should be interpreted as ADJ or (W) if no other operator is indicated. This is a logical default based on the way people talk. Other defaults in use are not nearly so logical.

A user-friendly system is consistent so that a user can anticipate how the system will behave, and can transfer that knowledge to other applications. For example, the SilverPlatter function keys always have the same function regardless of which database is being searched; if one wants to limit a Knowledge Index search to title words the command "/TI" is always used. A variety of bibliographic, full-text, or numeric databases can make consistency hard to achieve.

Finally, a user-friendly system should be impossible to crash no matter which key or combination of keys the end-user strikes. It should avoid the appearance of having crashed by indicating to the user that it is working on the query after the user strikes the ENTER key by flashing or repeating a message such as WAIT or PROCESSING or some other visual and obvious indicator. A user-friendly system should allow the user to cancel a query that, in the user's opinion, is taking too long (Pfaffenberger, 1990).

There are many systems that have these features and call themselves user-friendly, and yet they are not friendly enough to meet the end-users' expectations of them. Perhaps their expectations are colored by science fiction movies and television programs where computers really do interpret and analyze the questions and make value judgments on the answers they provide. As long as users have to restructure their questions to meet the computer's expectations and learn some kind of code that computers understand, there is no such thing as a truly user-friendly system. Experiments with artificial intelligence and expert systems, or systems that assign weights to word occurrences and rank the output accordingly, are trying to overcome the user-hostile elements inherent in automated information retrieval, but until these are perfected the patron who wants ten good citations on the national debt will be better served by a human librarian than by a computer.

End-User Online Services

BRS/After Dark and DIALOG's Knowledge Index are the best known of the end-user online services and have been available since 1982. Both are characterized by a user-friendly interface mounted on the host's mainframe computers, which accesses selected databases already available through the vendors' native modes. The services are only available during nonbusiness hours, usually after 5:00 p.m. local time on weekdays and most of the weekend hours. They are very inexpensive when compared to the services' native modes; a search that costs $50 during business hours can cost $5 on the off-hours systems. Knowledge Index charges a flat rate of $24 per hour on all databases; BRS/After Dark charges variable rates for the different databases, averaging about $18 per hour, and also charges citation fees for each citation printed. As with the business-hours services, new databases are added and occasionally some databases are deleted from the services, and some databases may be split according to ranges of publication years. In all, an average of a hundred or so databases are available through the two services to end-users. The success of the non-business-hours services led BRS and DIALOG to make end-user searching on user-friendly interfaces available during business hours, through BRS's Colleague or BRKTHRU systems or DIALOG's Business Connection for example, but the rates are much higher or the same as regular business-hour rates on each system.

The user-friendly interface is called a "front-end" system, because it intercepts the end-user's information request and translates it into the language and protocols the host computer normally processes. BRS and DIALOG have loaded the front-end systems on their host computers. Front-ends can also be purchased as software packages that can do the same thing—accept user-friendly input and translate it into the user-hostile protocols—but with the added advantage of allowing offline keyboarding and editing of input.

Wilsearch is an example of a front-end software package to be loaded on a local microcomputer with a modem and designed to interface with the WILSONLINE databank. Any of the WILSONLINE databases can be accessed either singly or in combinations specified by the user. Menus prompt the user to select databases, then the system presents a preformatted screen for query input. Once this screen is filled in, the front-end software dials the WILSONLINE computer and executes the search. If results are found the user is asked how many citations he or she wants, the citations are downloaded to the local microcomputer, and the front-end software then terminates the connection with the WILSONLINE mainframe. At this point the end-user can begin viewing the resulting citations. A very brief manual accompanies the software and explains to end-users how to structure a search. Wilsearch is inexpensive and there are a variety of contract options that can be negotiated. It sounds simple, but a number of user-hostile elements easily prevent an end-user from getting results. Once past the database selection menus, there is nothing intuitive about the system; the end-user must read the manual. The preformatted search screen presents the user with a variety of fields—subject, author, title, etc.—followed by blanks for the user to fill in. Most end-users are tempted to fill in as many blanks as they possibly can, unaware of the fact that the system is AND-ing all the fields together, and as a result the most frequent response of the system is to produce no citations. The front-end software signs off, and the end-user must start over again at the beginning with database selection. There is no interaction with the database and no way to revise a search without starting over.

Wilsearch allows user-friendly access only to WILSONLINE databases. Two other front-end software packages, Pro-Search and Sci-Mate, are more flexible. Pro-Search, available from Personal Bibliographic Software, Inc., is a front-end program for searching BRS and DIALOG. Included on the software are descriptions of most databases available from both vendors, which means that the software must be updated and almost immediately goes out of date as new databases are added. However, providing database descriptions is not the main purpose of the software, so this is a minor quibble. The software allows the end-user to construct a search strategy offline, makes the connection to the host computer and executes the search. The end-user does not have to know and remember the different protocols for BRS or for DIALOG. Once the search has been executed, the user remains connected to the host computer and can then interact with the database in the normal way, revise the search, view citations, and print or download selected citations. Windows and help screens assist the user in formulating or revising a search both offline and online.

Sci-Mate Searcher is available from the Institute of Scientific Information and allows access to BRS, DIALOG, NLM, ORBIT, and QUESTEL. It is a menu-driven system that assists with search strategy development, and it does include some information about the structures of selected databases on each of the hosts, namely record fields and their codes. As with Pro-Search, strategies are typed offline and uploaded, and the user can interact with the host computer.

Both Pro-Search and Sci-Mate Searcher are components of software packages that can be used to reformat or edit the downloaded citations. Sci-Mate Searcher, for example, is accompanied by Sci-Mate Manager and Sci-Mate Editor. A user can create in-house databases with citations downloaded via Searcher, or can edit the citations according to several different style manuals or in a style of the user's design. Either front-end package costs in the neighborhood of $400; either total package including the text editing modules costs around $1,000.

These front-end packages access the regular host computers at the regular business-hours rates. A library must have negotiated its own contracts with the host vendors before the front-end packages can access them. All of the host computer databases can be accessed through the front-ends even if the database description is not part of the package. End-user searching at regular business-hours rates cannot be inexpensive, but the offline typing of the search strategy does save some money, and end-users trained on front-end packages do not interact with the databases as much as end-users trained to search "live" user-friendly files. The front-end software requires a training period of at least two or three hours, and many end-users find them confusing since the front-end itself constitutes an extra intermediate step that must be learned along with the other components that make up the mental model of automated information retrieval. On occasion, something strange happens in the process of translating a host's protocols from the common command language of the front-end software, and unexplainable citations creep into the results. All searchers have had the experience of reviewing a set of citations and exclaiming, "How did that get in there?" over one or two of them; this seems to happen more frequently when front-end software is used.

The text editing components of the front-end packages appeal to researchers who have a lot of citations to manipulate. Front-ends are not limited to nonbusiness hours as are the vendors' user-friendly systems, and many more databases are available to end-users. The cost of accessing databases at regular rates, the cost of the front-end packages themselves, and the lengthy training period are the major disadvantages of front-end software.

Gateways are another path offering access for end-users. Gateways are a route through one host computer to other host computers. For example, a library with a WESTLAW contract can use the WESTLAW gateway to access DIALOG databases using WESTLAW searching protocols. A typical gateway serves as a front-end allowing end-users to search with commands that are already familiar, and one negotiates a contract with the gateway service, not with the multiple vendors the gateway accesses (Dewey, 1983). EASYNET is probably the most familiar gateway in academic libraries, providing access to some thirteen or so online vendors. EASYNET offers menu-driven help with database selection and search strategy development. The search strategy is typed and loaded in the EASYNET host, then uploaded and executed in the online vendor's host computer. There is a minimum charge of $8 per search for up to ten citations, and there are surcharges for some databases. For many end-user searches this is more expensive than a BRS/After Dark or Knowledge Index search; however, far more databases are available through EASYNET.

Another kind of gateway is available with certain CD-ROM products from Wilson and DIALOG. These allow end-users to search a database archived on compact disk and then execute the search for recent updates in the online file of the database. The end-user does not have to reformat the search suitable for the online mode, since the gateway acts as a front-end, user-friendly interface that dials the host mainframe, uploads the search, executes it, and downloads the results. The library must provide a telephone line for each workstation allowing such online updating and funds to cover the usually inexpensive costs (Benson and Weinberg (1988, McQueen (1990), and Tenopir (1986) list different access options for end-users).

Which method of end-user online access to provide depends on the type of end-user service the library envisions and how much money the library wants to spend or to charge back to the user. Online access for end-users requires a microcomputer with a printer (*not* a terminal) and a modem and telephone line, or multiple workstations if more than one end-user is to be served at a time. A hard disk microcomputer is required for the front-end software packages; it is preferable for any of the end-user access systems since a microcomputer allows downloading of results and can be programmed to provide password security.

The least expensive option is undoubtedly Wilsearch, if the library opts for the prepayment plan. A prepayment of $2,000 buys two thousand searches, a search being defined as a maximum of ten citations delivered. There is no charge if no citations are found. Note that this is "up front" money, which makes Wilsearch expensive to start up, especially if multiple users are to be served. Without the prepayment option, Wilsearch costs $5 per search. Either way, there is an annual licensing fee of $150 for the software. Wilsearch offers the additional advantage of allowing daytime access to any of the Wilson databases. The limited number of databases and limited searching capability are the disadvantages, especially for serious faculty and graduate level researchers.

Start up costs for the front-end packages, and ongoing costs at the regular online rates, are the main disadvantages of front-end systems, and it is not likely that the library will recover all these costs from end-users. Lengthy training is another disadvantage. Certainly undergraduates would not be willing to spend the time needed for training, and the infrequent searcher would not be able to maintain skills at a comfortable level. The text-editing components make front-ends such as Pro-Search and Sci-Mate most suitable for serious, frequent researchers, and yet if the library purchases the text-editing components the start-up costs are vastly increased, and library microcomputers would be put to a nonsearching use more suited to the researchers' office computers. Access to several hundred databases during business hours is the major advantage of the front-ends.

The limited night and weekend hours of BRS/After Dark and Knowledge Index can be seen as the major disadvantage of these services. Certainly faculty will be infrequent users, but students seem to appreciate the hours of availability. Library staff will not appreciate the hours, and staffing considerations will probably be the deciding factor in whether or not these end-user services are chosen. Easy search engines and very inexpensive access make these two most appealing to students, and enough databases are available to be of use to graduate level research. Naive end-users appreciate the ease of use and sophisticated end-users appreciate the more complex and interactive searching that can be done even on the user-friendly software. Faculty members are quite likely to delegate searching tasks to their graduate students anyway, so they will benefit indirectly. Start-up costs are quite low even for multiple passwords. BRS/After Dark does charge a monthly minimum of $12 per password.

A gateway such as EASYNET has moderate but unpredictable costs, makes hundreds of databases available during business hours, and uses an easy search engine. However, the search engine facilitates only the simplest of searches and gets in the way of any even moderately complex interactive search. The gateway interface frequently produces unexplainable results. The easy searches will cost more than the same search performed on BRS/After Dark or Knowledge Index; start-up costs are low.

If undergraduates are to be the primary clientele of the end-user service, the databases and low cost of Wilsearch will serve them well. If costs charged to the end-user get much above $5 or are unpredictable, undergraduates probably will not use the service. Undergraduates, graduate students, and faculty can be served by the choice of databases, ease of use, and low costs of Knowledge Index or BRS/After Dark. Staffing the service nights and weekends is the major drawback; costs can be controlled by limiting the number of workstations and the amount of time end-users are allowed online. Graduate students and faculty appreciate the wide choice of databases made available through front-end services and are usually willing to invest the time needed for training, but the high and unpredictable costs will keep them from becoming frequent searchers. The unpredictable costs, and most importantly the unpredictable results of EASYNET are major drawbacks. When results are unpredictable users learn nothing about the structure of automated information retrieval, and teaching end-users how to search should be one of the goals of any end-user service. However, EASYNET is widely available to home computer users outside the academic library environment and therefore is already familiar to many users.

Management of an End-User Online Service

An end-user online service should be accessible to the public, but due to the noise generated by printers and by talking, it should be shielded from other public areas. Security for equipment and for passwords make a separate room desirable, but locking rolltop cabinets can provide the appearance of security. It may be possible to use the mediated search service setting and equipment for end-users, especially if end-user services are only available nights and weekends, or end-users can be scheduled to use the equipment in between mediated searches. An end-user service is likely to become quite popular and well used, so the service manager should keep an eye on possibilities for expansion.

Each end-user workstation requires a microcomputer, a printer, a modem, and a telephone line. Microcomputers are preferable because they permit downloading of citations whereas terminals do not, and a hard disk microcomputer is preferable because it can store communications software, front-end software, and a large number of downloaded citations. Baud rate is a consideration when purchasing modems. The printer should be fast enough to handle at least 120 characters per second (cps) in draft mode, and it should be very reliable and not subject to frequent repairs. Online end-users must either print or download citations since off-line printing is not an option in end-user systems. Some end-user services do away with the printer and permit users to download only; users are required to bring their own formatted diskettes. Users can then print the citations if desired on their own equipment, or the library may make a single printer available for this purpose. End-users do print more citations usually than would be printed in a mediated search because they either do not know how to limit a search or they are afraid they might miss something valuable if they limited the search; therefore they print browsing lists to examine later at their leisure when the pressures of online time and costs are off. The library will incur considerable expense for paper and ink if printers are available; on the other hand, requiring users to download may turn away those users who do not have access to or do not feel comfortable with computer technology.

Bookshelf space must be provided for system documentation, database documentation, and thesauri. This is not a problem if the end-user searching area shares space with the mediated searching area. The majority of end-users probably will not use the documentation, but staff members helping end-users will, and it should not be denied to those sophisticated end-users who want to improve their searching skills. Staff members in the area will need a desk or other work surface to serve as a home base and for consulting with end-users.

End-User Services 147

Since online vendors are involved, most libraries require end-users to make an appointment and to prepare in advance, either by attending training sessions or by reading a training manual. Especially if multiple end-users are served, one completely untrained end-user can dominate the staff member's time and no doubt online funds. End-users can be required to show proof of advance preparation by submitting a written-out search strategy for approval and revision by the staff member (see Illustrations 6 and 7). Forms for this purpose should be provided by the service. The service manager must decide how much flexibility can be accommodated, whether drop-ins will be allowed to search, whether a search strategy is always required, whether service is strictly limited to students and faculty, and so on. Probably a new service just beginning should be rather hard-nosed at first until the routines are worked out.

Staffing patterns depend on the type of service offered. Staff must be trained to advise end-users on database selection, on search strategy development, and on search protocols. Staff will also be expected to troubleshoot the equipment

Illustration 6
End-User Worksheet

```
                           SEARCH PLANNER WORKSHEET
INSTRUCTIONS:  (1) Select database(s). Write database label(s) in the space provided.
               (2) Write your topic statement. Determine the concepts in the topic statement.
               (3) Write the keywords and synonyms of a single concept group within a single
                   box. Use the next box for the next concept group.
               (4) Decide which logical connectors will link your concept groups.

(1) DATABASE LABEL(S): _____  _____  _____  _____
(2) TOPIC: _____
           _____

            (3)
       ┌───────────┐  ┌───────────┐  ┌───────────┐  ┌───────────┐
       │ CONCEPT 1 │  │ CONCEPT 2 │  │ CONCEPT 3 │  │ CONCEPT 4 │
       ├───────────┤  ├───────────┤  ├───────────┤  ├───────────┤
       │    OR     │  │    OR     │  │    OR     │  │    OR     │
       ├───────────┤  ├───────────┤  ├───────────┤  ├───────────┤
       │    OR     │  │    OR     │  │    OR     │  │    OR     │
       ├───────────┤  ├───────────┤  ├───────────┤  ├───────────┤
       │    OR     │  │    OR     │  │    OR     │  │    OR     │
       └───────────┘  └───────────┘  └───────────┘  └───────────┘

You can have more than four concept groups or synonyms. Check with the After Dark staff before
your appointment. They will make suggestions to help refine your search strategy.
```

A worksheet intended to encourage end-users to plan search strategies before going online. Workshops, written manuals, or handouts can explain in more detail how the search strategy is planned.

Illustration 7
End-User Appointments and Logs

TIME 6:00	NAME	ID NUMBER	DEPT	STATUS		
	DATABASE: PRINTS:	DATABASE: PRINTS:	DATABASE: PRINTS:	DATABASE: PRINTS:	CONNECT COSTS: PRINT COSTS:	$ $
TIME 6:40	NAME	ID NUMBER	DEPT	STATUS		
	DATABASE: PRINTS:	DATABASE: PRINTS:	DATABASE: PRINTS:	DATABASE: PRINTS:	CONNECT COSTS: PRINT COSTS:	$ $
TIME 7:20	NAME	ID NUMBER	DEPT	STATUS		
	DATABASE: PRINTS:	DATABASE: PRINTS:	DATABASE: PRINTS:	DATABASE: PRINTS:	CONNECT COSTS: PRINT COSTS:	$ $

A combined End-User Appointment Form and End-User Statistics form. As searches are performed, the monitor or other staff member helping the end-users records the databases used and the number of citations printed from each database. The information can be transferred to a DBMS database.

when required. This means that staff must have the searching abilities of a sophisticated end-user at least, and ideally of a trained search analyst. The ideal is hard to achieve when night and weekend services are offered. In such a case, clerical or student workers may be the only staff available, and they should be trained to refer complicated search strategies to librarians. The service manager can consider having a business-hours consultation service to assist end-users with their search strategies (Janke, 1984). Search analysts or other trained librarians can be assigned to assist daytime end-users if there are enough to go around; otherwise, trained clerical or student assistants can monitor the search and call on a search analyst if difficulties arise.

Some end-user services may decide to keep online assistance to a bare minimum due to staffing problems. In such cases, the service manager provides training to end-users in classes and workshops during the day, and may provide business-hours consultation service for search strategies, but the end-user at the keyboard is pretty much on his own with nothing more than a monitor in the area to troubleshoot equipment problems and keep people to their appointments. It is, after all, an end-user service, and if staffing is such that expert help and consultation cannot be provided, at least the access is available to end-users.

Costs can be controlled by limiting the number of end-user appointments available and the online time of each end-user. Take, for example, an end-user service using Knowledge Index and available Sunday through Friday nights from 6:00 to 10:00 p.m. An end-user is allowed a maximum of thirty minutes online within a forty minute window. Appointments are scheduled at 6:00, 6:40, 7:20, 8:00, 8:40, and 9:20, for a total of six appointments each evening. The extra ten minutes are allowed for consultation before the search and as a cushion for those end-users who still have a few citations to print once their thirty minutes are up. Some end-users will not use the full thirty minutes and some will use a few minutes more, but in general a maximum of three hours online will be consumed per evening. Since Knowledge Index charges a flat rate per hour with no additional charges for citations, the cost is easily computed. If the library can afford more, a second or third searching station can be added; if the library can afford less, fewer appointments can be offered. The calculations become more complicated when services charge variable rates, but the principle remains the same. It is safer to compute the maximum charges possible and be pleasantly surprised when they fail to materialize.

If end-users are to be charged a fee the library can certainly afford to offer more searching stations and more appointments, but they may not be necessary because fees will drastically reduce the number of end-users (Anders and Jackson, 1988; Halperin and Pagell, 1985; Jaros et al., 1986). Even quite modest fees, such as a $1 or $2 flat rate, will convince some end-users that printed sources are better, and unpredictable fees based on business-hours connect rates and citation charges will turn away all but the most dedicated and well-heeled end-users. If a fee is to be charged, it is better if at all possible to charge a flat rate, because the user can better judge whether or not the search is worth the money. On the other hand, telling an end-user that a search can cost anywhere from $5 to $50 presents the user with something akin to gambling, and most will decline. Inexpensive flat rates are only possible with Wilsearch, BRS/After Dark, and Knowledge Index unless the library can afford to subsidize end-user searching on the more expensive and unpredictable EASYNET, Pro-Search, or Sci-Mate options. If the library can afford to partially subsidize costs there are several alternatives, such as:

— Library pays the first $25 (or $10, or whatever the library can afford), user pays any amount over. This option allows many end-users a totally subsidized search.
— Library pays connect costs, user pays any citation charges. This option encourages users to be far more selective in their searching and retrieval which, by the way, increases their online time and the library's connect costs.
— Library pays half, or one-third, or any other fraction that can be afforded. This puts the element of unpredictability back into the calculation, and it is frequently the unpredictability of the cost, rather than the cost itself, that turns away many end-users.

Any fee, no matter how reasonable, discourages use, and if there are other options available to end-users such as locally loaded or ondisk databases available at no charge, a fee for end-user online access can put the service out of business. There are hard choices to be made here. An online service such as BRS/After Dark or Knowledge Index offers far more databases to end-users than can be purchased as ondisk databases for the same price, and many of the databases are not available ondisk. Where does a library put its limited budget? In subscriptions to ondisk databases or subsidies for online end-user databases? Or possibly, the budget could subsidize mediated searches performed by trained search analysts who provide accurate, efficient searches rather than the frequently hit-or-miss affairs performed by end-users.

Ondisk Services

Databases on CD-ROM or optical disks are designed for end-users with a user-friendly search engine included as part of the package when the database is purchased. There are scores of databases available now and more databases, search engines, and vendors become available every month (Van Arsdale, 1986). There probably is not a database producer that is not considering an ondisk option, and there are some databases that are only available ondisk and not in print or online. The cost of an ondisk database, although frequently quite high, is predictable, and can serve more end-users than any business-hours end-user online access to the same database. Comparing the costs of ondisk databases to the off-hours services of BRS/After Dark and Knowledge Index is problematic, since the ondisk database is available to more users for more hours than the online services. A single ondisk database is probably less expensive than its online equivalent if the database serves a large population of end-users, but for the less-used databases and for the variety of databases offered the online services may be the less expensive alternative. Ondisk databases definitely have the advantage of being available to more users for more hours than any other option. They are the most attractive option for libraries that do not want to charge a fee for use.

They are expensive. The searching station consisting of a fast, hard disk microcomputer, a printer, and a CD-ROM drive costs around $5,000. Leasing equipment may be a less expensive option, and some vendors offer package deals that include equipment to go with the database, which can cost much less than independent purchases of database and equipment. These are good options for small operations, but a library with many ondisk workstations should strive for compatible, interchangeable equipment, which may not be possible through package deals. Most of the CD-ROM databases now require a hard disk microcomputer rather than a plain PC with floppy disk drives, and the 386 or faster machines retrieve data significantly, visibly faster than the slow machines. Many of the databases are themselves expensive, and there are many different pricing options. Most are subscriptions that merely lease the database; if the subscription lapses the library does not own the disks. Some databases are less expensive if the library maintains a subscription to the printed copy of the corresponding index or abstract, and will be more expensive if the library replaces the print subscription with an ondisk subscription. Many tack on a high licensing fee for those libraries that mount the database on a network.

There are many different search engines on the market, causing confusion for librarians and search analysts, not to mention end-users. The variety of databases is astounding. In addition to bibliographic databases there are full-text databases. In some full-text databases the text is stored on the compact disk as an optical image, therefore the text can be displayed and printed but not searched. UMI's Business Periodicals OnDisc is an example. Full-text databases such as Grolier's *Electronic Encyclopedia* or the *Oxford English Dictionary* ondisk database are designed to be searched in a fashion similar to bibliographic databases using free-text keywords or descriptors and logical operators. Some databases combine the text storage capabilities of compact disks with the computing capabilities of the microcomputer to store, search, and manipulate combined numeric and text data, such as Lotus OneSource and Compact Disclosure.

Deciding which ondisk databases to purchase becomes problematic when so many and so many kinds are available, and the potential for wasting a hefty chunk of the library's budget on an underutilized database is great. If the library already has an online operation for end-users, an examination of the statistics from the program will indicate which databases are most frequently accessed by end-users, and these will be good candidates for ondisk databases. Many vendors will provide the compact disk and software of a database for a one-month free trial, which can be useful for determining if there is interest in the database, although one month is hardly sufficient for word to get out to all those who might be interested. Once a subscription has been placed, the database should be monitored closely to see if it is being used enough to justify the subscription price, or if pay-as-you-go online access is the cheaper alternative.

There are many ways to set up an ondisk service. Originally the database producers and vendors and most libraries envisioned one database per searching station, and for a database that is in nearly constant use all day this is still a good option. However, when a library owns several ondisk databases, equipment costs can quickly get out of hand. It is possible to mount several ondisk databases on one searching station by loading the search engine softwares on the hard disk of the microcomputer and devising a system for accessing the individual compact disks. This can be done by physically placing the compact disk in the CD drive when a patron requests it and changing disks as needed, by daisy-chaining several CD drives together, or by installing a disk-changer drive that holds multiple disks such as Pioneer's 6-disk CD-ROM Mini-Changer. If the compact disk products are from various vendors and therefore use different search engines, some programming skills will be needed to get the different software packages to reside together on the hard disk and to establish routes to daisy-chained or multiple disk drives. This solution reduces access to the individual databases; while one patron is searching database A, another patron will have to wait until the workstation is free to search database B. The solution is ideal for large databases loaded on multiple compact disks.

Another option for multiple CD-ROM databases is a local area network (Au and Borisovets, 1990; Butcher, 1990; Flanders, 1990). This is practical only if there are multiple workstations, but one does not need a workstation for each database. In brief, a LAN or local area network works like this: All the compact disks are mounted on individual CD drives in a single unit, usually called a tower. One powerful microcomputer is designated as a "file server" or essentially a switchboard that routes traffic among the various microcomputer searching stations cabled to it and the tower where the compact disks reside. A patron can approach any of the searching stations and search any database mounted in the tower. The LAN equipment is expensive in itself, and many database producers require a licensing fee if their databases are mounted on a LAN. Furthermore, installing a LAN is not something a typical librarian without extensive computer hardware and software experience would care to tackle; in fact, SilverPlatter's LAN purchase price includes the services of engineers who will come to the site to install the LAN.

Ondisk workstations can be centralized in one location (centralization is necessary if they are mounted on a LAN) or dispersed in the library. It is necessary to provide assistance to end-users, so the availability of staff is sometimes the deciding factor in the arrangement of the workstations. Security for the equipment and databases should also be considered. A dispersed arrangement works well if the databases are mounted one per workstation and if the workstations are close to a reference desk. Multiple databases on one workstation are confusing to end-users, who may not be aware that they need to select the correct database for their needs, and who may attempt to load the compact disk incorrectly; loading the compact disk in the floppy disk drive of the microcomputer is such a common mistake that experienced service managers know to look in the floppy drive whenever a compact disk is reported missing. When the workstations are configured one database per workstation, experienced users can help themselves without having to stop at the reference desk to fetch a disk, but help is at hand for inexperienced users. A dispersed arrangement resembles the typical arrangement of indexes and abstracts in a reference area, and in fact some libraries place the ondisk workstation adjacent to the paper copy of the corresponding index.

If there is more than one database mounted per workstation and more than one workstation, it is probably better to bring the workstations together in a centralized arrangement. This can be a location near the reference desk, in which case staff assigned to the desk can assist end-users, or it can be a separate location removed from the reference desk, in which case staff must be assigned to the area (Tucker et al., 1988). In essence, the ondisk area becomes another service point that must be staffed for long hours and on weekends. This is the major disadvantage of a centralized arrangement. On the other hand, there are several advantages, including noise control. A busy ondisk operation can be quite noisy with printers operating and keyboards clicking, the frequent consultations between end-users and staff, and conversations among end-users themselves, especially those who are waiting to use a database. If one piece of equipment malfunctions the database can be mounted on a neighboring workstation rather than taken out of service for as long as it takes to repair the equipment; this cannot be done easily in a dispersed arrangement. It is advisable to have compatible, interchangeable equipment. Staff on duty in the area encourages end-users to ask for help, whereas in a dispersed arrangement the end-user is not likely to get up and leave a workstation to ask for help, and if an end-user leaves a workstation to go to the reference desk to ask for assistance another end-user is likely to take over the workstation. Staff patrolling the area can see when an end-user is in difficulty and offer assistance before the end-user has to ask for help.

Traffic management is easier in a centralized arrangement. A busy ondisk operation will need appointments or waiting lists and timers to keep one user from monopolizing a database for hours, and it may be possible to accommodate and contain people who are waiting to use the databases. This is almost impossible to manage in a dispersed arrangement. Usage statistics, security for the equipment and compact disks, troubleshooting equipment, and keeping printers supplied are all easier to manage in a centralized operation. As the number of databases and workstations increases, the centralized operation looks like the better option. If staff is being kept away from the reference desk for long periods of time to help ondisk users in a dispersed arrangement, the library should consider centralizing the operation.

Staff must be able to assist end-users with database selection, search strategy development, search engine operation, and general reference assistance when the patron has produced a printout and needs to know how to find material in the library, or when the patron is unsuccessful and needs advice on alternative sources. Staff will also be called upon to replenish printer supplies and to perform some equipment troubleshooting, usually paper jams in printers, loose connections, and sometimes crashed systems requiring a reboot. Trained search analysts and other trained librarians are ideal if there are enough of them available. Clerical staff and student assistants can be trained to provide most of the forms of assistance needed, but search strategy development and advice on alternative databases will need to be referred to the professional staff. As with an end-user online operation, it may be necessary to establish a business-hours consulting service to provide this assistance.

Traffic management in a busy ondisk operation is an important component of the staff duties. If there are many workstations a first-come, first-served method works nicely, but a system of waiting lists will be necessary for high-demand databases, and the service will need timers to be sure no one user monopolizes a database. If some workstations serve multiple databases, the staff member will need a system for checking out compact disks and mounting them, unless they are already mounted in disk-changers or daisy-chained drives, in which case the staff will need to be sure that the end-user has selected the correct database. Some services have successfully allowed end-users to handle and change the compact disks themselves, but this can lead to scratches on the disks that make them unreadable, and there is always the danger that a naive end-user will put the compact disk in the floppy drive of the microcomputer. If there are many databases and very few workstations, the service may want to consider taking appointments for use. Appointments will definitely cut down the amount of use the service achieves and increase the amount of paperwork the staff has to deal with, and they interfere with the perception that the system is user-friendly. Appointments are not friendly; instead they are formal and limiting and require advance planning and punctuality. One makes appointments with one's dentist. Ondisk databases are so amenable to the first-come, first-served mode of operation that it seems a shame to require users to make appointments for them. One of the major advantages of an ondisk database over an online database is that it is inviting, easy to use, and ready to use, encouraging patrons to become familiar with it and by extension with the universe of automated information retrieval. Such a service should consider spending money on more workstations rather than more databases.

It should go without saying that fees will make an ondisk database less inviting as well, but, due to the expense of the database subscription and the equipment, some libraries find it necessary to charge fees if they are to make the database available at all (Duggan, 1990). A library can attempt to recover some costs on a voluntary basis. A sign beside the database explains the expenses, for example stating that paper costs five cents a sheet, and invites end-users to contribute payment. It is surprising how much money can be collected this way, and it also cuts down on the end-users' propensity to print citations indiscriminately. The keyboard of the workstation can be wired through a VendaCard machine, such that the keyboard will not function until a debit card is inserted in the machine (Schloman et al., 1990). Any other method of collecting fees from users will vastly increase the amount of paperwork the staff must handle and almost force the use of appointments to insure that patrons know what they are getting into and to insure collection of the fees.

A clear and precise policy statement is absolutely necessary if fees are collected. Even without fees, a policy statement explaining patron access issues such as waiting lists, time limits, and user priorities (can librarians bump end-users from a system, do academic users have priority over community users, is a valid ID a prerequisite for use, etc.) is necessary to prevent or resolve conflicts.

TRAINING END-USERS

A user-friendly system encourages users to believe that no advance instruction or training is necessary. Ondisk systems especially, sitting in an open, public area and inviting users to sit down and start typing, promote this belief and, in fact, a user will get some sort of response out of an ondisk system. When asked on evaluation forms to rate a system for ease of use, very few end-users will rate it as difficult to use. User-friendly systems are indeed easy to use and hard to master. Furthermore, end-users frequently do not recognize help when they receive it. On evaluation forms they answer "No" to the question "Did you have to ask for help," but staff in the area see something quite different. Probably the end-user read the introductory screen or perhaps consulted some written instructions. Perhaps a staff member advised the user on the correct truncation symbol, or perhaps the user asked how to print citations. But the end-user does not recognize this as receiving help. No one should assume that user-friendly systems are so friendly that some sort of instruction is not needed, and certainly end-users should not be allowed to assume so. Assistance should be offered actively, almost aggressively, rather than waiting until it is summoned. The techniques of automated information retrieval are not intuitive—they do not come naturally.

The Training End-Users Need

Based on the typical end-user misconceptions and mistakes, what areas of instruction do end-users need? The naive end-user who sits down to an ondisk database for the first time most frequently asks, "How do I make this machine work?" whether the question is asked aloud or not. In other words, the end-user wants to know which buttons to punch. It is an unsophisticated question and is best answered by point-of-use, over-the-shoulder instruction with the user's hands on the keyboard. As users get more exposure to computers in public schools, in their own homes, and in the library, this kind of question goes away and becomes, "How do I get information out of this machine?"

End-users are most likely to recognize that they need instruction in system-specific searching commands, that is, how to use the search engine of a particular database. For example, an end-user working with a SilverPlatter ondisk database may know absolutely nothing about Boolean logic or search strategies, but immediately recognizes that he or she needs instruction on how to use the function keys, where to type the "FIND" command, and how to get a printout. If the results are satisfactory the end-user will not recognize a need for any further instruction. If not, the end-user is ready for training in search strategy development and Boolean logic.

The end-user may progress to a sophisticated level of searching that requires a knowledge of the database's structure, such as limiting to fields or an understanding of the use of a controlled vocabulary. By this time the end-user recognizes that a search strategy must be evaluated and revised so that it works with a particular search engine and a particular database structure, and now is ready to apply this knowledge in a variety of databases. The end-user has now achieved an appropriate mental model of automated information retrieval.

This step-by-step progression, from wondering which button to punch to an adequate understanding of automated information retrieval, is ideally suited to ondisk databases that are readily available on demand and do not have any connect time or costs attached to them. The patron can learn when he wants and at his own pace without pressure. Essential to this scenario are readily available, trained, and sympathetic staff who can patiently lead a variety of users step by step and who can recognize the moment when a patron recognizes that more information is needed. Readily available does not describe a librarian helping a patron at the reference desk and also "keeping an eye" on the ondisk workstation. If an ondisk installation is expected to perform this kind of teaching role, it must be staffed and it must be centralized so that the existence of other databases can be explained and demonstrated on the neighboring workstation. Not all patrons will make this steady progress. For every patron who wants to know why the controlled vocabulary of the Psychological Abstracts database is different from the controlled vocabulary of the Sociological Abstracts database, there are dozens of patrons who are perfectly happy to type in one free-text search term and browse through the results for two or three good citations. There is some controversy as to what, if anything, should be done about the latter. If they are happy with the results, perhaps they should be left alone rather than having instruction crammed down their throats. However, even these users will be more likely to ask for instruction or at least listen in if they see and hear a knowledgeable staff member giving good advice on redefining a search to the user at the neighboring workstation. Surveys and experience have shown that end-users prefer one-on-one, point-of-use assistance (Allen, 1990a; Sewell and Teitelbaum, 1986).

The areas in which end-users need, and frequently recognize that they need, instructions are as follows:

— System-specific, search-engine-specific, or database-specific operations;
— Search strategy design;
— Boolean logic;
— Evaluating and revising searches;
— General overview of information management to develop a mental model of automated information retrieval.

Arguably, this last item in the list may be the most important to the formation of a lasting understanding of database searching and indeed of library collection manipulation in general, but unfortunately it is not likely to be greeted with any enthusiasm. End-users will not be clamoring for a general overview.

Methods of Training End-Users

The methods of instruction for end-users include *individualized instruction*, either point of use or by appointment; *self-study*, including printed handouts, printed instruction manuals or workbooks, computer-assisted instruction, and help screens; and *group instruction*, including workshops, demonstrations, and classroom lectures.

It is probably obvious that this author favors individualized, point-of-use instruction for an ondisk operation. Individualized instruction by appointment is valuable for, and appreciated by, a faculty member or a graduate assistant who will be using automated databases extensively. The appointment can be made with a search analyst as if for a mediated search, and with a good supply of handouts, adequate database-specific or search-engine-specific instruction can be delivered in an hour. Individual appointments with a search analyst to discuss a difficult search strategy to be performed by an end-user are also appreciated, and staff who work with end-users should refer patrons to an individual appointment when needed. As more end-user options become available to the library's clientele, the demand for mediated searches will be reduced and more of the search analysts' time will be freed for these consultations; they may become a significant way to maintain the search analysts' skills (Lewontin, 1991).

Refusing to read the instructions is a notorious trait of end-users, and one can hardly blame them when most of the documentation supplied by the database producers and vendors goes into far more detail than even the librarians want to read. The service manager should produce (or assign others to produce) simplified handouts for end-users. If possible, each handout should be no more than the front and back of a single sheet; anything longer will most likely be ignored by the end-users. A system of modular handouts is in order. For example, an ondisk database could have a series of individual handouts explaining the content of the database and the searchable fields, the search engine and the use of function keys, Boolean logic, search strategy development, and so forth. The modular handouts can be delivered as an end-user works up to the point of needing instruction, or they can be bound together to form a manual for classes and demonstrations.

If online services are available to end-users, a more extensive form of instruction is in order. Online searching costs money, so end-users must be as prepared as possible before they are allowed to use it. Some libraries require online end-users to attend classes or workshops, and issue coupons to attendees that they must produce before they can make an appointment. Others may require the end-user to read a workbook or instruction manual that details database selection, search strategy development, and search engine operation. Once the manual is read the end-user fills out a search strategy worksheet, which must be presented and approved or revised before the end-user can go online.

Computer-assisted instruction (CAI) and help screens present a particular problem. The faults of help screens—too long, linear paging, not context-sensitive—have already been detailed. Many vendors of end-user services do have CAI packages that are quite well done, and lead the end-user step by step through the searching process for a particular database or search engine. A library may want to produce its own CAI that covers the gaps in the vendor-produced packages, such as database selection and search strategy (Grotophorst, 1984). The problem with CAI is that it has to be performed on a microcomputer. In a busy end-user service where waiting lines develop and users are limited to thirty minutes when others are waiting, no one has time to read the help screens or work through a CAI program. That time spent searching the database will produce some sort of result whereas reading the help screens produces nothing. A service might set aside a microcomputer to be used exclusively for CAI, but there would be a strong temptation and pressure to mount a database on it and let people use it for searching. Recognizing that end-users want to spend their time searching, not learning, some libraries have opted for the low-tech printed materials and individualized instruction rather than CAI. Libraries that have tried both CAI and printed instructions have found very little difference in the amount of material learned by the end-users (Hutchins et al., 1987).

Demonstrations to groups or classes are effective for introducing the concepts of automated information retrieval. A demonstration can show how efficiently and quickly information can be retrieved from a computerized database, and gives the group some idea of the complexities involved. In combination with handouts explaining specific commands for the search engine and the database content and structure, a demonstration can give individuals the confidence to attempt a search on their own. Demonstration, handouts, and a lecture can begin to develop a correct mental model of automated information retrieval. However, learning to search requires hands-on experience. Searching requires not only the background knowledge of techniques and theory, but also the ability to manipulate a keyboard, and the ability to recognize and analyze information as it is displayed on the screen. The sensori-motor skills must be learned by doing. Information acquired by experience stays with the learner longer than information gleaned from a lecture or a demonstration. A good CAI package attempts to incorporate this sensori-motor component by requiring the learner to analyze information presented on the screen and to strike appropriate keys in response, but most CAI packages merely tell the learner when a mistake has been made rather than allowing him or her to see the consequences of a mistake. For example, the learner types "CATS *AND* DOGS *AND* HORSES" instead of the correct command "*CATS OR DOGS OR HORSES*" and the CAI simply prompts the learner to use the correct Boolean operator, whereas a hands-on experience with the database produces an unexpected result that the learner must analyze and correct. The learner has a better chance of recognizing this mistake the next time it is made.

Workshops incorporating demonstrations, lectures, handouts, and hands-on experience are an excellent way to instruct end-users. The demonstration illustrates the search engine- or database-specific operations; lectures and paper exercises teach search strategy design and Boolean logic; hands-on exercise reinforces the previous material and introduces the concept of evaluating and revising a search. All the information presented in the workshop builds a correct mental model of automated information retrieval. Modular handouts compiled into a workbook or manual stay with the students and provide prompts or review material as they start searching on their own. The workshop covers all the areas of instruction end-users need and incorporates all the various methods of instruction (Steffen, 1986).

Workshops are not easy to provide. Access to equipment can put an immediate stop to any plans for workshops. Learners can work in teams of two or three people at one workstation, and in such small groups they can help each other learn. But if the groups are larger the less assertive members of the group will never get their hands on the keyboard, some of the group may not be able to see the screen displays, and interaction among the group members will be less effective. The people farthest away from the workstation are more likely to start talking about their physics class than about automated information retrieval. Ideally a workshop should have access to enough workstations so that no more than three people are using a workstation during the hands-on exercises. If multiple workstations are used, there must be multiple passwords or ondisk databases available.

Preparing for a workshop takes a great deal of the instructor's time. Modular handouts help, but the instructor must prepare lectures, devise effective sample searches and exercises, and possibly prepare pre- and posttests that must be graded and evaluated. The amount of material to be covered in a workshop means the workshop itself will take at least two hours, and the small size of the workshop group insures that the session must be repeated frequently—provided the workshop has attendees at all. Students quite naturally avoid taking any more classes than they must, and faculty are sometimes reluctant to admit that they need instruction. Publicity for the workshops should emphasize the benefits to be gained and possibly include a "hook" such as a free search or a search strategy consultation to tempt people to attend. Workshop attendance can be required, especially for online systems available to end-users, with some sort of coupon or other identification issued to prove that the workshop was attended.

The Realities of End-User Training

Unless training is required before an end-user is allowed to use any online or ondisk system, most people will bypass the training. For every end-user who receives training, dozens will not, because they are attracted by the assurances that end-user systems are easy to use, because their information needs are immediate and they do not have time to spend on instruction, and because end-user systems nearly always produce some kind of result that the end-user does not question, not realizing that there are other and better ways to search the system. The lectures, workshops, demonstrations, instruction manuals, handouts, and CAI packages will be used by a few and ignored by the majority. Furthermore, the naive end-user who has read the instructions or seen a demonstration will sit down to the workstation for the first time and invariably ask, "What do I do now?" The instruction is not fully assimilated until the end-user applies it to his or her own information needs. For this reason, point-of-use instruction must be available. The trained end-user who needs a nudge to get started or assistance with a complex search question, and the untrained end-user who must be told which buttons to punch can be helped by a trained staff member who provides over-the-shoulder assistance.

Most end-users are infrequent searchers who forget commands and techniques between searching sessions. Having performed searches before, they by-pass instruction and approach the workstation confidently, but may come upon difficulties during the search. The end-user who is quite competent on Knowledge Index databases is stumped by the SilverPlatter search engine; the engineering student searches COMPENDEX confidently but when confronted with a term paper assignment for an English composition class is totally confused by the MLA Bibliography database. The individual who has a home computer and uses COMPUSERVE frequently will be bored by workshops covering keyboarding, function keys, and online connections but needs help selecting appropriate databases. It is impossible to design workshops, demonstrations, and handouts to cover all these variables, and impossible to insure that these methods of instruction are available when the end-user needs them. Once again, point-of-use instruction is the only way to provide the correct instruction in the right amount and at the right time when and where it is needed.

Automated information management has become a necessary and integral part of business and professional fields, and many academic librarians feel that providing end-users with a comfortable level of exposure to these tools is incumbent upon them—that it is yet another teaching function needed to prepare students for the "real world." On the other hand, computers are so familiar to students who have used them since elementary school and may have their own microcomputers, that some librarians feel it is not necessary to design special programs to teach people how to use end-user systems, especially when user-friendly interfaces become friendlier and more like expert systems with each new update (Eadie, 1990; Pavelsek, 1991). Once again, the middle ground is point-of-use instruction.

Providing point-of-use assistance will require considerable staff time and training. Take as an example a centralized ondisk service of a dozen or so databases and workstations using four or five different search engines. Potentially a dozen patrons can be accessing databases at the same time and some of them will need assistance at any time the service is available to the public. The staff member in the area must be familiar with all the search engines and databases in order to provide specific assistance for each one, and should be able to refer users to alternative or better sources beyond those in the ondisk installation. Probably the staff member will be called upon to troubleshoot equipment. Certainly the staff member must have an appropriate mental model of automated information retrieval in order to assist patrons, but this concept is difficult to teach in the brief and specific interaction of point-of-use instruction; it serves as a background for referrals to other sources of information. The staff member must be able to assist with Boolean logic, search strategy design, and evaluating searches with an eye to revising them. This sounds like a job for a trained search analyst; however, an ondisk operation can be available to the public from the moment the building opens until it closes, long beyond the normal working hours of most search analysts. Therefore, it is not always possible to staff with appropriately trained librarians at all times.

The service manager may spend more time training the staff who work with end-users rather than training the end-users themselves. Although end-users cannot be forced to attend workshops, the staff should be, and they provide a good testing ground for the design and effectiveness of workshops that may be offered to the public. Along with search engines, search strategies, and Boolean operators, staff should be trained in referral techniques, especially referring end-users to a search analyst for consultation on a complex search strategy.

THE IMPACTS OF END-USER SERVICES

As more end-user options are offered to the public, there will be less demand for mediated searches. This is especially true if the options are locally loaded databases or ondisk databases because, unfortunately, most end-users will assume that all their information needs are being met by the readily available sources, and even those who get zero or irrelevant results will assume that the answer is definitive and there are no alternatives. Search analysts will find that more of their time is being spent in teaching and advising end-users rather than providing mediated searches. Certainly some of their time, and indeed some of all librarians' time, should be spent in educating users to the many alternatives available.

The use of printed indexes will decrease drastically as the automated alternatives are made available to end-users. Especially when ondisk workstations are placed beside the printed equivalent of the database, librarians have seen that users will line up and wait to use the automated database and deliberately, consciously reject the printed equivalent. Noticing a long line developing, the librarian points out the printed index and even offers to help users interpret it, but the user's response is "No thank you, I would rather use the computer." Patrons will try to force inappropriate automated databases to meet their needs rather than use appropriate printed tools; thus all printed indexes suffer and not just the ones having an automated equivalent.

The use of the library's journal collection increases with the increased access provided by automated information retrieval. Use of interlibrary loan will increase as well. Most end-users assume that information retrieved from the database is held in the library's collections; when they discover that this is not the case they will demand that titles covered by the automated sources be added to the collection. Furthermore, patrons will demand more automated databases. Patrons whose subjects are not covered by the automated sources available to them will demand that their databases be added; patrons who had to wait for a turn at an ondisk database will demand more copies of the database. These demands for more journal coverage, more databases, and more access put tremendous pressure on the library's budget.

Almost as soon as access to databases is made available in the library, users demand remote access. "How can I search this from my office computer?" the users ask. Remote access puts more demands on the budget for licensing fees and networks, demands that frankly cannot be met by most library budgets. Yet this demand for remote access is insistent and persistent and exposes a definite trend for the future.

Vendors are responding to feedback from libraries and from users by constantly upgrading their search engines. User-hostile elements are identified and removed and the friendliness of the interface is increased, sometimes by interposing more menus and more context-sensitive help screens. System reliability and speed of access have also been increased, frequently by requiring more powerful and more expensive equipment for mounting the databases. This means that library staff must constantly relearn the search engines and revise their handouts and other instruction for end-users. The user-friendly products are definitely getting better. There seems to be a trend toward incorporating expert systems or knowledge-based programming so that the products more and more resemble something like artificial intelligence. As this trend continues, the products may come to resemble the end-user's mental model of a database that analyzes the end-user's information request and evaluates or ranks the output.

Consider what such a database would look like. It would be small, turning away from the superdatabase models such as COMPENDEX or MEDLINE that strive for comprehensive coverage rather than selective coverage. The larger the database, the more irrelevant material end-users retrieve due to a lack of skill in limiting and refining the search strategy; furthermore, large databases include far more items than are available in the local collection and thus produce irrelevant citations because the material is not readily available to the end-user. Both kinds of irrelevance are frustrating and irritating to end-users. Boolean logic also frustrates end-users, so it would not be required in such a system and neither would a controlled vocabulary, which is endlessly confusing to end-users.

Instead, in these future "smart" databases, the end-user merely types in keywords and the system retrieves citations ranked according to the number of times those keywords co-occur and according to the proximity in which they co-occur. The more co-occurrences and the more proximate the co-occurrences, the higher retrieved citations rank on the list until, toward the bottom of the list, are citations that contain keywords occurring singly rather than in combinations. Thus the system appears to have evaluated the results and presents the end-user with a ranked browsing list. It is not a long list because the database is small (Cleverdon, 1984).

Experienced search analysts are grinding their teeth. "What about known-item searches?" they cry. "What about synonyms?" And most important to librarians, researchers, publishers, and the public, "Who gets to select the selective coverage in the small database?" End-users would probably be happy to use such a system, and, as now, librarians would be required to educate the public as to the existence of alternative sources and alternative ways of finding information.

REFERENCES

Allen, Gillian. "CD-ROM training: what do the patron's want?" *RQ* 30 (Fall, 1990a): 88-93. The author asked new and experienced CD-ROM users in what areas they felt they needed instruction—Boolean logic, search strategy development, etc.—and in what format they would prefer instruction.

Allen, Gillian. "Database selection by patrons using CD-ROM." *College and Research Libraries* 51 (January, 1990b): 69-75. A fascinating study that points out the fact that end-users and library patrons in general really do not understand that there are different databases and different indexes for different subjects.

Anders, Vicki and Kathy Jackson. "Online vs. CD-ROM: the impact of CD-ROM databases upon a large online searching program." *Online* 12 (November, 1988): 24-32. Statistics from a mediated service and an end-user online service show decreased use of online databases only a few months after the ondisk products were purchased. End-user evaluation forms made it clear that free access—meaning no charge and no appointment necessary—was preferred by the users.

Ankeny, Melvon L. "Evaluating end-user services: success or satisfaction." *Journal of Academic Librarianship* 16 (March, 1991): 352-356. End-users express satisfaction with automated database searching even when the results of the search are not satisfactory. In a well-designed procedure for evaluating end-user services, the author discovered that end-users could distinguish a successful search from an unsuccessful one but still expressed great satisfaction with the automated means of searching regardless of success.

Au, Ka-Neng and Natalie Borisovets. "The changing LANdscape of undergraduate research: The Rutgers-Newark experience." In *Public Access CD-ROMS in Libraries: Case Studies*, edited by Linda Stewart. 217–233. Westport, Conn.: Meckler Corporation, 1990. Provides a list of networking options and describes the CD-ROM installation at the Rutgers-Newark campus.

Belanger, Anne-Marie and Sandra D. Hoffman. "Factors related to frequency of use of CD-ROM: a study of ERIC in an academic library." *College and Research Libraries* 51 (March, 1990): 153–162. The authors investigated gender, age, previous computer experience, and student status as factors affecting CD-ROM use, with the intention of tailoring instructional sessions for groups identified as nonusers. As with other studies, they found that women and older users typically use computerized products such as OPACs and automated databases less frequently.

Beltran, Ann Bristow. "InfoTrac at Indiana University: a second look." *Database* 10 (February, 1987): 49–50.

Beltran, Ann Bristow. "Use of InfoTrac in a university library." *Database* 9 (June, 1986): 63–66. Two articles describing the use and enthusiastic acceptance of InfoTrac, especially by undergraduates.

Benson, James A. and Bella Hass Weinberg, eds. *Gateway Software and Natural Language Interfaces: Options for Online Searching*. Ann Arbor: Pierian Press. 1988. This useful introduction to and directory of gateways and front-ends is in the *Library Hi Tech* Special Studies Series.

Borgman, Christine. *The User's Mental Model of an Information Retrieval System: Effects on Performance*. Dissertation. Stanford University, 1984. Conceptual training—assisting the student to develop an appropriate mental model—is superior to procedural training in the mechanics of a system, in this case a prototype bibliographic database using Boolean logic. The author notes that one-third of the subjects failed to reach a minimum competency level and suggests that Boolean difficulties were the problem.

Butcher, Karyle S. "The rewards and trials of networking." *Database* 13 (August, 1990): 103–105. A case-study type of article describing the CD-ROM installation at Oregon State University's Kerr Library, and the problems involved in setting up a local area network.

Charles, Susan K. and Katharine E. Clark. "Enhancing CD-ROM searches with online updates: an examination of end-user needs, strategies and problems." *College and Research Libraries* 51 (July, 1990): 321–328. The authors found that most CD-ROM end-users did not perceive the difference in dates covered between the CD product and online, and while observing their searches concluded that the majority of end-users did not understand the basic concepts of searching despite the ready availability of point-of-use assistance, handouts, and instruction manuals, and despite the fact that the end-users considered their searches to be successful.

Cleverdon, Cyril. "Optimizing convenient online access to bibliographic databases." *Information Services and Use* 4 (April, 1984): 37–47. A fascinating paper arguing against the large, comprehensive databases and standard Boolean logic because they are user-hostile. Citing the 80/20 rule, the author argues that a less comprehensive, broad-coverage database using "quorum function" searching is ideal for end-users.

Cuadra, C. A. "History offers clues to the future: user control returns." *Online* 11 (January, 1987): 46–48. "We are edging into an era where both computer power and database power will be firmly in the hands of the users," the author claims. Front-ends, gateways, CD-ROM, and downloading are factors in putting control in the hands of users.

de Stricker, Ulla. "How do end users search?" *CD ROM Enduser* 2 (August, 1990a): 68.

de Stricker, Ulla. "User training for CD-ROM, or: it's so easy, anyone can do it." *CD ROM Enduser* 2 (August, 1990b): 35–36. In two articles for this issue of *CD ROM Enduser* de Stricker promotes the idea that end-users need a conceptual model of searching before they can perform effective searches.

Des Chene, D. "Online searching by end users." *RQ* 25 (Fall, 1985): 89–95. Following a brief review of end-user issues is a bibliography of over one hundred items covering all aspects of interest to librarians serving end-users.

Dewey, Patrick R. "A professional librarian looks at the consumer online services: the Source, CompuServe, Apple Bulletin Board, et al." *Online* 7 (September, 1983): 36–41. The author compares the electronic mail and bulletin board features to reading "a wall of graffiti," and comments on the ease of use of all systems. The review makes no recommendations.

Duggan, Mary Kay, ed. *CD-ROM in the Library, Today and Tomorrow.* Boston: G. K. Hall, 1990. A conference bringing together "a varied group of presenters from academic, public, and corporate settings to talk about CD-ROM's impact on information service and management."

Eadie, Tom. "Immodest proposals." *Library Journal* 115 (October 15, 1990): 42. The author's immodest proposal is that user instruction for students does not work and is therefore (whisper this quietly) a waste of librarians' time. See Pavelsek (1991) for a slightly more modest variation of this theme.

Eaton, Nancy L., Linda Brew MacDonald and Mara R. Saule. *CD-ROM and Other Optical Information Systems: Implementation Issues for Libraries.* Phoenix: Oryx Press, 1989. A thorough text, with chapters on the technical specifications of optical disk technology, public service considerations, hardware and software considerations, and case studies from nine installations.

End-user Searching Services. SPEC Kit 122. Washington, D.C.: Association of Research Libraries, Office of Management Studies Systems and Procedures Exchange Center, 1986.

Ernest, Douglas J. and Jennifer Monath. "User reaction to a computerized periodical index." *College and Research Libraries News* 47 (May, 1986): 315–318. They loved it, of course. Ernest points out a few of InfoTrac's faults, such as the system's propensity for crashing and patron misconceptions about the system.

Flanders, Bruce L. "Spinning the hits: CD-ROM networks in libraries." *American Libraries* 21 (December, 1990): 1032–1033. A useful review of the networking equipment, and the advantages and disadvantages of mounting a CD-ROM installation on a local area network.

Friend, Linda. "Independence at the terminal: training student end users to do online literature searching." *Journal of Academic Librarianship* 11 (July, 1985): 136–141. A lecture/demonstration format was used by Penn State librarians to teach graduate level students the rudiments of BRS/After Dark searching. Responses to a postsearch questionnaire, cost figures, and discussion of typical end-user errors are included in the report.

Grotophorst, Clyde, W. "Training university faculty as end-user searchers: a CAI approach." In *National Online Meeting Proceedings, 1984.* 77–82. Medford, N.J.:

Learned Information, 1984. Grotophorst developed a "freeware" CAI package for BRS/After Dark searching protocols, which some libraries adopted and adapted to their own needs. After using the CAI, faculty end-users consulted with search analysts to refine search strategies and database selection.

Hall, Cynthia, Harriet Talan and Barbara Pease. "InfoTrac in academic libraries: what's missing in the new technology?" *Database* 10 (February, 1987): 52-56. The authors compare InfoTrac to junk food in that its coverage of popular magazines and inadequate indexing, yet ease of access, make it attractive but not nourishing.

Halperin, M. and R. A. Pagell. "Free do it yourself online searching—what to expect." *Online* 9 (March, 1985): 82-84. Lippincott Library at the University of Pennsylvania subsidizes the costs of BRS/After Dark searching by end-users. The authors note staffing needs, average costs, and typical errors, and also note the impact or "pressures" end-user searching places on the library.

Hutchins, Geraldine, Joe Jaros and Vicki Anders. "End-user perceptions of teaching methods." In *National Online Meeting Proceedings, 1987.* 183-190. Medford, N.J.: Learned Information, 1987. The authors tried a slide-tape presentation, CAI, and a locally produced instruction manual to train BRS/After Dark end-users, and monitored each initial search after training. Regardless of the training method, end-users made the same typical mistakes, and all expressed equal satisfaction with the results of their searches.

Jackson, Kathy M., Evelyn M. King, and Jean Kellough. "How to organize an extensive laserdisk installation: the Texas A&M experience." *Online* 12 (March, 1988): 51-60. A generous donor made the installation of an ondisk unit possible. This article describes the process of working with the donor, selecting the equipment and databases, and setting up the unit.

Jakobovits, Leon A. and Diane Nahl-Jakobovits. "Measuring information searching competence." *College and Research Libraries* 51 (Spring, 1990): 448-462. An interesting study that concentrates on teaching affective skills—directing the way students feel about the library—as a necessary precursor to teaching the cognitive and sensorimotor skills of searching, in this case searching an OPAC.

Janke, Richard V. "BRS/After Dark: the birth of online self-service." *Online* 7 (September, 1983): 12-29. Compares and evaluates BRS/After Dark and Knowledge Index for database coverage, ease of use, commands, hours of access, and cost. The author describes a pilot project offering BRS/After Dark to end-users. Examples of end-user and librarian evaluation forms are included.

Janke, Richard V. "Online after six: end-user searching comes of age." *Online* 8 (November, 1984): 15-29. In this second of two articles, Janke details the installation of an end-user online service and some of the insights gleaned from a year's operation. Examples of forms and details on costs and procedures make the articles valuable.

Jaros, Joe, Vicki Anders, and Geri Hutchins. "Subsidized end-user searching in an academic library." In *National Online Meeting Proceedings, 1986.* 223-229. Medford, N.J.: Learned Information, 1986. Evans Library at Texas A&M University set aside funds to provide free end-user searching on BRS/After Dark. Usage increased so much that additional searching stations were required to meet vociferous demand, and when fees were reinstated usage fell off drastically. The study includes cost and use figures.

Johnson, Mary E. and Barbara S. Rosen. "CD-ROM end-user instruction: a planning model." *Laserdisk Professional* 3 (March, 1990): 35-40. "Successful end-user instruction depends upon a knowledgeable staff," the authors state, stressing the importance of the staff's familiarity and comfort with CD-ROM databases if they are to assist users. Classes, handouts, help screens, and one-on-one assistance are some of the methods mentioned.

Kesselman, Martin and Sarah B. Watstein, eds. *End-User Searching: Services and Providers.* Chicago: ALA, 1988. A collection of contributed papers devoted mainly to online end-user services, with separate papers on the different service providers, gateways and front-ends, training, end-users, etc.

Kleiner, Jane P. "InfoTrac: an evaluation of system use and potential in research libraries." *RQ* 27 (Winter, 1987): 252-263. An example of a thorough evaluation of an optical disk database system, in this case InfoTrac. The author concludes that such systems put appropriate or superior research tools in the hands of the users.

Kupferberg, Natalie. "End-users: how are they doing? A librarian interviews six do it yourself searchers." *Online* 10 (March, 1986): 24-30. The end-users interviewed are working professionals rather than students or faculty. All agreed that online searching saves them considerable time and most mentioned their appreciation of the fact that the time is no longer spent in the library.

LaBorie, Tim and Leslie Donnelly. "Vending database searching with public access terminals." *Library Hi Tech* 4 (Summer, 1986): 7-10. "A computer control device manufactured by CompuVend Computer Systems, Inc. provides password security, automatic log-on and charging, and frees the reference staff from having to monitor the terminal." The article describes the equipment used, training sessions, and charging policies.

Lewontin, Amy. "Providing online services to end users outside the library." *College and Research Libraries News* 52 (January, 1991): 21-22. A small business college library allows end-users from home or office computers to access LEXIS, NAARS, and the Dow Jones News Retrieval Service using library passwords.

Machovec, George S. "Administrative issues in planning a library end-user searching program." ERIC ED278416. Syracuse: ERIC Clearinghouse on Information Resources, 1986. The author stresses that libraries must participate in end-user services or be left behind. Needs assessment, hardware, software, training, budgeting, systems options, publicity, policies, and procedures are some of the management issues addressed.

McQueen, Howard. "Accessing databases." *CD ROM End-User* 2 (September, 1990): 54-55. The author discusses DAPS—database access platforms—comparing online, locally loaded, and CD-ROM databases.

Management of CD-ROM Databases in ARL Libraries. SPEC Kit 169. Washington, D.C.: Association of Research Libraries, Office of Management Studies Systems and Procedures Exchange Center, 1990.

Pavelsek, Mary Jean. "A case against instructing users of computerized retrieval systems." *College and Research Libraries News* 52 (May, 1991): 297-301. Having conducted both mandatory and voluntary workshops for end-users, the author concludes that user-friendly systems and the increasing computer sophistication of students makes such end-user instruction unnecessary. A short handout and hands-on experience are the best instructors.

Penhale, S. J. and N. Taylor. "Integrating end-user searching into a bibliographic instruction program." *RQ* 27 (Winter, 1987): 212-220. Bibliographic instruction librarians are an important source of instructors for end-users and certainly should include training in automated information retrieval in their programs if end-user services are available. The article describes a program at Earlham College to instruct users of BRS/After Dark.

Pfaffenberger, Bryan. *Democratizing Information: Online Databases and the Rise of End-User Searching*. Boston: G. K. Hall, 1990. The author asks if end-user searching is likely to become as common as using the telephone and answers, "not yet." The barriers he identifies include end-user reluctance to study and develop the specialized skills required, and the end-user's failure to perceive a need for the information available.

Phillips, Linda L. and Rita H. Smith. "Online searching for undergraduates." In *Academic Libraries: Myths and Realities*, edited by Suzanne C. Dodson and Gary L. Menges. 395-399. Chicago: American Library Association, 1984. Recognizing that the costs of mediated searches put them out of reach for most undergraduates, the authors undertook a study of an early end-user service (IAC's Search Helper) to determine its potential use by undergraduates.

"Planning for end-user searching: a checklist of questions." RASD Occasional Papers No. 1 (1987). Needs assessment, administrative issues such as staff resources and budgets, scope of system being considered, software, and hardware are the major divisions of this three-page checklist.

Puttapithakporn, Somporn. "Interface design and user problems and errors: a case study of novice searchers." *RQ* 30 (Winter, 1990): 195-204. The author tested SilverPlatter's 1.4 search engine software on students enrolled in a library science class and noted the types of errors they made, proving once again that no system is so user-friendly that instruction in its use is not necessary.

Reese, Carol. "Manual indexes versus computer-aided indexes: comparing the *Readers' Guide to Periodical Literature* to InfoTrac II." *RQ* 28 (Spring, 1988): 384-389. Describes an experimental study undertaken at Brookdale Community College in New Jersey in which students were asked to find citations in both indexes for a list of questions. Statistically, *Readers' Guide* was the more effective index, although users clearly preferred the automated database.

Richardson, Robert J. "End-user online searching in a high-technology engineering environment." *Online* 5 (October, 1981): 44-57. In this early study of end-user training, the author concludes that his highly specialized group of working engineers could be taught to perform successful searches on their own, and many expressed a desire and an interest in searching, yet less than half continued to search after the training was complete.

Schloman, Barbara F., Jeffrey N. Gatten and Greg Byerly. "Fee-based CD-ROM at Kent State University." In *Public Access CD-ROMs in Libraries: Case Studies*, edited by Linda Stewart, Katherine S. Chiang and Bill Coons, 207-216. Westport, Conn.: Meckler Corp., 1990. Kent State successfully recovered the subscription costs of CD-ROM by charging users fifteen cents per minute of use. Workstation keyboards were wired through a VendaCard box.

Sewell, Winifred and Sandra Teitelbaum. "Observations of end-user online searching behavior over eleven years." *JASIS* 37 (July, 1986): 234-245. NLM (National Library of Medicine) databases searched by end-users are the subject of this article. Typical end-user behavior—the "quick fix" with no advance preparation, very simple keyword searches, and a preference for point-of-use assistance—have characterized end-users for a decade and probably will continue to do so.

Shill, Harold B. "Bibliographic instruction: planning for the electronic information environment." *College and Research Libraries* 48 (September, 1987): 433–453. The article "is intended to convey the importance of strategic thinking and planning for developing bibliographic instruction programs that will provide information-retrieval skills and to demonstrate to administrators the importance of including patron instruction programs in libraries' long-range planning activities."

Steffen, Susan Swords. "College faculty goes online: training faculty end-users." *Journal of Academic Librarianship* 12 (July, 1986): 147–151. A program to see if "with limited resources, end users from a wide variety of fields could be trained to use a standard search system." The author reaches some enlightened conclusions on the future role of librarians as teachers and as searching consultants.

Stewart, Linda, Katherine S. Chiang and Bill Coons, eds. *Public Access CD-ROMs in Libraries*. Westport, Conn.: Meckler Corp., 1990. Twenty-one cases from a variety of libraries illustrating a variety of options for selecting, installing, and servicing CD-ROM databases and instructing patrons in their use.

Sullivan, Michael V., Cristine L. Borgman and Dorothy Wippern. "End-user, mediated searches, and front-end assistance programs on DIALOG: a comparison of learning, performance, and satisfaction." *JASIS* 41 (January, 1990): 27–42. Describes a workshop training environment using a front-end system to access DIALOG databases. End-users can be trained to search to the point where they are as satisfied with their own results as they are with the results of a mediated search. An excellent literature review and bibliography characterize this research project.

Tenopir, Carol. "Four options for end-user searching." *Library Journal* 111 (July, 1986): 56–57. The options are: end-user systems offered by the major online vendors, front-end software, gateways, and locally loaded databases, especially ondisk databases.

Tucker, Sandra, Vicki Anders, Katharine Clark and William R. Kinyon. "How to manage an extensive laserdisk installation: the Texas A&M experience." *Online* 12 (May, 1988): 34–46. Describes the day-to-day operation of a centralized ondisk installation. Staffing, statistics, traffic management, and troubleshooting are some of the aspects discussed in the article.

Van Arsdale, William O. "The rush to optical discs." *Library Journal* 111 (October 1, 1986): 53–55. Lack of industry standards, wildly variable and high prices, and non-compatible search engines in the optical disk industry prompted the author to encourage librarians to vote with their budgets in an effort to force some standards on the industry.

6

Databases and Vendors

The information industry is a growth industry. To those of us who work with information access tools in libraries every day it would seem to be a major industry, and yet its customer base is quite small and specialized. The industry itself is trying to change and expand its customer base by looking beyond the libraries and information specialists who have traditionally purchased the product and aiming their marketing strategies at purchasers of personal microcomputers. The home user with a COMPUSERVE or PRODIGY account who accesses EASYNET probably does not realize that he or she has become a customer of the information industry and is thus contributing to its growth, and is using tools that only a decade ago were thought to be the exclusive domain of information professionals. However, when compared to the number of personal computers currently in use, database access services and compact disks have not yet penetrated the market to any great extent. The customer base is still small and rather exclusive.

The information industry is making a profit (*Information Industry Factbook*, 1990; Williams, 1985). Database producers are finding a growing percentage of their income switching away from the printed products to the online or ondisk versions of databases. It is becoming difficult for new producers to break into the market, and the number of producers is growing very slowly. There are few subjects that are not already covered by a database, and the cost of hiring and training a production staff is prohibitive; therefore most new databases are being introduced by established producers who already have the indexing infrastructure in place. Mergers and acquisitions characterize the database vendor market in recent years. Although profitable for Lockheed, DIALOG Information Services did not fit in with the parent company's aerospace development and construction industry focus. After several years of trying to sell DIALOG, Lockheed finally found a buyer in Knight-Ridder. Recently, both BRS and ORBIT were purchased by Maxwell. The only new online vendor to emerge recently is OCLC's developing EPIC and FIRSTSEARCH services (Arnold, 1990).

Compact disk databases displayed a fantastic spurt of growth between 1987 and 1989, which has leveled off recently but remains high. Originally, established databases that had been available online were distributed on compact disk but the format invited experimentation. Collections of literature, collections of microcomputer programs, and even nationwide telephone directories are available on CD-ROM, and there is a steady private market using compact disks to store a business's records, inventories, and other papers. Commercial sales are mainly to libraries, and mainly to academic libraries; special libraries remain cautious about adopting ondisk databases while public and school libraries find the costs prohibitive. Equipment costs and database costs insure that most private users will stay away, but this is changing. Currently there are microcomputers with internal CD-ROM drives on the market that cost no more than a 40MG hard drive microcomputer cost just a few years ago, so it is no longer necessary to buy a separate CD drive and go to the bother of installing the interface card and cabling the drive to the microcomputer. Some standard reference tools such as encyclopedias, almanacs, and dictionaries are inexpensive enough to appeal to the affluent home market, and the average price of all CD databases is dropping slightly since the time they were first introduced. Bibliographic databases, the mainstay of library CD collections, are still quite expensive, and in fact most ondisk versions of bibliographic databases are almost twice as expensive as the print equivalent. This is not surprising, since the ondisk database comes with powerful search engine software, printed documentation, and frequently a support staff available by telephone; nonetheless, the cost is high (Chen, 1990; Nicholls, 1989).

The price of information products always has been and remains a controversial issue. (The literature on price, costs, and cost savings is extensive. The following works provide a sampling: Barker (1984), Cavanagh (1990), Fischer (1988), Garman et al. (1990a and 1990b), Jack (1990), Kostenbauder (1988), Quint (1990a), Saffady (1985 and 1988), and Trudell (1988).) Since the 1970s when online access became widely available, information professionals have been predicting that the price of access will come down. It has not. Faster modems and telecommunications access, the use of microcomputers for uploading and downloading, and more skilled search analysts applying advanced techniques have brought the actual cost of any one search down, but the industry has responded by raising its prices or by changing the pricing structure entirely in order to keep its profit up, as has Chemical Abstracts Service for CAS Online. The cost of an ondisk database is high because the producers assume that online usage for the database will drop once a library purchases the ondisk version, and the library may drop its subscription to the printed version as well. All producers and vendors are currently looking at the ways they charge for access to information. Their goal is to keep the industry profitable and to increase profits if possible. It is a small and interconnected industry and a change by one of its participants, such as CAS Online, affects everyone involved. The consumers of the information products—mainly libraries—try to find the most economical and efficient way to access the information, sometimes by preferring online access to a little-used database, or by purchasing an ondisk or locally loaded version of a heavily used database, or by opting for the printed version when automated access is prohibitively expensive or does not significantly increase efficient access.

Everyone is juggling costs and benefits and profit margins. The library's patrons undoubtedly prefer automated access; once they are exposed to it through OPACs, ondisk databases, or online end-user services, they demand more, and they would certainly prefer it to be free. The need of the producers and vendors to make a profit insures that automated access will be expensive. The cost can come down only if producers and vendors expand their market beyond the limited library market where the customer base is small and static and traditionally pennypinching. Libraries continue to pinch pennies while making hard choices among hundreds of vendors and thousands of databases and several different database formats. Statistics from the end of 1990 indicate that there are nearly five thousand commercially available databases containing some five billion records. Around two thousand database producers make their products available through over seven hundred online services and nearly one hundred gateways (*Directory of Online Databases*, 1991, no. 1). Hard choices, indeed.

THE DATABASES

Database Producers

The producers create the machine-readable file of data that can then be used to produce a printed product, or can be sold to a vendor who makes the file accessible to the public, or the producer can vend its own product. A good percentage of database producers in this country are government or quasi-government agencies; for example, AGRICOLA is produced by the National Agricultural Library, CENDATA is produced by the Census Bureau, and ERIC and NTIS are produced under U.S. government contract. Government sponsored databases are typically less expensive to access than databases from other producers. Currently, the U.S. government is producing a great many compact disk databases, many of them full-text.

Nonprofit organizations associated with scientific or professional societies produce around 40 percent of the commercially available databases. MLA Bibliography from the Modern Language Association, GEOREF from the American Geological Institute, and MATHSCI from the American Mathematical Society are examples. For-profit organizations produce another 40 percent of the databases. Predicasts produces several text and numeric files, Bowker and University Microfilms produce bibliographic files.

Some database producers are their own vendors as well, making up the socalled integrated companies. The National Library of Medicine, University Microfilms International, and Information Access Company are examples of organizations that produce databases and sell them through their own online or ondisk services, and also sell their tapes to other vendors. The H. W. Wilson

Company has been the sole vendor for its online and ondisk databases, but in mid-1991 agreed to make its databases available through BRS. In addition, there are many very small or very specialized databases only available via the host computer of the database producer. One example is FAPRS, the Federal Assistance Program Retrieval Service, which is the online equivalent of the *Catalog of Federal Domestic Assistance*.

Many of these database producers have been in the business of producing printed indexes and abstracts and other printed resources for many years and began using computers to produce the printed tools in the 1960s when the technology became available. Bibliographic database producers were the first to offer their products through online vendors, and these databases remain the major tools of most libraries. A bibliographic database producer must first determine that there is a market for yet another database and then select the sources that will be included in the bibliography. Next, the producer must devise an indexing scheme and a structure for the entries, making decisions regarding abbreviations, the use of a controlled vocabulary, whether or not abstracts will be included, and the frequency of updates. A staff is hired and trained to produce the index, to assign controlled vocabulary subject headings and possibly to write abstracts, and the producer hopes to keep the trained staff on hand since high staff turnover means inconsistent indexing and subject heading assignment. Finally, the producer must distribute the database, perhaps in paper copies or perhaps as an automated file either online or ondisk or as a tape to be locally loaded. These are the responsibilities of the bibliographic database producer (Tenopir 1990).

There are very few subject areas that are not already covered by a bibliographic database and very few source publications that are not already indexed. This explains why the number of database producers remains rather static. The exception is Information Access Company, which recognized a need and a market for a series of general indexes in online and ondisk formats and boldly leaped into the business while Wilson was rather slowly and methodically developing its own general indexes for automated access. Wilson's decision to be its own vendor rather than mounting its databases through established vendors clinched a prominent position for IAC databases. Such niches in the information industry marketplace are hard to identify and even harder to exploit in a timely fashion as IAC did. Of all the subjects covered by bibliographic databases, only the humanities are poorly represented, especially the periodical publications for ancient literature, archaeology, and pre-1500 A.D. history.

The database producers expect to recover the costs of producing the databases, and for-profit producers naturally enough want to make a profit from their efforts. Producers who distribute their tapes through the major vendors expect to receive royalty payments that can be calculated based on the amount of time the database is accessed and/or the number of citations printed. The royalty payments are included in the price the vendor charges to the library or end-user accessing the database, and it is frequently very difficult to determine what percentage of the price is a royalty payment. Some database producers will lease or sell their tapes to libraries for local loading, and some of these require royalty payments for access time and citations printed in addition to the cost of leasing the tape.

Types of Databases

With nearly five thousand commercially available databases to choose from, there would seem to be very little data that is not contained in some sort of database. Libraries typically deal with four types of databases on a regular basis: bibliographic databases, full-text databases, numeric databases, and database indexes.

Bibliographic databases have been the bread and butter of libraries, the type most frequently used and most familiar to both librarians and end-users. They provide what is called "surrogate" information—a citation to an article or other publication, possibly with an abstract, but not the full publication itself. A good many of them began life as printed indexes although a few, notably some from IAC, have no print counterparts. The structure of the printed indexes is very evident in the automated versions: the use of controlled vocabularies and the choice of fields that can be searched can make automated searching not much different from print-version searching. However, most bibliographic databases have enhanced access by providing more searchable fields and by providing free-text searching. Thus, in the automated index one can look for terms not part of the controlled vocabulary, or search in more fields than the printed index allows, or limit retrieved items by language, or by source publication, or by document type in certain indexes. In addition to enhanced access points, the capabilities of the machinery for speed and printed output make the automated version more attractive to the user of the information retrieved. The documentation provided by both producers and vendors makes bibliographic database searching easier and more certain; one is less likely to get unexpected and unexplainable results from a search of a bibliographic database.

Bibliographic databases range from the "superdatabases" containing millions of records and striving to be comprehensive, such as COMPENDEX or MEDLINE, to smaller and more exclusive or selective databases such as Meteorological and Geoastrophysical Abstracts or Linguistics and Language Behavior Abstracts, each with fewer than 150,000 records. Some cover a particular type of publication such as books (LC MARC—BOOKS), technical reports (NTIS), congressional publications and documents (CIS Index), or papers delivered at meetings (Conference Papers Index). The preponderance of bibliographic databases are in the scientific and technical fields; less than 5 percent cover humanities subjects.

Full-text databases, as their name implies, contain the complete text of publications rather than the surrogate information of a bibliographic citation and possibly an abstract. Some full-text databases have been enhanced by the addition of surrogate information to aid indexing and access, some have tagged fields to aid access, and some others that claim to be full-text are actually less than complete, to-cover text. Although some full-text databases can be hard to classify, it into the following categories.

ECTORIES, such as the American Library Directory or the Electronic Yellow Pages or PHONEDISC. Like their print counterparts, these can be used for "look-up" information, for example, finding the telephone number of XYZ Library. They are useful for fact finding rather than providing reading material in full-text. But the automated versions allow access points and sorting capabilities that are impossible in the printed versions. Using the Electronic Yellow Pages, one can list the names and addresses of businesses engaged in a certain activity based on SIC code for a region of the country based on a range of ZIP codes, and print only those that employ a certain number of people. Usually, automated directories have far more uses than their printed counterparts.

HANDBOOKS, ENCYCLOPEDIAS, *and other reference tools*, such as Merck Index Online or Kirk-Othmer Encyclopedia of Chemical Technology. As with the automated directories, added access points provided by free-text searching and sorting capabilities enhance the use of these tools far beyond what is possible in the printed version, and in fact the automated version can be used as an index to articles in the printed version. Especially for expensive and seldom-used reference tools, online access on-demand can be an economical alternative to purchasing the printed tool for some libraries.

PUBLICATIONS IN FULL-TEXT, such as *Consumer Reports* or *Harvard Business Review* and several hundred other publications. Unlike the directories and other reference tools mentioned above, the intention here is to provide a reading copy of the full text rather than fact-finding or sorted output. They can be used to provide on-demand access to articles that are not held in the library's printed materials collection and sometimes to provide access before the paper copy reaches the library's collection. Newspapers, journals, and magazines make up the bulk of this material.

The phrase "full-text" must be taken with a grain of salt. Charts, graphs, photographs, and other illustrations frequently are not included in full-text databases, which have been keyboarded to convert them to machine-readable format, and frequently letters, editorial columns, and advertisements are left out. It can be difficult to pin down a producer or vendor claiming to have a full-text product as to what constitutes full text, and the definition can change from month to month. It may depend on the manner in which the text was digitized or converted to machine-readable format, either by keyboarding or as a digitized image. If the text was keyboarded, obviously illustrations and most graphs cannot be included. Text-digitizing by optical scanner can handle alpha-numeric characters adequately but has problems with anything else. In both of these cases the text itself has been made machine-readable and therefore can be searched as a collection of free-text terms in the same way that words in the abstracts of bibliographic databases can be searched. A digitized image, on the other hand, is a machine-readable photograph of text. All of the illustrations can be stored along with the text, but the text itself is not searchable—only an image of words on a page has been stored in the computer, not the words themselves. This optical storage technique has been used by University Microfilms International in their Business Periodicals Ondisc product. With a laser printer attached to the microcomputer, even photographs from texts can be reproduced beautifully, and the entire cover-to-cover text—including the covers—is stored and can be printed. However, the text itself cannot be searched; access to the individual articles is provided by UMI's ABI/INFORM database which refers the user to the appropriate disk where the image of the article is stored.

Full-text searching presents special problems (Basch, 1989). There are too many words. In a full-text newspaper file consisting of thousands of records and each record being the equivalent of a typical newspaper article, the standard Boolean operator AND is practically useless. Searching for "IBM AND LAYOFFS" as free-text terms produces results that have nothing to do with personnel layoffs at an IBM plant. The standard technique of limiting word occurrences to titles does not work in newspapers because the titles of articles are composed to be short and catchy and frequently nondescriptive; alliterative titles are more attractive to browsers than descriptive, but dull, ones. Ideally one could limit the terms to the descriptor field but unfortunately many full-text files are not indexed; there are no descriptors. Good full-text newspaper files set off the lead paragraph of the story as a searchable tagged field; some have brief abstracts of the stories that can be searched. Full-text reference tools such as encyclopedias and handbooks have somewhat better indexing, but if a computer is being used to search the tool it is probably because the indexing in the paper copy produced zero results and the term in question must be searched as a free-text term. Search analysts soon learn to use positional operators rather than AND, to check the documentation to see if the record structure can be used to limit a search, or to use BRS's Occurrence Tables or other searching features that help to limit and refine a search. However, infrequent searchers and end-users are usually unaware of these refinements and will always have problems with too large a retrieved set and low precision ratios in full-text files.

Keeping the library's staff and patrons aware of the publications available as full-text sources is another problem, and in fact it is difficult enough for the service manager and the search analysts to keep up to date with the growing number of full-text sources available from many different vendors. No doubt there are many patrons who are told that the library does not have a particular resource when in fact it is available online in a full-text database, and no doubt there are hundreds of interlibrary loan requests placed for items that could be retrieved immediately from a full-text file. It is the service manger's job to keep the staff informed and to remind them of the possibilities of full-text files. The policy and procedures manual should have a statement regarding the use of full-text files when needed resources are not in the library's collection, and reference and interlibrary loan staff should be trained to check for the availability of a full-text source online rather than automatically telling a patron the resource is not available and a two to three week wait is necessary to get the resource from another library.

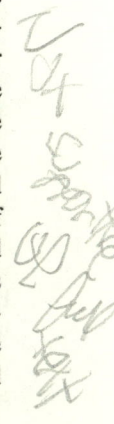

LEXIS and WESTLAW are two specialized vendors and producers of full-text databases related to law. Law journals, court reporters from the states and federal courts, texts and dictionaries, and state and federal statutes are some of the full-text documents available. One expects to find LEXIS or WESTLAW in a law library, but they have a place as well in the academic library that does not serve a law school. The paper copies of the resources available through either service are incredibly expensive, take a great deal of shelf space, and receive limited but significant use from the faculty and students in business and public policy curricula. Online access on demand can serve these users and save the library money and space. Both vendors have various contract options for academic libraries or government agencies and both have relatively easy search engines designed for end-users. NEXIS, the companion to LEXIS, provides access to full-text news resources. WESTLAW provides gateway access to DIALOG and VU/TEXT.

Numeric databases fall for the most part into three categories: *NUMERIC*, consisting of raw data such as census figures, statistical data, etc.; *PROPERTIES*, consisting of handbook-type data, usually in the physical sciences, engineering, and technology fields; and *TEXTUAL/NUMERIC*, consisting of text fields and numeric fields, often in the form of charts or graphs.

It is the last two types that are most familiar in libraries. The strictly numeric databases are not widely available through the standard online vendors except in abbreviated of predigested forms. For example, one can purchase census tapes from the Census Bureau, Labor Statistics tapes and so forth, but they must be mounted on a mainframe computer and manipulated with sophisticated and powerful programs. The manipulation is best done by the researcher who is using the data; this is not the kind of situation where the researcher explains his or her needs to an intermediary who interprets and performs the functions necessary. The researcher needs to interact with the data, not with the intermediary. The CENDATA file from the Census Bureau contains the results of such manipulations in reports where the numeric data has been compiled and arranged in tables. PTS TIME SERIES and ECONBASE are examples of numeric databases available through DIALOG.

Properties databases are most frequently used for "look-up"-type information and as such would seem to be most useful to the researcher without the intervention of an intermediary. Databases such as BEILSTEIN ONLINE and HAZARDLINE can be searched by numeric input to identify boiling points, densities, and other properties of chemicals. Technically these are textual/numeric databases, the type most familiar to search analysts, since they are the type available through the standard vendors. They include such online databases as those available from PTS and the ondisk products Compact Disclosure and Lotus OneSource. They are characterized by the ability to define parameters and produce numeric reports in which the data has been extracted from several records and several fields within a record; the printed output is a manipulation of the data rather than a collection of individual records as in a bibliographic or full-text file.

Most numeric databases are heavily coded, so access to and familiarity with the database documentation is essential. The exceptions are the ondisk products mentioned above, designed for end-users with menu-driven interfaces, which really are quite easy to use. Numeric databases are underutilized in most libraries, probably because librarians do not feel comfortable with them and because the search analyst intermediary is actually a barrier between the researcher and the data (Bellardo and Stephenson, 1986; Chen and Hernon, 1984).

Another very special type of database is the database index such as DIALINDEX from DIALOG, CROS from BRS, or DATABASE INDEX from ORBIT. These are master indexes to all or to selected categories of the databases loaded with each vendor. When the patron has no preference as to databases searched and the search analyst is not sure which databases are likely to contain the most or the best information, a master index search is in order. The search statement is entered, and the system responds by indicating the number of hits in each database from the category selected. The results can help the search analyst decide which database will produce the largest recall, and sometimes give an indication that a search strategy needs to be restated. It is very easy for a search analyst to get into the habit of searching the same ten or twenty databases. The service manager should encourage analysts to use the master indexes frequently; they demonstrate the possible choices graphically to the patron who is then less likely to feel that something may have been missed, and they broaden the database repertoire of the search analysts.

Evaluating Databases

With five thousand databases to choose from, the question of which database is the best for a particular query will inevitably arise. The master indexes described above will give an indication of which databases produce the most hits, but not which one produces the best hits. Recall ratio is only one of the criteria for evaluating a database; precision ratio, ease of access, date coverage, amount and quality of information, and cost are other factors to consider. (Articles that provide different frameworks for evaluating and comparing databases include LaBorie (1981), Rice (1985), Tenopir (1982), and Watkins (1981).)

There is considerable overlap among bibliographic databases, since all of them are attempting to cover a finite body of literature. The superdatabases that attempt comprehensive coverage, such as COMPENDEX, have a different goal and purpose than a more selective database such as Engineered Materials Abstracts, and yet both index many of the same publications. If the goal of the search is high recall, in other words, to find everything available on a subject, many users will opt to search all the relevant databases even though the search will produce many duplicate citations, which must be paid for and sifted through. DIALOG's recent "duplicate detection" innovation makes this less of a problem if all the databases to be searched are available through DIALOG. If the goal of the search is to produce a high precision ratio, the superdatabase may not be the best choice, since the likelihood of producing false drops (citations in which the search terms occur but the subject matter of the item retrieved is not relevant to the topic being researched) is greater in the larger databases. The expectations of the patron should have been determined in the interview preceding the search, but unless the search analyst has a thorough familiarity with the relevant databases he or she will have no basis for choosing among them. The problem is compounded when working with end-users who probably have fewer choices of databases available to them and who cannot be expected to have a broad knowledge of other databases.

A master index search will provide a starting place by indicating which databases have hits on the subject in question. An examination of the database documentation will provide some hints on the precision ratio one can expect from the database. Specifically, one should look for:

Source publication coverage. The patron or end-user will probably be the best judge to determine if the publications covered by the database are likely to produce the expected results. When helping undergraduates, the librarian may need to steer the patron to less technical sources or those that are most likely to be in the library's local collection—Wilson or IAC databases, for example.

Date coverage and currency. Some very large files are divided into groups of years covered. If the patron has date limits, searching a smaller file will produce faster and more precise results.

Amount and quality of information. The availability of abstracts provides more access points for free-text searching and provides more information to the patron upon which to base decisions regarding the relevance of the citations. Free-text searching allows access to terms or concepts that are not part of a controlled vocabulary; on the other hand, free-text searching can lead to imprecise results if the terms to be searched are not unique and definitive.

Ease of access/availability. This is largely determined by the structure of the record and its division into searchable fields. If the patron wants only literature review articles, searching a database that does not allow access by document type will be frustrating and imprecise. Searching the descriptor field for controlled vocabulary terms improves precision. In textual/numeric databases, the ability to search a range of numbers may be critical. Checking the brief database guides the vendors produce is always a good idea; they provide clues to ways that databases can be searched most efficiently, often ways that the searcher has never tried before. The DIALOG BlueSheets are available as on online file, providing an easy way to see which databases are searchable by document type or have other coded fields.

Controlled vocabulary and codes. As every librarian knows, some controlled vocabularies are better than others. If the patron's concept is precisely defined by a controlled vocabulary term in a particular database, that database is an obvious choice. In combination with free-text terms, controlled vocabularies and codes can limit an imprecise and large retrieval set.

Cost. This may or may not be a factor, but any patron will appreciate some effort at keeping costs as low as possible. A small, specialized database may have a higher per-hour charge than one of the superdatabases, but the faster access time and lower, more precise retrieval can make the bottom line cost of searching it less expensive than the larger databases.

These evaluative criteria help a searcher decide which online databases are likely to produce the best results, but they can also be used to decide which ondisk or locally loaded databases to purchase. In this case, the search engine that comes with the database is another evaluation that must be performed, using the evaluative criteria listed below for vendors (Haar et al., 1990; Miller, 1987; Nicholls, 1990; Nicholls et al., 1990).

Ultimately, the best, and sometimes the only, way to determine if a database has the information needed is to search it. If a library charges fees for searches, there should be some provision in the library budget allowing search analysts to test a database or practice in it to see if it is suitable for a particular question, or the library budget should absorb the costs of databases mistakenly accessed because the search analyst was not familiar enough with them to know that they were inappropriate.

Database Directories and Selection Tools

The major vendors add new databases to their services practically every month, and sometimes an old and familiar database dies and goes away. Search analysts are often asked to advise library staff and patrons on the availability and use of databases even though they may not be asked to provide a search of the database. Keeping up with the proliferation of databases and the formats they come in would be impossible without the following tools:

CD-ROMs in Print: An International Guide. Westport, Conn.: Meckler. This has been published annually since 1987 and seems to double in size each year. In addition to a full bibliographic citation of each database, hardware and software specifications are given, along with price and restrictions information, and a brief description.

Computer Readable Databases: A Directory and Sourcebook. Detroit: Gale Research. This is now an annual publication, although in the early years it was not updated so frequently. It has also changed its format considerably from early years. There is a separate index for CD-ROM databases. Also available as File 230 on DIALOG, which provides a midyear update.

Directory of Online Databases. New York: Cuadra/Elsevier. Published twice a year. Databases are listed alphabetically, with an indication when appropriate that the database is available on CD or mag tape. This is an indication to consult.

Directory of Portable Databases. New York: Cuadra/ Elsevier. A new entry that first appeared in 1990. The databases are thoroughly covered in lengthy descriptions. Databases distributed on CD-ROM or other optical devices, on diskette, and on mag tape are included.

Fulltext Sources Online. Needham Heights, Mass.: Bibliodata. Published twice yearly in January and July since 1989. Journals are listed alphabetically by title. Each entry lists the vendors that carry full-text, the name of the file, frequency of updates and time lag if any, span of coverage, and an indication of less than full-text coverage when appropriate.

Ulrich's International Periodicals Directory. New York: Bowker. This venerable favorite now indicates when a publication is available online in full-text. Very little information about span of coverage and so forth is given, but it does provide a useful hint when a librarian should check further. Ulrich's is available online as ULRI in BRS and as File 480 on DIALOG.

In addition to these directories, individual vendors publish newsletters that announce new databases added to the service, or enhancements and reloads of old databases, price changes, restrictions, and the deaths of a few databases. Newsletters should be routed to the searching staff and maintained on file with other documentation from vendors and producers. Some vendors also have online announcements, which should be checked by the service manager at least daily.

THE VENDORS

The vendor makes a database available to the public. Some database producers are their own vendors, such as the National Library of Medicine or H. W. Wilson; others are supermarkets making the databases of several producers available through a single system. A few who are primarily vendors also produce databases. DIALOG, for example, has its BlueSheets, Chronolog Newsletter, and Journal Name Finder as online databases.

The vendor devises the search engine that will be used to search all the databases mounted on the vendor's system. This consists of the database management and retrieval program and a user interface that allows nonprogrammers to communicate with the program. The vendor negotiates agreements with database producers for their machine-readable tapes, under which the vendor purchases or leases the tapes and in many cases agrees to collect royalty fees for the producers based on the total time a database is accessed and the number of citations printed. Next, the vendor must manipulate the data on the tapes so that it conforms to the design specifications of the search engine. For example, the author field of each record must be delimited—set off from the other fields in the record and identified with a code in such a way that the search engine can recognize it—and the same must be done for every other field in the record. Stop words must be coded and indexes built that identify the record number and field and word order for each significant word in every record. This would be a daunting task if it had to be done manually, but most of it can be handled by a computer program.

Online vendors then mount the tapes on mainframe computers that provide the storage and processing capabilities to apply the search engine program. Multiple telecommunication ports allow users to dial up the computer and manipulate the program via the user interface. Most online vendors have printing facilities to provide offline prints. The mainframe tracks usage based on the user numbers of the individuals who dial in to the computer and computes the bill for each user. Ondisk vendors package the search engine as software that is sent with the ondisk database and loaded on the local user's microcomputer.

These, then, are the basic functions a vendor performs: devising a search engine, acquiring machine-readable databases, editing the database to work with the search engine, and packaging the search engine and database together so that they are accessible to a customer base. The fact that there are so many different online and ondisk vendors should point out an alarming problem: the proliferation of search engines. Each vendor must invent a new search engine—specifically the user interface—that is sufficiently different from other, existing programs to be copyrightable, or else pay a hefty fee to the original compiler of the search engine program and frequently a royalty to the original compiler each time the search engine program is distributed. This cuts into the vendor's profits enough so that it is more economical to reinvent the wheel, and thus there are hundreds of search engines. In the ondisk industry especially, the majority of these search engines apply to only one or two databases.

This presents a problem, a major headache, to academic libraries especially. A library may have one search engine for its OPAC, multiple contracts with several online vendors each with its own search engine, and several ondisk products. A competent search analyst can easily keep four or five different command structures straight and apply the appropriate one when searching a particular vendor, but when there are ten or fifteen search engines in use, the search analyst slows down, and must stop and think or consult the manual to figure out the correct command, even for something as simple and basic as a truncation symbol. Many end-users simply do not understand the reason for multiple search engines; to them it is merely inefficient, and they blame the library. Search engine programmers keep promising that certain conventions will develop but so far the only one that seems to apply in nearly all search engines is the use of the F1 key to summon the help screens. For librarians, the proliferation of search engines means less efficient access to data and more work—more instruction, more one-on-one assistance, and more handouts. For search analysts, the proliferation of search engines can lead to a deteriorating ability to search any one of them efficiently. For end-users, it is inconvenient and frustrating and frankly looks like a mistake.

Librarians do have a chance to select a particular search engine because there are some databases that are widely available from several different online and ondisk vendors. A branch library specializing in a particular subject area may be able to keep the number of search engines down to one or two by careful shopping among the options available. However, the search engine is only one of the criteria to consider in selecting a vendor, and it may not be the most important one. Beyond the basic functions of a vendor described above, there are a variety of services and options to weigh (Nichol, 1983).

The selection of databases a vendor offers is usually the prime consideration for any library, since the library must match the information needs of the community it serves. DIALOG offers by far the most databases in all subject areas.

However, access to all those databases may not be necessary and may be outweighed by other considerations. BRS specializes in medical and biosciences databases and offers the added advantage of MEDSPELL, which automatically retrieves American and British spellings, the full-text sources in its Comprehensive Core Medical Library, and LINK, which retrieves the full-text sources when citations to them are found in other BRS databases. ORBIT specializes in technology, materials sciences, and patent databases. WILSONLINE offers the H. W. Wilson databases only, but the sources for these databases were selected by a panel of librarians and therefore are more likely to be found in a large academic library's collection, which cuts down considerably the frustrations and delays in trying to obtain sources outside the collection. Each vendor offers unique databases that are not available through the others, and it is for this reason that most academic libraries have found it necessary to maintain contracts with multiple vendors.

The cost of the service and the contract options available are points to consider in selecting a vendor. It is difficult to compare costs per search among the major vendors. One may have a lower connect charge per hour for a particular database but charge more for online and offline citations; another may have a high connect charge per hour but process searches slightly faster, making the cost for any one search somewhat lower than or the same as its competitors. A library may find that one service is more economical for ready-reference searches where only a few citations are printed online, and another service is more economical for mediated searches producing long printouts printed offline (Griffith, 1987 and 1989). On a bad day when the telephone lines are noisy and it seems that every library in the country is accessing the same vendor, no search is economical. Although several articles have been written comparing the costs of various vendors, individual libraries will have different experiences based on the equipment they use, the proficiency level of the search analysts, and the types of searches they typically perform. It is better to compare the contract options and the fees not related to searching (Buckel, 1982; Eskola, 1990; Maloney, 1987). Some of these pricing options are:

Start-up fee: This is a flat fee required before a user ID allowing access to the system is issued. Sometimes the fee covers only the issuing of the ID, sometimes it covers the cost of basic documentation such as a user's manual, and it may include one or two hours of free online time, sometimes limited to a practice database. The start-up fee may be charged for each user ID issued, or it may cover multiple IDs. Some services require an annual fee.

Open-access rate: This has different names from different vendors, but it refers to the usually high rate charged to a user who makes no guarantees such as a monthly minimum or a deposit account. The user can access the system as often or as seldom as needed and pays only for searches performed. If there is no searching activity in any month, the user is not billed. Most often these rates are the highest charged, but a library that does not expect to use a system frequently can save money by choosing open access rates.

Guaranteed minimum: The library guarantees to perform searches at least up to a stated amount. If a library guarantees $300 worth of searches every month and only performs $10 worth of searches in one month, the library will be billed $300. If the library performs $500 worth of searches it will be billed $500. In return for the guaranteed minimum, the vendor reduces the rate to below the open access rates by a certain percentage so that the library is paying less for each search. For some services, the guaranteed minimum is not optional; for example, BRS/After Dark requires a monthly minimum of $12 per user ID. For some services, the guaranteed minimum is charged in addition to searching activity charges; in other words, the library pays what amounts to a monthly service charge and also pays for any searching done that month, but at the reduced rate guaranteed by the contract.

Prepaid deposit: Prepayment of a certain amount reduces the rate at which the library pays; in some cases a larger prepayment causes a larger percentage of reduction from the open access rates. In addition to reduced rates, a prepaid deposit can have other advantages such as multiple user IDs without additional charge. A library's searches are debited from the deposit account until it is exhausted; thereafter, the library is billed for searches but at the same reduced rate. Sometimes the amount of money required for the prepaid deposit is rather high. Library networks such as AMIGOS or SOLINET sometimes negotiate prepaid deposits for the member libraries and thus collect the total amount needed for the highest discount rate through smaller payments from each individual library.

Multiple copy discounts: Some ondisk vendors charge lower rates per copy when multiple copies of a disk are purchased. On the other hand, some databases have such high licensing fees for mounting a database on a local area network that the fee is equal the cost of a second copy of the database.

In addition to these contract options some vendors may offer special rates to academic institutions or government agencies; many have quite low rates for classroom instruction use. A library may qualify for discounts on certain databases if the library subscribes to the print copy of the database; for example, the Institute for Scientific Information databases, GEOREF, and TULSA offer discounts for online database access, and several ondisk databases have lower rates for subscribers. It can be time-consuming tracking down all the contract options and discounts that may apply to a particular library, but the reduced costs for a frequently used system or database are certainly worth the effort.

The special services and features a vendor offers should be examined to find the closest fit to the library's needs. Not all vendors offer every feature, and some features will never be used by a particular library. Among the services to look for are:

Training: The location and frequency of vendor-sponsored training sessions should be examined, because a library will not find it economical to send search analysts several hundred miles to attend training sessions offered two or three times a year. Some vendors offer online CAI training packages that vary in quality and vary in price ranging from telecommunications only to several dollar per hour. Practice files and their costs are another feature to look for. Some vendors have programmed instruction manuals or microcomputer CAI packages available; these may be included in the start-up fee price or they may carry an additional charge.

Documentation: Good documentation is critical to successful searching. At a minimum there should be a system manual explaining the commands and other system features, and database documentation showing the database record structure and searchable fields. The documentation should be updated when necessary and distributed to users in a timely fashion. Some vendors publish newsletters to keep users informed of new system features and new databases.

Help screens: Often a user does not get a chance to evaluate help screens until the contract has been signed and the product paid for. Help screens should be brief, informative, easily navigated, context-sensitive, and should return the user to the point of the search at which help was summoned. Unfortunately, very few help screen features meet these criteria. Most are wordy and must be paged through in a linear fashion, are difficult to exit, and frequently interrupt the search when help is summoned. Some ondisk products substitute help screens for printed documentation, forcing the user to make paper copies of all the help screens in order to have a system manual and database guide.

Customer support: A toll-free telephone help number is a feature of the best vendors. It should be available for a reasonable number of hours since most libraries do not shut down at 5:00 p.m. Eastern time. This is especially important for end-user systems available only during nonbusiness hours. Expert help should be available for troubleshooting, assistance with system commands, and questions related to the business aspects of dealing with the vendor. Some vendors offer expert assistance with search strategy development and database-specific advice. With ondisk products especially, being able to talk to an engineer or technician who can assist with programming or equipment-related questions is very helpful.

Output options: A variety of output formats and the ability to tailor output in the detail and the order suited to the user's needs are valuable features. Online vendors have shown more flexibility in this area than ondisk vendors. Sorted and customized printouts and reports are available for some products and are promised for many more. Online vendors offer online prints and offline prints either printed at the host computer and sent through the mail or dumped into a reduced-price file for later printing or downloading by the requesting library on its own equipment. Some databases have different rates for online and offline prints, which can make a difference in the cost to the consumer who prefers downloaded output or who prefers immediate output. Online vendors should offer a no-charge browsing format, usually consisting of titles and descriptors, so that searchers can check the precision of the retrieved set without incurring a penalty other than the connect time spent reading through the list. Viewing, printing, and downloading from ondisk databases should require no more than a few simple keystrokes, but unfortunately some user interfaces make output delivery much more difficult than it needs to be.

Saved searches: The ability to store either temporarily or permanently a search strategy in the host computer's memory and execute it in different databases or at intervals is a useful feature. Automatic execution of saved searches to create SDIs (selective dissemination of information) is offered by many online vendors. There may be charges for the different types of saves, and SDIs especially can get very expensive when they are run against databases that are updated frequently. Charges for saved searches appear on the monthly invoices from online vendors, and the service manager should check these at intervals to be sure the saved search is still needed. DIALOG's ONESEARCH feature is a special kind of temporarily saved search running in multiple databases and combining the postings from all databases into a single set. ONESEARCH combined with the duplicate detection feature can save quite a bit of money.

Extras: Automatic plurals, internal and left-hand truncation, the ability to save or delete selected search statements, access to E-mail and document delivery services are some of the useful features that are not shared by all vendors. Unfortunately, one never knows just how useful they can be until one has experienced the services of several different vendors and notes the lack of a favorite feature from one or more of them. Gateway access to other vendors' databases is an extra that should be looked for because it can save a library the bother and expense of negotiating yet another contract with yet another vendor. BRS, ORBIT, and PERGAMON INFOLINE have been owned by the same parent company Maxwell Online for some time now and gateways from one to another's databases have been promised but are not yet available.

Consistency and change: Search commands should be applied consistently across all the databases available from a single vendor. Naturally, the structure of an individual database can make this difficult and can require more editing of the producer's tape than the vendor had planned on, but the command "PY=1986" should produce the same results in all databases and should not be structured as "YR=1986" or "PY=86" in a few databases where the meaning and intent of the command is exactly the same.

On the other hand, vendors should be willing to change when change improves the product. Ondisk vendors have shown a much greater willingness to change their search engines and especially the user interface than online vendors, so much so that the early UMI search engine is practically unrecognizable in the much improved PROSEARCH software UMI uses today. SilverPlatter has updated its software several times, incorporating suggestions from librarians and end-users and at the same time keeping a fairly consistent product that does not require major retraining and relearning with each new update. The online vendors are much slower to change, but enhancements such as DIALOG's ONESEARCH and duplicate detection features are so major and so valuable that they should shake up the whole industry.

In reality, a library may not always have an option in selecting a vendor, since it is the availability of the databases that forces the vendors upon us. A large academic library serving the entire academic community will probably have contracts with four or five of the major vendors at least, and many have contracts with a dozen or more. The problem this creates due to multiple search engines has already been mentioned. Another problem is the increase in paperwork. Each vendor sends a monthly invoice or multiple invoices if the library has multiple passwords. Some of the contracts have to be renewed every year with service fees or prepaid deposits, or possibly the monthly minimum has to be renegotiated because searching activity with that particular vendor has slacked off. Password security becomes a problem; even keeping track of all the passwords is a problem. Checking dozens of invoices every month against every recorded search to be sure a password has not been stolen becomes impossible.

Search analysts can develop a preference for a certain search engine that is not because of any inherent superiority of one search engine over another but because it was the first one they learned and the one they feel most competent in using. When another vendor has only one or two unique databases, the analysts will understandably resist using it even when those unique databases are the most appropriate ones to search. There will be some systems that are searched so seldom that all the searchers will have to brush up by reading the manual before they can use it. At some point the service manager will have to question whether it is worth the extra paperwork, the money, and the time spent on learning to add another vendor in order to make a few more databases available for searching.

Gateways may be able to solve the problem. An EASYNET contract allows access to several vendors without negotiating separate contracts with each vendor, and there is only one search engine to learn (Quint, 1990b). The search engine is not optimal and search analysts will find it frustrating, but it does provide access, which may be enough for databases that will be searched less than a dozen times a year. An existing contract may already have gateway access to other vendors; it is worth checking out. Alternatively, it may be possible to farm out a search request to an information broker or to a neighboring library that does have the appropriate access (See Burwell, 1984).

Names and addresses of vendors can be found in many of the directories listed for databases earlier in this chapter. Below are the names and addresses of the major supermarket vendors providing access to a number of different databases:

BRS INFORMATION TECHNOLOGIES
8000 Westpark Drive
McLean, VA 22102
(800) 289-4277

BRS specializes in medical and biosciences databases and offers databases in all other subjects. BRS/After Dark offers user-friendly access at reduced rates during nonbusiness hours. BRS COLLEAGUE is a business-hours, user-friendly system. The standard search engine is easy to learn and use. MEDSPELL and automatic plurals are special features. BRS provides simplified AidPages and more detailed database chapters for each database. The *BRS Bulletin* is a newsletter published every two months.

DATATIMES CORPORATION
Suite 450
14000 Quail Springs Parkway
Oklahoma City, OK 73134
(800) 642-2525

DataTimes provides access to full-text newspapers, mainly major U.S. newspapers and some Canadian and European papers as well. DataTimes also serves as a gateway to Dow Jones News Service. The search engine has been revised several times over the years and is now simple to use and powerful. Controlled vocabulary indexing is provided for some newspapers.

DIALOG INFORMATION SERVICES, INC.
3460 Hillview Avenue
Palo Alto, CA 94304
(800) 334-2564

DIALOG provides access to the most databases by far, with a powerful and flexible search engine. Knowledge Index is the nonbusiness-hours, user-friendly version, and most of the business-hours databases are accessible through a user-friendly interface called MENUS. DIALOG is a vendor of several ondisk databases as well. DIALOG publishes BlueSheets and database chapters and its monthly newsletter CHRONOLOG.

MEAD DATA CENTRAL
P.O. Box 933
Dayton, OH 45401
(800) 227-4908

Mead Data provides access to LEXIS, a full-text law database, and NEXIS, a full-text news and journal database. The interface was originally designed to be used by lawyers and other law professionals with very little training, so it is moderately user-friendly. Several contract options are available.

ORBIT SEARCH SERVICES
8000 Westpark Drive, Suite 400
McLean, VA 22102
(800) 456-7428

Orbit specializes in technology, materials science, and patent databases. The search engine is powerful and flexible and includes the GET command, which allows some bibliometric analysis. Quick Reference Guides are available for each database, and the vendor publishes a monthly newsletter called *Searchlight*.

STN INTERNATIONAL
c/o Chemical Abstracts Service
2540 Olentangy River Road
P.O. Box 3012
Columbus, OH 43210
(800) 848-6533

STN specializes in scientific and technical databases and is the "home" vendor of Chemical Abstracts databases. Complicated chemical structure and numeric searching capabilities are special features. A user-friendly interface is available as a separately purchased front-end software package called STN EXPRESS. STN makes non-business-hours access to CA available at reduced rates through its academic account program.

SILVERPLATTER INFORMATION, INC.
One Newton Executive Park
Newton Lower Falls, MA 02162
(800) 343-0064

SilverPlatter provides a powerful yet user-friendly search engine for several ondisk databases. Documentation consists of the standard SilverPlatter manual and command cards for the individual databases. One can order package deals of databases and equipment from SilverPlatter. MultiPlatter is a local area network system developed and installed by SilverPlatter technicians.

VU/TEXT INFORMATION SERVICES, INC.
325 Chestnut Street, Suite 1300
Philadelphia, PA 19106
(800) 323-2940

VU/TEXT, a division of Knight-Ridder, provides access to full-text newspapers, newswires, some major magazines, and other sources. Gateway access to VU/TEXT is available through several different online services.

WEST PUBLISHING CO.
50 West Kellogg Blvd.
P.O. Box 64526
St. Paul, MN 55164
(800) 328-0109

Access to WESTLAW, a full-text law and law journal collection of databases, is provided. Designed for use in law offices, the native search engine is fairly user-friendly, and WESTLAW also provides EZ ACCESS, a menu-driven interface that is even friendlier. WESTLAW provides gateway access to DIALOG.

H. W. Wilson Co.
950 University Avenue
Bronx, NY 10452
(800) 367-6770

WILSONLINE, Wilsearch, and WilsonDisc are automated information retrieval products providing access to the Wilson databases. Wilsearch is user-friendly and inexpensive enough to be provided to end-users. The ondisk products have four interface modes that can serve novice and expert searchers.

There are non-United States vendors that provide access to databases not otherwise available. Dealing with a foreign vendor can be tricky; the service manager will want to investigate hours of availability, telephone access and reliability, training and the language of the documentation, and the currency in which the invoices are payable, among other things, and will want to check the database directories thoroughly to be sure that access is available only through a foreign vendor. The major foreign vendors are:

CAN/OLE
Canadian Online Enquiry Service
National Research Council Canada
Ottawa, Ontario K1A 0S2
Canada

DATA-STAR
D-S Marketing Limited
Plaza Suite
114 Jermyn Street
London SW1Y 6HJ
England

DIMDI
Weisshausstrasse 27
Postfach 420580
5000 Cologne 4I
Federal Republic of Germany

ESA-IRS
European Space Agency—Information Retrieval Service
Via Galileo Galilei
00044 Frascati
Italy

QUESTEL
83-85 boulevard Vincent Auriol
75013 Paris
France

SELECTING THE FORMAT

Automated information retrieval users constantly choose among databases, deciding which database is most suited to provide a fast, thorough, and economical answer to a question. Would Applied Science and Technology Index answer the question, or would COMPENDEX be a better choice? Occasionally a choice of search engines is offered; would the search analyst prefer to search COMPENDEX on BRS, DIALOG, ORBIT, or STN today?

Now the choice of format complicates the issue (Hewins, 1990). If COMPENDEX is to be searched by trained search analysts, any of the four major vendors can provide access. If COMPENDEX is to be searched by end-users, Knowledge Index offers a user-friendly interface for online access, or the library can opt for the DIALOG Ondisk version of COMPENDEX, which would increase the cost but also increase the hours of access to the database. On the other hand, the library may be worried about downtime due to hardware failure, or the durability of the CD-ROM format (Marshall and Voedisch, 1990). Perhaps a gateway or front-end software could provide the hours of access needed without requiring the library to purchase the specialized hardware needed by ondisk databases, and to find room for it in the library. Perhaps the library has determined that online access is needed for the earliest citations or the most recent citations, whereas the ondisk format will serve the most users with the latest five years worth of indexing (Williamson, 1990). Or, it may be that COMPENDEX is so much in demand that the library decides to mount it as a locally loaded tape, entailing great cost to the library but providing great convenience to the users. If the database is made available to end-users, who will instruct them, and how, and when? The variables driving the decisions to be made are the database, the search engine, and the cost.

It is hoped that the automated information retrieval service has kept a good set of statistics on database usage. An online database that has shown a consistently high or increasing level of use is a possible candidate for becoming a "portable" database as the *Directory of Portable Databases* calls them, a database available in the local environment on optical disk, diskette, or magnetic tape. Statistics will show how much money has been spent accessing the online database and printing from it, and it may be that an ondisk subscription and the necessary equipment, or locally loading the tape, can provide less expensive access to far more users. Usage will increase once the database is available without the appointments necessary in an online environment, and it will increase far more if the database is available at no charge to the users. Despite the usage statistics, some libraries may question whether or not a particular database is suitable for the end-users of a particular institution. For example, COMPENDEX may be well used in a small college library that has online services exclusively from DIALOG because that is what has been made available, but users might be better served by Applied Science and Technology Index via Wilsearch or as an ondisk or locally loaded database. Highly coded databases and full-text newspaper or journal databases probably are not suitable for end-users because they do not have the knowledge and training necessary to use them efficiently and most are not willing to spend the time learning. On the other hand, some databases are not suited to the "intermediary as translator" format of a mediated search; when the user needs to interact with the data as with many numeric databases, or can easily and quickly look up reference-type information from a full-text encyclopedia or directory, the database is more suited to end-users.

Once it has been determined that a database is available and suited to the library's needs, the type of search engine must be determined. If the database is suitable for end-users, and usage statistics show that it will be used, a user-friendly search engine will be necessary. User-friendly means different things to different users. Trained search analysts find the frequent and wordy instructions, the warnings, and the pop-up menus of some user-friendly search engines to be irritating—they are barriers rather than facilitators, to achieving the wanted result. A novice user may prefer to browse through a list of controlled vocabulary terms since this is the familiar format of printed indexes. If library users have been exposed to an OPAC, they already have some familiarity with automated information retrieval and probably will prefer a more advanced user-friendly search engine. In fact, they would prefer the ready access and familiarity of a locally loaded database that uses the OPAC's search engine.

The library must decide between online or local access. If costs must be controlled or charged back to the user, the appointment format of online access is preferable. The choice then becomes one of front-ends, gateways, or the non-business-hours services from BRS/After Dark and Knowledge Index. If the goal is to serve the most users, a locally loaded or ondisk database is preferable. Providing local access to a database limits the choice of search engine, since only a few databases such as ERIC, NTIS, and AGRICOLA are available from multiple ondisk vendors.

The cost of providing access must be considered (Porter, 1991). If the goal is to make many databases available, either to end-users or through mediated searches, online access is the cheaper alternative. However, online access limits the number of users. Far more users can be served by local access, but the number of databases is severely limited by the high costs of leasing and mounting locally loaded databases and the high cost of providing multiple search stations and LANs for ondisk databases. Any sort of end-user access carries hidden costs for instruction, handouts, one-on-one assistance, and the increased usage of the library's facilities and collections in general. If costs must be recovered, a mediated search service provides a ready format to handle billing and the record-keeping involved, and also provides the most efficient and cost-effective searches. If end-user searchers must be billed, the record-keeping and user-monitoring tasks of the staff are greatly increased and usage of the databases is greatly decreased.

Provided the library has selected end-user databases carefully, based on the users' needs as determined by statistical analysis or even a close attention to general perceptions, locally loaded or ondisk databases will be used. A clumsy and irritating search engine will be overcome by any number of persistent end-users who need access to the database. But a fee for use will stop a good many of them dead in their tracks. No one wants to pay for access to information in a library; nearly everyone perceives such payments to be against the nature of "free" libraries. The hard choice for libraries is to select from the databases, search engines, and formats available the configuration that the library can afford without forcing the users to pay for it.

REFERENCES

ALA Yearbook of Library and Information Services. Chicago: American Library Association. This annual publication usually includes an article ("Databases, Computer Readable") reviewing the year's activities and innovations in the information industry.

Arnold, Stephen E. "Marketing electronic information: theory, practice and challenges, 1980–1990." *Annual Review of Information Science and Technology* 25 (1990): 87–144. Electronic information is relatively new to marketers. The history and scope of electronic information marketing is covered in this typical ARIST article, which includes a literature review and extensive bibliography.

Barker, Frances H. "Pricing of information products." *ASLIB Proceedings* 36 (July/August, 1984): 289–297. A review of the considerations and options in establishing the price of an online database, from the database producer's point of view.

Basch, Reva. "The seven deadly sins of full-text searching." *Database* 12 (August, 1989): 15–23. A humorous review of the problems inherent in searching full-text files through several different vendors. The bibliography provides a good list of other sources to consult.

Bellardo, Trudi and Judy Stephenson. "The use of online numeric databases in academic libraries: a report of a survey." *Journal of Academic Librarianship* 12 (July, 1986): 152–157. Fifty-five academic libraries, all members of the Association of Research Libraries, were surveyed. The study found that use of numeric databases is increasing, especially if the database is available through one of the major vendors such as DIALOG.

Buckel, William L. "Literature searching services—choosing the contract with the best discount plan." *Online* 6 (September, 1982): 59–64. Discusses the contract options and discounts available from DIALOG and shows how one library reduced its costs by performing "spreadsheet"-type analysis of the various options.

Burwell, Helen. *Directory of Fee-Based Information Services*. Houston: Burwell Enterprises, 1984–. An annual listing of information brokers, fee-based services, and freelancers arranged by state. Entries frequently include information about the systems available and any subject specialties.

Cavanagh, Joseph M. A. "Pricing CD-ROM products; possible winning strategies for producers, distributors and users." In *National Online Meeting Proceedings 1990*. 63–66. Medford, N.J.: Learned Information, 1990. The author recommends that ondisk database producers and vendors expand the market for their products and switch to a per-use pricing policy, which would lower the price for everyone.

Chen, Ching-chih and Peter Hernon, eds. *Numeric Databases*. Norwood, N.J.: Ablex, 1984. A collection of contributed articles providing background information on the types and use of numeric databases, and case studies from a few academic and research libraries.

Chen, Ching-chih. *Optical Discs in Libraries: Uses and Trends*. Medford, N.J.: Learned Information, 1990.

Directory of Online Databases. Santa Monica, Cal.: Cuadra Associates, 1979– . Lists databases, vendors, producers, gateway services, and practically everything else connected with the online industry. Introductory pages frequently include statistical information.

Elias, A. W. "Pricing strategies and impacts on producers, vendors and users." *Information Services and Use* 1, no. 6 (1982): 351–357. The author admits that there is no way to bring a logical structure to this topic as he goes on to detail how database producers and database vendors price their products and how consumers attempt to find economical ways to buy the products.

Eskola, Pirkko and Eero Sormunen. "Cost comparison of online searching in four hosts: DATA-STAR, DIALOG, ESA-IRS, and STN." *Online Review* 14 (October, 1990): 303–316. In a series of graphs and tables the authors present the results of their experiment comparing six databases available through the four hosts. The effect of baud rate is one of the factors examined.

Fenichel, Carol H. "Databases and database producers and vendors." In *Online Searching: Technique and Management*, edited by James J. Maloney. 26–34. Chicago: American Library Association, 1983. A succinct review of the online information industry structure with addresses and advice on selecting vendors. The date of the publication precludes inclusion of CD-ROM vendors.

Fischer, Margaret T. "Overview of pricing strategies in the electronic information industry." *Information Services and Use* 8, nos. 2/3/4 (1988): 73–78. While admitting that there is no industry norm, the author suggests ten rules for pricing, among which are flexible prices based on the market to which the data is sold, charging for information rather than access, and predictable pricing, which libraries would certainly appreciate.

Garman, Nancy and R. K. Summit. "DIALOG discusses pricing: an interview with DIALOG's president Roger K. Summit." *Online* 14 (January, 1990): 40–43. DIALOG's president would prefer that the database producers get their cut from citations printed or displayed while the vendor gets the connect time income. The obstacles to changing the pricing structure of online searching are discussed.

Garman, Nancy, M. F. Saksida, M. Johnson, and P. Walters. "Online pricing: an interview with Marino F. Saksida of ESA-IRS." *Online* 14 (January, 1990): 30–34. ESA-IRS has virtually eliminated connect time charges and now bases its prices on "use"—search terms input and citations printed or displayed. User reactions are included in this article.

Griffith, Cary. "Cost effective computer-assisted legal research, or when two are better than one." *Legal Reference Services Quarterly* 7 (Spring, 1987): 3–13. LEXIS and WESTLAW are compared as to their costs, searching methods, and content. The author found that WESTLAW is least expensive for ready-reference type searches while LEXIS is least expensive for longer research.

Griffith, Cary. "The cost effective use of LEXIS and WESTLAW." *Information Today* 6 (June, 1989): 32–33. The author continues an interesting and repeatable comparison of two vendors offering the same type of product, and proposes six rules for choosing between them that will lower costs.

Haar, John, Juleigh Clark, Sally Jacobs, and Frank Campbell. "Choosing CD-ROM products." *College and Research Libraries News* 51 (October, 1990): 839–841. The authors provide a checklist for evaluating the costs and features of an ondisk product before purchase.

Hewins, Elizabeth T. "Information need and use studies." *Annual Review of Information Science and Technology* 25 (1990): 145–172. This is the eleventh in a series of articles appearing in ARIST providing a literature review of information need and use studies. User modeling, interface design, and methodology are some of the topics covered.

Information Industry Factbook. Stamford, Conn.: Digital Information Group, 1990. "Trends in online services" and "Trends in CD-ROM publishing" are features of this issue of an annual publication providing financial data and analysis of the information industry.

Jack, Robert F. "The new ESA-IRS pricing scheme: a comparison with DIALOG." *Online* 14 (January, 1990): 35–39. Charge rates for 78 ESA-IRS databases are detailed. Thirty-six databases common to ESA-IRS and DIALOG are compared as to total costs per search, and so are different baud rates on each vendor.

Kostenbauder, Scott. "Pricing issues: user perspectives of database pricing, deep pockets and empty wallets." *Information Services and Use* 8, nos. 2/3/4 (1988): 85–90. The author suggests that more reasonable costs will increase the numbers of users of online databases, and increased users will lead to more reasonable costs. End-user markets should be expanded.

LaBorie, Tim and Michael Halperin. "The ERIC and LISA databases: how the sources of library science literature compare." *Database* 4 (September, 1981): 32–37. By comparing retrieval of known items from a manual search of the two print-counterpart indexes, the authors examine recall and precision ratios in the online versions. They were surprised to find recall ratios hovering in the 50 percent range.

Maloney, James J. "Contract options for lowering the cost of online searching." In *Dollars and Sense*, edited by Bernard F. Pasqualini. 22–28. Chicago: American Library Association, 1987. A *Consumer Report*-type checklist and explanation of the discounts and contract options offered by vendors, with an eye toward reducing libraries' costs for online services.

Marshall, Mary E. and Ginni Voedisch. "Compact discs: permanence and irretrievability may be synonymous in libraries as well as in Roget's." In *National Online Meeting Proceedings 1990.* 249–254. Medford, N.J.: Learned Information, 1990. "CD rot" and other hazards can cause data stored on compact disk to be irretrievable. The authors explain the hazards and offer guidelines for CD care and recommendations to CD vendors for more frequent updates.

Miller, David C. "Evaluating CD-ROMS: to buy or what to buy . . . ?" *Database* 10 (June, 1987): 36–42. Standards, hardware requirements, operating system, user interface, search software, postprocessing support, product support and documentation, price, and content are the evaluative criteria the author examines in detail. A "CD-ROM evaluation checklist" concludes the article.

National Online Meeting Proceedings. Medford, N.J.: Learned Information. This annual publication includes a "Highlights of the Online Database Industry" article by Martha Williams in each volume.

Nelson, M. L. "High database prices and their impact on information access: is there a solution?" *Journal of Academic Librarianship* 13 (July, 1987): 158–162. The author finds automated information retrieval to be the best way to deliver information to academic researchers, and, like most librarians, would like to deliver the service without charging the user but finds the cost impossible to absorb in the library budget. Some solutions are proposed.

Nichol, K. M. "Database proliferation: implications for libraries." *Special Libraries* 74 (April, 1983): 110–118. Search analysts are confused "not only by the proliferation of new databases but also by the availability of more systems." Standardization, vendor contracts, training, restrictions, and duplicate citations are some of the problems identified, primarily in business and social sciences databases.

Nicholls, Paul T. *CD-ROM Collection Builder's Toolkit: The Complete Handbook of Tools for Evaluating CD-ROMS*. Weston, Conn.: Pemberton Press, 1990. This very useful book provides background information on the CD-ROM industry, evaluation and selection criteria, and extensive bibliographies. The bulk of the book consists of CD-ROM product reviews based on the system used in *CD-ROM Professional*.

Nicholls, Paul T. "The cost of information: comparative economics of print, online and laserdisk full-text media." *Laserdisk Professional* 2 (July, 1989): 116–122. With tables showing actual costs and graphs, Nicholls shows that full-text reference tools on CD-ROM compare favorably in cost to printed tools. The online alternative is initially more economical than ondisk but soon goes through the roof as more searches are performed.

Nicholls, Paul T., Isaac Han, Karen Stafford and Katherine Whitridge. "A framework for evaluating CD-ROM retrieval software." *Laserdisk Professional* 3 (March, 1990): 41–46. A brief literature review and a discussion of the proliferation of CD-ROM retrieval software precede a thorough, two-page checklist of features one should evaluate when considering the search engines of CD products.

Porter, G. Margaret. "What does electronic access to bibliographic information cost?" *College and Research Libraries News* 52 (February, 1991): 90–92. Locally loaded database tapes, networked CD-ROMs, and gateway access costs are compared in this article. Actual costs are given when available, although the author warns that variable costs based on the size of the potential user population can make a big difference.

Quint, Barbara E. "Online pricing breakthroughs." *Wilson Library Bulletin* 65 (September, 1990a): 85–88. From her "Connect Time" column in WLB. Quint urges librarians to vote with their wallets and force online vendors to charge for a service rather than a product. Vendors should aim for a high volume product since the market is there to be exploited.

Quint, Barbara E. "The right tool." *Wilson Library Bulletin* 64 (February, 1990b): 71–72. Another of the author's "Connect Time" columns discusses accessing databases through EASYNET and other gateways when the library does not have a contract with a particular database's host vendor.

Rice, Barbara A. "Evaluation of online databases and their uses in collection evaluation." *Library Trends* 33 (Winter, 1985): 297–325. The article discusses evaluation of vendors and databases for possible inclusion in a search service, and also how database access can be used to evaluate the print collection. The article is valuable for the extensive literature review and bibliography.

Saffady, William. "Availability and cost of online search services." *Library Technology Reports* 21 (January/February, 1985): 1–111.

Saffady, William. "The Availability and cost of online search services." *Library Technology Reports* 24 (May/June, 1988): 291–502. Another article was published in the September, 1979 issue of LTR. The articles compare connect time charges from various vendors, price changes, etc. The competitive positions of various databases, costs of library-based online searching, fixed and variable costs, and cost differences associated with different search services are analyzed.

Tenopir, Carol. "Evaluation of database coverage: a comparison of two methodologies." *Online Review* 6 (October, 1982): 423–441. The author compares the "bibliography method"—using specialized bibliographies or review articles—and the subject profile method—developing a subject search strategy—to compare coverage of similar databases, in this example GEOREF and GeoArchive.

Tenopir, Carol. "Value-added searching." *Library Journal* 115 (April 1, 1990): 79–80. Value-added means something added by human intellectual effort to the basic bibliographic or textual information in a database, such as subject descriptors or codes, classification schemes, abstracts, or index terms added to a full-text database. Tenopir discusses the particular value each adds and notes the trade-offs in time and costs.

Trudell, Libby. "Pricing online information in the 90s: an online service viewpoint." *Information Services and Use* 8, nos. 2/3/4 (1988): 79–83. Another advocate of expanding the online market in order to reduce prices. The author strongly suggests that prices should be simple, predictable, and controllable.

Watkins, Steven G. "The IRL Life Sciences Collection and BIOSIS: a comparison of online access to the literature of biology." *Database* 4 (September, 1981): 39–59. In this comparison of databases, the author ignored precision and recall ratios in favor of comparing coverage overlap and currency.

Williams, Martha E. ed. *Information Market Indicators*. Monticello, Ill.: Information Market Indicators, Inc., 1984–. An annual survey that monitors revenues and usage/connect time of online vendors, database producers, and specific databases.

Williams, Martha E. "Usage and revenue data for the online database industry." *Online Review* 9 (June, 1985): 205–210. A description of how the data in the *Information Market Indicators* database is collected and analyzed. The author includes some usage and revenue figures for the early 1980s extracted from the data collected from IMI.

Williamson, Robin. "CD-ROM and online compared." *Libri* 40 (March, 1990): 19–27. The database being compared is CELEX, the official legal database of the European Community, available through different online hosts and on CD-ROM. Online offers up-to-date information but at the cost of high prices for online time and complex command language, whereas the ondisk version uses a user-friendly interface and, of course, has no ongoing costs. The author concludes that there is room for both versions.

Wolff-Terroine, M., L. Ghirardi and B. Marx. "Main trends in royalty policy of database producers." *Online Review* 7 (April, 1983): 101–110. As the result of a survey, the authors found interesting differences between European and North American database producers that affect the amount and type of royalties they charge. For example, far more databases are produced by government agencies in North America.

7

The Technology: Hardware and Software

Especially for the library planning to install multiple CD-ROM searching stations, it is quite likely that more funds will be spent on equipment than on access to databases. It is possible that the service manager will spend more time fiddling and fretting with machines and software than searching databases. When some glitch prevents access to a database, it is more likely to be a hardware or software problem than a problem with the database. For these reasons it is essential to give careful consideration to the technology decisions that must be made before any database can be searched.

GENERALITIES

Only a decade ago librarians searched remote databases on 300 baud terminals and were quite happy to do so. The search analyst probably typed slowly because correcting errors on a printing terminal was difficult and required a special combination of keystrokes to move the printhead aside so that the characters just typed could be seen. The result was a printout on brittle, grey thermal paper that the patron could cut and paste onto index cards and squint at as the gray characters faded into the grey background of the paper. Today, the ten year old technology seems as ancient and cumbersome as Guttenberg's printing press.

Today, the microcomputer is the preferred technology for a searching station because of the assistance it provides before, during, and after the searching process. A microcomputer can automate the telephone connection and log-on procedures; search analysts no longer need to memorize a long list of telephone numbers and passwords and logon protocols. Searches can be typed and proofed and edited offline before a connection is made and before the meter starts ticking. The results can be stored electronically—downloaded—and edited, sorted, or culled electronically with word processing or database management software, without the hassle of scissors and tape and index cards. Or, the search results can be forwarded electronically from one microcomputer to another. The statistics that justify the search service manager's request for next year's budget can be accumulated automatically and almost painlessly.

Microcomputers make end-user searching possible. Passwords to online services can be masked with automated log-on procedures that simplify the connection to a single keystroke; typing error detection and correction is simple and direct. Stand-alone CD-ROM databases must be mounted on microcomputers.

Microcomputers are flexible. The same machine can be used for mediated searches, for end-user searches, and for access to CD-ROM databases, the online catalog, and the campus network if the right peripherals and connections are available. It is the microcomputer's potential for use in many different applications that makes it the machine of choice as a searching station. Dumb terminals may be making a comeback in a CD-ROM local area network configuration, but even there one or two very fast, very powerful microcomputers are needed to make the network operate. Therefore, this chapter will concentrate on microcomputers and the software and peripherals needed for automated information retrieval (Kilpatrick, 1990).

The Campus Computing Environment

If the faculty and students on campus are committed to MacIntosh computers and the library installs IBM PC-type machines, the library has created a barrier to accessing data. It is not an insurmountable barrier, but certainly the library staff will hear many complaints from patrons about the extra steps involved in converting data from one operating system to another, and some patrons will find the barrier too troublesome to bother with. The data from databases should be easily transportable to the operating system environment that prevails in the community to be served, so it is essential to set aside one's personal preference in favor of the majority preference. For now, that majority preference is for the IBM and IBM-compatible family of microcomputers and for the MS-DOS operating system, although the MacIntosh is making gains and so is IBM's OS/2 operating system. The PC is designed to handle large volumes of text accurately and quickly, and this makes it the tool of choice in an academic community where large volumes of text, rather than graphic images, are the norm.

There will always be users who prefer a different type of machine that is incompatible with the library's choice, and it is possible to accommodate them if the library can assume the expense. A common problem at present is the choice of 5.25 inch or 3.5 inch diskettes, both in common use on PC-type machines. Microcomputers can be purchased with disk drives of both sizes, although the second disk drive costs extra. Translating data from the MS-DOS operating system to the MacIntosh operating system is more problematic and requires a software program and a second disk drive to perform the operation. Providing different sizes of disk drives and software on every searching station will be very expensive, so the library may consider making available one fully equipped machine that is set aside for the purpose of converting data to meet the users' needs. A survey of users to determine potential need is in order before this expensive step is taken.

Applications

Once the microcomputing family and operating system have been decided upon, the service manager needs to determine the uses to which the machines will be put. An online searching station to be used exclusively by trained search analysts does not need to be a particularly fancy, fast, or powerful machine. It must be equipped with a modem, and the simplest of communications software is all that is absolutely required. But if end-users are to perform online searches the communications software must be far more sophisticated and preferably stored on a hard disk with password protection, and a fast, reliable printer capable of enduring hard and continuous use is needed. A microcomputer used as a CD-ROM searching station requires a capacious hard disk, at least 640K RAM memory, special software, expansion slots for the CD drive controller card, and preferably a "fast chip" to speed up the searching process. A search service that has been in business and expanding over the years may have several different models and configurations of machines, ranging from an old dual-floppy used on occasion by the search analysts for practice and training to the latest 486-based machine with 2MB RAM and expansion slots for network boards and a couple of six-disk CD-ROM drives. If the fancy machine breaks down, the service manager cannot simply dust off the old dual-floppy machine as a replacement.

Ideally, every machine in the search service manager's inventory will be compatible with every other machine, and the parts and peripherals will be interchangeable, flexible enough to allow one component to replace another when the inevitable breakdowns occur. Ideally, someone on the staff will know how to take the CD-ROM control card out of a nonworking machine and install it in another, compatible machine so that a database is not out of service for weeks while the nonworking machine is being repaired. The ideal is difficult and expensive to achieve, but the service manager should strive to assemble hardware that has compatibility, flexibility, and connectivity in common.

Compatibility means making a conscious decision to favor one family of microcomputers over another and sticking with the decision. A few years ago this was an easy, almost automatic, decision, since the majority of necessary software packages such as DIALOGLINK and Sci-Mate were made exclusively for IBM-compatible machines, and CD-ROM applications were exclusively IBM-compatible. Recently, the MacIntosh has entered the library picture with the release of such software packages as MacSPIRS from SilverPlatter for CD-ROM applications. The NeXT microcomputer is a very attractive machine rapidly gaining adherents among the "scholars' workstation" users. Certainly the local community of users should be surveyed to determine what is the dominant choice, but a library will not be making a mistake by favoring the IBM-compatible family of microcomputers, since it is currently thoroughly entrenched in business and academic computing. It is the data retrieved via the microcomputers that is of interest to the library's clientele, and it appears likely that software solutions will be found to make data compatible and transferable among operating systems and families of microcomputers. The service manager must be more concerned with hardware compatibility among the search service machines so that parts and peripherals such as printers, modems, monitors, CPUs, and CD-ROM drives are interchangeable and can be switched from one workstation to another to keep the critical components of the search service operating. Downtime is minimized when the hardware is compatible and interchangeable. It is possible to keep spare components on hand, which the service manager can be sure will work where they are needed when a part breaks down.

Flexibility is another facet of compatibility that focuses on the CPU—the central processing unit of the microcomputer. A flexible machine can be plugged in to any compatible peripheral, and this is largely a matter of the number of expansion slots available in the CPU. For example, here is a list of peripherals commonly found on a search service microcomputer.

— A modem, necessary for online connections;
— A printer, probably a dot matrix printer for providing hard copies of citations;
— Another printer, this time a laser printer for printing graphics or for printing full-text documents stored as graphic images rather than as digitized text;
— A mouse, necessary for using increasingly popular graphic user-interface software packages;
— CD-ROM drive, requiring a controller card installed in an expansion slot in the CPU;
— Extra disk drives to allow for 5.25 and 3.5 inch disks;
— A network card allowing a CD-ROM workstation to operate on a LAN;
— Another network card, this one allowing the computer to interface with the campus E-mail network;
— Fax boards, memory upgrades, special graphics cards, and math coprocessors are other possibilities.

A microcomputer equipped with all of the above would be a very fancy and expensive machine, but it is certainly within the realm of possibility. The point is, one can never have too many expansion slots on a microcomputer, but unfortunately the industry standard is two-and-a-half expansion slots for most machines. At a minimum, a search service machine should come equipped with one or two serial ports for a modem and possibly a serial printer or a mouse, and one or two parallel ports for printers, making a minimum total of three ports already installed on the machine. If the machine already has a capacious hard disk, two sizes of floppy disk drives and a VGA color graphics card installed, and 2MB RAM, the standard two-and-a-half expansion slots will be just enough to add a CD-ROM drive and network cards.

Connectivity is the third major concern. Connectivity is the ability of one logical device—a microcomputer or terminal—to transfer data or commands to another logical device. It is the major factor in transforming a library into a service rather than a building (Brandt, 1991a and 1991b; Mangrum, 1990; Rosenberg, 1985). A local area network connecting CD-ROM searching stations is one form of connectivity. A LAN allows a user to search any database mounted on the LAN from a single workstation rather than physically moving from one station to another. It can also allow researchers in their offices and homes to use the campus network to search databases mounted in the library. A workstation with enough connections can search the online catalog and any locally mounted databases, can send E-mail messages to the interlibrary loan office or full-text documents from the interlibrary loan office to the terminals of individual researchers, and can even transmit documents between interlibrary loan offices in libraries across the country. Connectivity is currently a problem in the process of being solved. Disparate equipment in the researchers' offices and in the library must be able to communicate with each other through different networking protocols and using different communications software. There is no standard at present, and this makes the choice of network configurations and networking hardware difficult. However, library clientele increasingly demand remote access to computerized databases in the library, and librarians recognize that it is a reasonable demand. Computers can communicate with each other, and it is unreasonable to expect that users will be satisfied to come into the library building to use automated information resources for too much longer.

Compatibility, flexibility, and connectivity are the qualities to consider when selecting search service hardware. Lifespan is another consideration. Ten year old dual floppy PCs are still around and still operating, perhaps as word processing machines in the office or even as "dumb terminals" for online searching, but anyone who has used a fast and powerful modern machine realizes that the old ones do not work well. The machine to buy is the one that will be capable of performing the tasks expected of it at least five years from now, and this requires some gazing into a crystal ball. Inevitably, the crystal ball tells us to buy the fastest, most powerful machines the budget will allow (Grosch, 1989 and 1991; Rumsey, 1990).

Speed is a definite plus when searching CD-ROM databases. A 386 or faster machine accesses and displays data from CD-ROM databases noticeably faster than any of its predecessors. Furthermore, the 386 machine does a better job of memory management, an important feature in CD-ROM applications mounted on a LAN where the operating system software, the search engine, and the network software all require a great deal of RAM memory. Most CD-ROM software requires a minimum of 640K RAM, and if more than one CD drive is mounted on the machine or if the machine is networked, more RAM is required, leading inevitably to the conclusion that megabytes of RAM will be needed on many machines. A hard disk is a minimum requirement for most CD-ROM databases. It allows multiple software packages to be loaded on one machine and moreover provides security for the software; therefore hard disks are necessary.

New software developments employ more graphics than in the past, such as GUI—graphic user interfaces using icons and images as memory-jogging devices to take the place of commands that must be memorized. More graphics will require VGA (Video Graphics Array) monitors. Another future development quite useful in database searching is multitasking, allowing a set of citations to be printed or downloaded while the user continues searching, or allowing the user to edit retrieved citations in a window while the system is searching. This requires RAM memory and sophisticated software. Connectivity is another future development that will require fast, powerful, and flexible machines.

It is not quite time to throw out the old dual-floppy PCs or PC/XTs. They can be used as terminals in a CD-ROM local area network if a powerful 386 machine is used as a file server and CD drive server. Old hard disk machines can be used for online searching where speed is controlled largely by the telecommunications network, the modem, or the host mainframe. Adding more memory to an older hard disk machine may make it suitable for a CD-ROM workstation, although it will be slow. However, issues of speed, graphics, connectivity, and the flexibility to support multiple peripherals or other applications will eventually make the older machines suitable for little more than dumb terminal duties wherein they merely receive and display data from a more powerful host.

Management and Maintenance

As more machines are added to the search service inventory, more of the manager's time will be consumed by maintaining the machines in working order (King, 1989). A machine that does not work, no matter what the reason, will be the manager's responsibility, and he or she must be able to solve the problem one way or another. This means that the manager must be able to analyze a problem and decide how it can be solved; it does not mean that the manager must become a microcomputer whiz able to fix the problem with a screwdriver and a piece of tape. A computer technician on the staff is a great asset and can keep downtime to a minimum by performing simple repairs or program "fixes" in-house rather than sending the machine to the repair shop. The following minimal skills are absolutely necessary:

— An understanding of and ability to use DOS (or other operating system) commands;
— Ability to run a diagnostic utility;
— Ability to cable the basic components of a workstation together, such as the monitor, modem, printer, CD drive, etc.;
— Ability to install a board or card in an expansion slot;
— Ability to perform simple maintenance such as vacuuming and cleaning of the basic components.

An inventory of hardware and software is essential. A file should be created for each item that includes a copy of the purchase order and the invoice or shipping bill so that warranty dates can be confirmed if necessary. The file should also include a description of the item's use, location, and attachments; for example, a microcomputer used as an online searching station located at the reference desk and attached to printer #10 and modem #2. If an annual inventory of equipment is required by the organization, such a file will be invaluable for tracking down all the pieces, especially if components have been moved around from workstation to workstation as replacements for parts under repair. The file should include repair records and invoices as well. The inventory can be maintained as a database management system program, although a physical file for purchase orders and invoices will need to be kept. Software should be inventoried as well, to keep track of the machines it has been installed upon and to keep track of the versions in use. Outdated software, if it is kept, should be clearly labeled and stored separate from the active versions of software currently used. It is a good idea to keep a copy of outdated software on hand in case a problem develops with the current version, although it is not always possible to substitute the older version.

Only the search service manager should perform or authorize any changes to machine configurations, such as switching or removing components, or to software installations. This is to insure that the inventories and other records are kept up to date, and to insure that all the functions the search service is expected to perform can be performed on the equipment on hand. Probably the service manager should be rather hard-nosed about this; someone who casually borrows a modem or tries out a new software package on a search service workstation can ruin a day's business.

Simple maintenance procedures performed on a routine basis will stop many problems before they start. Microcomputers and their components are rather picky about their environments. An adequate supply of electrical outlets and surge protection should be in place before any microcomputer is installed. If an area must be rewired to allow multiple workstations, the service manager should be sure that the electricians are not merely running extensions off the existing wiring without allowing for sufficient amperage. The technical specifications for the various pieces of hardware state the power consumption for each unit, and this should be added up and possibly multiplied by a small "fudge factor" to provide a safe margin for the equipment. Especially in carpeted areas, static may be a problem and can be controlled by aerosols sold at computer supply stores, or by a bottle of fabric softener in a pinch. If the screen crackles when it is touched, static is building up and should be controlled.

The purchase of a vacuum cleaner especially designed for cleaning computer components is a good investment. Workstations for public use should be vacuumed regularly to keep dust and lint from building up underneath and around the CPU and in the keyboard. Printers that operate almost continuously quickly build up an accumulation of paper dust that can clog up tractor feeds and platens. When vacuuming the machines, it is a good idea to keep an eye out for insects. Ants have been known to build nests inside microcomputers.

The hard disks should be "cleaned" at regular intervals, as well. End-users especially are guilty of misdirecting a download to the hard disk rather than to a floppy disk, and more often than not they do not realize they have done so until they have left the library and try to work with the data in their offices or homes. Search analysts sometimes leave search strategies or downloaded searches on the hard disk, and on occasion something entirely unexpected and unexplained appears on the hard disk, especially on machines used by the public. These files should be deleted, and the service manager may want to run a hard disk utility program to load more efficiently the programs and data that must remain on the machine. Virus detection is another hygienic practice that should be observed on machines used by the public. The manager may want to institute a practice of requiring that any disk brought by the public to be used on library machines be inspected by virus detecting and cleaning software packages.

Keeping up to date with the latest developments in hardware and software is the responsibility of the search service manager, and it can be a time-consuming job. It is an essential job in order to be sure that one is not buying equipment or software that cannot perform the tasks expected of it and to talk intelligently with a public that is increasingly computer literate and increasingly demanding of automated services in the library. Scanning the publications listed below will keep the service manager at least as literate as the public:

Advanced Technology Libraries. White Plains, N.Y.: Knowledge Industry Publications. A monthly newsletter format publication. Watch for announcements of forthcoming databases, software updates, and new releases.

CD-ROM Professional. Weston, Conn.: Pemberton Press. Formerly titled *Laserdisk Professional*, this bimonthly publication is valuable for hardware and software reviews and articles describing first-hand solutions to installation and operation problems of CD-ROM technology.

Computers in Libraries. Westport, Conn.: Meckler Corp. Published eleven times a year. Automated information retrieval is not the main thrust of this publication but it is valuable for keeping up with hardware developments. Formerly titled *Small Computers in Libraries*.

Datapro Directory of Microcomputer Hardware. Delran, N.J.: Datapro Research Corp. A looseleaf publication with monthly updates providing descriptions, specifications, and price ranges for microcomputers and peripherals. This is invaluable when one is trying to identify just the right type of printer or other equipment. Data arranged in tables allows easy comparison of products. Hardware mentioned in this chapter can be found in this and other, similar directories.

Datapro Directory of Microcomputer Software. Delran, N.J.: Datapro Research Corp. Another looseleaf publication with a format similar to the above.

The Electronic Library. Medford, N.J.: Learned Information. Subtitled "The International Journal for Minicomputer, Microcomputer, and Software Applications in Libraries." Published six times a year. Look for the "Hardware Corner" column for announcements and reviews of new products, including LAN adapter boards and file servers for computer networks in recent issues.

Information Retrieval and Library Automation. Mt. Airy, Md.: Lomond Systems. A monthly newsletter format reporting major issues discussed at recent meetings and seminars, new or updated databases and hardware, optical disk technology news, etc.

Library Software Review. Westport, Conn.: Meckler Corp. A bimonthly publication. Recent issues have included articles and reviews of LAN software and other software items of interest to a search service manager.

Online. Weston, Conn.: Online, Inc. Published six times a year. A "must read" for search service managers and search analysts. Online searching, end-user searching, and ondisk searching issues are covered.

PC Magazine. New York: PC Communications Corp. For IBM and compatibles users. Just browsing the advertisements is an education. As a bonus, subscribers receive freeware utility programs that can be quite useful and are usually well done, such as opening menus and password protection programs mentioned in this chapter.

ONLINE SEARCHING: HARDWARE AND SOFTWARE

An online searching microcomputer can be the simplest of dual-floppy PCs with a serial port for the modem and another port for the printer. DOS or another operating system and communications software complete the picture. Nothing else is needed to permit connection to a host system, searching, and printing or downloading. The communications software can be a no-frills freeware package downloaded from a bulletin board. This will get the job done, but a few enhancements will make the job much easier.

A hard disk machine saves the bother of carrying around the communications software on a floppy disk, and for an end-user searching station it is essential. Depending on the communications package used, it is possible to store the telephone numbers, passwords, and sign-on protocols on the communications software floppy disk so that connections to the host mainframes are accomplished by a single keystroke. This makes the connection easy enough for end-users but it also makes the passwords extremely vulnerable to theft; all one has to do is remove the floppy disk from the drive. A hard disk makes it more difficult to find the passwords and remove them. Extra RAM memory on the microcomputer makes it possible to manage additional software packages and to store long searches. A fast printer capable of printing 120 characters per second if communications are performed at 1200 baud, or 240 cps for 2400 baud communications, will make a hard copy of the search at the same rate as information scrolling on the screen; therefore one does not have to wait for the printer to catch up and thus spend online connect time and money doing nothing but watch the printer work: If the online station is for pubic use, it is worthwhile to spend extra money for a reliable and sturdy printer able to endure hard and continuous operation. A capacious buffer on the printer can take the place of speed; the printer's buffer is a memory device rather like the RAM of the microcomputer that stores data until the printer can catch up. When considering printers for purchase, one should look at the draft mode cps—characters per second—and a buffer of at least 2K. Another hardware enhancement to consider is a pair of floppy disk drives, one for 5.25 inch diskettes and one for 3.5 inch diskettes.

Once the online searching station is equipped with a hard drive, the search manager can consider software enhancements. A good communications software package can transform the PC from a dumb terminal into a machine that assists and promotes the searching process (Clancy et al., 1990; Koga, 1989). Good communications software should have programmable macros that reduce a long string of commands to a single keystroke. For example, a typical logon sequence involves dialing the network, identifying the host system to be accessed, and sending at least one password, at a minimum. If this sequence can be programmed on the communications software, scores of keystrokes are reduced to one, and the search analyst's memory is not clogged with multiple telephone numbers, logon protocols, and passwords for several different hosts. The software should allow communications parameters such as parity, duplex, and baud rate to be configured separately for each host and stored in memory so that they do not have to be reset when a different host is accessed.

The way in which the communications software captures data is an important point to consider. One should be able to print or download as the search is proceeding rather than after the connection to the host mainframe is broken. Characters should display on the screen as soon as they are typed at the keyboard; for some hosts and local networks, this may require various "terminal emulation" settings. All input and output should be loaded to RAM memory; this allows the redisplay of text after it has scrolled off the screen by using the cursor control keys or the "PgUp, PgDn" keys. One must be sure that the microcomputer is equipped with sufficient RAM to handle long searches. Printing and downloading from text stored in RAM should be simple and controlled by function keys.

It should be possible to upload stored search strategies so that searches can be typed, proofed, and edited before the online connection is made. This is accomplished by text editor software, frequently included as a part of the communications software, but sometimes it is necessary to use the text editor program of the operating system software. Front-end interfaces that translate the commands of one search engine into the commands of another are features of some software packages such as Pro-Search and Sci-Mate. Other features to look for include the capture of accounting or statistical data, scripting languages allowing simple programming, a "break key" function to terminate processing, DOS utilities resident in the background, and real-time status lines that show elapsed time of the connection or RAM memory consumed.

It is important to select carefully communications software intended for end-users (Bell, 1989 and 1990). In fact, end-users should not be bothered with the communications software at all; it should be invisible to them. Keying through a series of pop-up menus in order to find the right keystroke to turn on the printer is especially irritating and time-consuming for end-users. Single keystroke commands for connections, printing functions, and downloading functions are essential. The service manager may want to have different communications packages loaded on the hard disk for search analysts and for end-users, but one should not go overboard and consume hard disk storage with a dozen or so communications packages.

The hard disk can store other software packages to assist the searching and postprocessing functions. An opening menu should allow the user to select the software options available. A machine open to the public should have a password program to prevent access to the passwords stored on the hard disk, and to prevent unauthorized use of the communications software to access online services. DOS utilities to allow formatting of disks and the deleting of files such as misdirected downloads are necessary. The PC may also have a text editor for typing search strategies to be uploaded (Nielsen, 1990), and a word processing package for the editing of downloads. Database management software may be needed for the creation of local databases from downloaded data, or for collecting statistics. All of these software options can easily be loaded on a 10MB hard disk, therefore an older XT/AT-type machine equipped with 640K RAM will make a perfectly adequate online searching station.

CD-ROM HARDWARE AND SOFTWARE

Although there are still some ondisk databases that can be operated from an old, slow, dual-floppy machine, the larger bibliographic databases in common use in libraries require a 10MB hard disk and 640K RAM at a minimum for a stand-alone searching station (Nickerson, 1991; Roscoe, 1990a and 1990b). The microcomputer must have a printer port and an open expansion slot for the installation of the CD drive control card; a printer and the CD drive complete the hardware requirements. The software required includes the search engine software supplied with the database, DOS, and usually a special software package called MSCDEX—the MicroSoft CD Extensions. MSCDEX is basically a "device driver," a program that instructs the microcomputer how to interact with the CD-ROM drive and also extends DOS file sizes to accommodate the search engine software. Some CD-ROM software comes with a device driver program loaded, and the installation manual instructs the purchaser to use DOS commands to change file size and buffer configurations, but most now require the separate MSCDEX software. MSCDEX also allows the loading of different search engines on the same microcomputer and easy switching among multiple CD-ROM drives installed on the same microcomputer. It is essential for a local area network installation ("MicroSoft CD-ROM extensions," 1990).

The first enhancement to the basic CD-ROM configuration should be an upgrade to a 386 or faster machine, which searches noticeably faster than older models. Some CD-ROM databases, such as those from Wilson and DIALOG, allow online access to the host for easy updating of searches, and thus require a modem to be installed on the machine. Large databases on multiple disks can be installed on multiple CD-ROM drives either by daisy-chaining the drives to each other or by purchasing drive units containing multiple CD drives. Multiple drives have the advantage of preserving the compact disks, which can be scratched and damaged if they must be switched in and out of a single CD drive. Two nice but not necessary enhancements include an internal clock that prints the current date on any output, and custom key caps labeled with the appropriate command such as PRINT, SHOW, SEARCH, and so forth and snapped on to the function keys.

Software enhancements should include an opening menu that allows a user to select easily the correct database or portion of databases loaded on multiple drives and any other software option installed on the machine. Other software can include DOS utilities allowing end-users to format diskettes or check for adequate memory on a floppy to be sure it is capable of accepting a download, and virus detecting and cleaning software, which is practically essential on any public access microcomputer. Screen saver software will preserve the life of the monitor by preventing images from burning in. The best screen saver programs keep a moving image on the screen rather than simply blanking the screen completely; a blank screen can lead end-users to believe that the machine is turned off, and they may either leave without asking for assistance or they may fiddle with the ON/OFF switch. The opening menu program should also provide password protection for programs loaded on the hard disk to prevent casual hackers from fiddling with search engine software or loading unwanted programs such as a home-grown virus.

The ultimate enhancement to a CD-ROM installation is a LAN—a local area network linking the individual searching stations such that any station can access any database loaded on the LAN. A CD-ROM LAN consists of multiple microcomputer workstations (which do not have to be powerful or even hard disk machines), a very powerful microcomputer with extended memory that is the file server or control device operating the LAN, a CD-ROM server that links the CD drives, the cables that link the components together via network boards installed in the microcomputer expansion slots, and the networking software packages that make the components work together. There may also be a dial-in module that allows remote users to access the databases mounted on the LAN.

A LAN maximizes use of the ondisk databases. A very popular database can be accessed by multiple users at the same time rather than requiring users to wait in line for a stand-alone searching station. It is possible to mount more databases on fewer workstations, thus saving the high cost of separate workstations for each database in a stand-alone configuration. The disks are permanently mounted in the CD drives and thus are protected from scratches and theft. Searching stations located at remote sites in the library can be cabled into the LAN, thus allowing librarians at service desks to use the databases without bumping an end-user. The advantages of a LAN are many. (For books and articles on LANs, see Butcher (1990), Carey and Massey-Burzio (1989), Flanders (1990), Florence (1989), Kriz et al. (1991), Leggott (1989), and Wright (1990).

The problems are many as well. Networks are tricky to install and thus far have required continual fiddling to keep them up and running. Estimates of staff time required for LAN maintenance vary from a minimum of ten hours per week to a full-time position, and the staff member who fills the position must be a microcomputer enthusiast who is happiest when solving hardware and software problems. A passing acquaintance with DOS commands and an ability to install boards is definitely not enough to keep a LAN running, let alone install one. Some vendors, such as SilverPlatter and Meridian Data offer turnkey installations in which a company engineer visits the site to install the network, and they offer continuing technical support via telephone. Other problems include incompatible databases and search engines—not all databases will work together on the same network—and site licensing fees. Most of the major database publishers charge a fee for the privilege of networking their databases, and the fee usually doubles the purchase price of the single CD-ROM disk. Some vendors base the site licensing fee on the number of potential users, easily counted if access is limited to the workstations physically cabled to the network, but if remote access through dial-up or through campus networks is allowed, the fees are prohibitive. Libraries may consider cost-sharing plans with campus users in which the library supports the equipment and network maintenance costs, and those departments on campus desiring remote access to databases pay the site licensing fees.

EXTRAS

A library with a busy and active automated information retrieval service soon discovers needs for equipment beyond the minimums required to operate an online or CD-ROM searching station. Enhancements such as bigger and faster microcomputers, daisy-chained CD drives, or more printers help up to a certain point, but then the operation bogs down for want of a better, different solution. Something extra is required.

Search output is the end product desired by users of automated information retrieval, and it is output that slows the operation down. An automated database can tell the user that it has found fifteen citations meeting the user's requirements in a matter of seconds, but printing the fifteen citations can take several minutes, during which time the microcomputer is frozen and cannot be used for further searching. An end-user twiddles his thumbs and watches the CD-ROM workstation printer do its thing while other users grind their teeth in frustration as they wait for a chance to use the same database. The computer can send the output data to the printer much faster than the printer can print it, so a possible solution is to do away with individual printers at each workstation and direct the output elsewhere. The search service may require users to download data to a floppy disk that is then transported to a separate stand-alone workstation devoted to printing, or a buffer or spoolers can accept output. The waiting line is redirected to an output device and away from the database. A buffer is an external storage device, a "black box" that accepts data from the computer and stores it in memory until a printer is ready to accept it. Spoolers are software solutions, programs that direct output into the computer's RAM or to a disk file where it is stored and directed to the printer at a rate the printer can accept. Being software, spoolers may not be compatible with the search engine software, and they eat RAM that the search engine software needs. A buffer is an extra piece of equipment that costs money, but there are usually no compatibility problems (Phillips, 1989).

Teaching end-users how, when, and why to search automated databases is a continuing task. One-on-one instruction at the point of use is an effective way of teaching end-users, but it is not efficient. Teaching a class or other group requires either multiple workstations for the students or special equipment to enlarge the image from a single workstation so that all in the class can see. If instruction is to be taken to the students' classrooms, large screen projection equipment is the best answer. CD-ROM databases are portable and can be taken to a classroom without worrying about the availability of a suitable telephone line, which is needed for online demonstrations, but both can be accomplished with the appropriate equipment. A portable hard disk computer with extended memory, an internal modem, and an internal CD drive is needed. The hard disk provides the most efficient way to store communications software and search engine software for various CD-ROM products; without the hard disk the various software packages must be stored on numerous floppies, which add to the transport problems and are likely to be misplaced. The most portable projection system is a projection pad such as a Kodak Datashow or Telex Magnabyte. These are LCD (liquid crystal display) devices that cable into a graphics card installed in the microcomputer; the pad is placed on an overhead projector that projects the enlarged image onto a screen. Only the overhead projector is inexpensive, and probably it is already available wherever an automated database is likely to be displayed. The cost of the specially equipped portable microcomputer and the projection pad hovers around $4,000, but this cost should be weighed against the hours and hours of staff time spent on individualized point of use instruction (Jaros and Clark, 1989).

A recently developed "extra" promises considerable utility for the future. This is the fax board, a telefacsimile device that fits into a microcomputer's expansion slot. It allows digitized data to be transmitted from the microcomputer over telephone lines to any fax machine, or a fax machine can send a digitized image to the microcomputer. The requirements are a 20MB hard disk machine with at least 2MB RAM, an expansion slot for the board, and an extra serial port, since the fax board operates as a specialized modem. The extended memory and the memory handling capabilities of a 386 or faster machine allow the fax board to send or receive data "in background," without interrupting work in progress on the microcomputer. The fax board solves the problem of delivering a good, clean copy of search output to a remote user. The search analyst performs a search as usual, downloads the output, and transmits it via fax board to a remote user's fax machine. Special software and hardware for OCR (optical character recognition) can transform the microcomputer into a standard fax machine capable of scanning and transmitting any printed document as well (Walton, 1990; Welsch, 1989; Wilson, 1989).

Finally, with eyes firmly focused on the future, the truly progressive and well-endowed search service may want to consider CDC—cellular data communications (Bell, 1991). By combining a laptop computer, an internal cellular modem, and a hand-held cellular telephone, one can take online searching anywhere, into the classroom or a faculty office, or even take it home for those search analysts truly dedicated to automated information retrieval. The future looks very interesting.

REFERENCES

Bell, Steven J. "Customizing communications software for end-users." *Online* 13 (March, 1989): 62–66.

Bell, Steven J. "Communications software for end-users." *Online* 14 (November, 1990): 40–43. The author emphasizes that novice end-users can be stumped by an unfriendly communications package as well as an unfriendly search engine. He recommends communications software that is command-driven and programmable to make it friendly for end-users, and in the 1989 article provides how-to advice for customizing commercially available software packages.

Bell, Steven J. "Online without the line: cellular technology for searching on the go." *Online* 15 (September, 1991): 15–25. A thorough description of CDC (cellular data communications) using laptop micros and cellular communications links. The author suggests applications for online searching such as classroom instruction, searching from a client's office, and as a backup when the usual telephone links are down. A buyer's guide is included.

Bjorner, Susan N. "Controlling delivery charges." *Online* 14 (January, 1990): 79–82. The author attempts to determine the most cost-effective method of receiving search output within twenty-four hours using various downloading options.

Brandt, D. Scott. "Making library files accessible in a campus network environment." *Academic and Library Computing* 8 (May, 1991a): 8–10.

Brandt, D. Scott. "The workstation in the academic research library setting." *Academic and Library Computing* 8 (April, 1991b): 8–11. From the author's "Library in Academic Computing" column. A good review of the problems encountered in achieving "connectivity"—or in other words, "Can my computer talk to your computer?" One problem emphasized is making the campus community aware of library databases available through the campus network and how to use them correctly.

Butcher, Karyle S. "The rewards and trials of networking." *Database* 14 (August, 1990): 103–105. This brief article presents an excellent summary of the decision-making process and the problems encountered in setting up a CD-ROM LAN using Meridian Data CD NET equipment. "Networking is costly and time consuming," the author warns, and site licensing fees make the blood boil, but ultimately a LAN is worth the effort.

Carey, Joan and Virginia Massey-Burzio. "Installing a local area compact disk network." *College and Research Libraries News* 50 (December, 1989): 988–992. Describes the installation of SilverPlatter's MultiPlatter CD-ROM LAN. Four different types of microcomputers and five different CD search engines were made to work together in this example, after the usual initial difficulties involving "frozen" workstations and heartbreaking licensing fees.

Clancy, Steve, Brian Nielsen, James Koga, Steven J. Bell, and Stephen F. Palincsar. "Communications software for online searching on a PC." *Online* 14 (November, 1990): 36–46. The authors provide a list of selection criteria to be considered before purchasing communications software, and review the major commercially available software packages. The "Suggested Readings" section lists reviews and how-to articles for different packages.

"Five experts' top choices: communications software for online searching." *Online* 14 (November, 1990): 44–46. Professionals involved in online searching list their favorite communications software packages and their advantages. The article is a good introduction to the options available.

Flanders, Bruce L. "Spinning the hits: CD-ROM networks in libraries." *American Libraries* 21 (December, 1990): 1032–1033. In two pages the author describes a typical CD-ROM LAN configuration and the trials and tribulations to expect if one is considering a LAN installation. Database incompatibility and site licensing fees can be the greatest obstacles to overcome.

Florence, Donne. *Local Area Networks: Developing Your System for Business*. New York: J. Wiley & Sons, 1989. Although directed at business managers rather than library managers, this small book provides an excellent introduction to LAN uses, environments, and equipment, and provides the definitions (with pictures) and background allowing a librarian to communicate intelligently with the engineers installing a local area network.

Grosch, Audrey N. "Microcomputer decisions for the 1990's." *Online* 13 (July, 1989): 15–26. The author feels certain that IBM PC-type microcomputers will remain the system of choice in academic libraries, and gives sound advice for upgrading older machines and purchasing new ones. Definitions help the novice keep it all straight.

Grosch, Audrey N. "Micros for the 1990's: an update." *Online* 15 (September, 1991): 63–67. The author revises her earlier recommendations about upgrading dual-floppy 8088-based machines and instead advises using them as access hosts until they fall apart. New software developments require speedy machines, big memories, and good graphics.

Intner, Sheila S. and Jane Anne Hannigan, eds. *The Library Microcomputer Environment: Management Issues*. Phoenix: Oryx Press, 1988. A collection of readings, primarily about software in libraries both for the public to use and for library applications. Also included are articles on LANs, CD-ROM, training for online, etc.

Jaros, Joe and Katharine E. Clark. "Taking it on the road: demonstrating CD-ROM databases using large screen projectors." *Laserdisk Professional* 2 (November, 1989): 35–42. Portable Compaq computers and large-screen projection pads allow Texas A&M librarians to take CD-ROM technology to the classroom where demonstrations and instruction can be given to large groups. The equipment is expensive, but surely not as expensive as hours and hours of individual instruction.

Kilpatrick, Thomas L. *Microcomputers and Libraries: A Bibliographic Sourcebook, 1986–1989*. Metuchen, N.J.: Scarecrow Press, 1990. A very large book containing citations to library microcomputing literature arranged in broad subject divisions, with an author and proper name index. If nothing else, the 1,000+ pages of this book illustrate the explosion of interest and concern about microcomputers in libraries.

King, Alan. "The seven deadly sins of online microcomputing." *Online* 13 (July, 1989): 40–44. Readers who have spent a few years working with PCs will immediately think of additions to this list, which provides a good introduction to the management and maintenance of microcomputers.

Koga, James S. "DIALOGLINK: shortcuts and quick tips." *Online* 13 (January, 1989): 32–39. For new users of DIALOGLINK, the logon macros for other online services at the conclusion of this article will be especially useful. The article also provides a sound introduction to using and programming DIALOGLINK.

Kriz, Harry M., Nikhil Jain and E. Alan Armstrong. "An environmental approach to CD-ROM networking using off-the-shelf components." *CD-ROM Professional* 4 (July, 1991): 24–31. LANtastic, an inexpensive alternative to turnkey systems, was installed at Virginia Tech Libraries, and older PCs and PC/XT-type machines were used as workstations. Microcomputer enthusiasts on the library staff got the LAN up and running with help via telephone from vendors and manufacturers.

Learn, Larry L. "Peeking inside the black box: a look at the private life of your modem." *Library Hi Tech News* 82 (June, 1991): 10–18. Quite detailed and technical, this article explains (possibly in more detail than most librarians will want) what modems do and how. The author does a remarkable job of making understandable statements such as "more than one bit will have to be carried by each baud."

Leggott, Mark. "CD-ROM and LAN: some practical considerations." *CD-ROM Enduser* 1 (July, 1989): 26–28. Price is the number one practical consideration, especially the cost of licensing fees, which the author predicts and prays will become less of an issue as producers and vendors realize the value of introducing their products to more users.

Machovec, George S. *Telecommunications and Networking Glossary.* Chicago: American Library Association, 1990. A brief handbook providing nontechnical definitions of telecommunications terms, networking terms, acronyms, etc. A librarian delving into the literature of networking for the first time will want to have this small book close by.

Mangrum, Rikki. "Networking information products on campus: local area networks and campus broadband." In *ASIS '90: Proceedings of the 53rd ASIS Annual Meeting.* 279–283. Medford, N.J.: Learned Information. 1990. Describes the equipment used to allow access to MRDF (machine-readable data file) databases mounted on a campus mainframe and to several CD-ROM databases mounted on a Meridian Data CD-NET installation in the library. The article makes some fascinating points on the future of librarians in a "paperless, electronic library" environment.

"MicroSoft CD-ROM extensions software explained." *OCLC Micro* 6 (April, 1990): 4. For the most succinct and nontechnical article explaining why the extensions are necessary and what they do, this brief article is the one to read.

Nickerson, Gord. "The CD-ROM workstation: what it is and what to look for." *CD-ROM Professional* 4 (May, 1991: 40–41. the author calls this two-page article a "Hardware Beginner's Guide." It is a sound introduction to the hardware components required for CD-ROM applications.

Nielsen, Brian. "Forget the taxi meter and ride in style." *Online* 14 (January, 1990): 86–89. This column offers practical, how-to advice on using a text editor to type out a search strategy before going online and uploading it to the communications software, thus saving online time and the hassles caused by the inevitable typo.

Phillips, Brian. "Printing without waiting: buffers and spoolers." *Online* 13 (March, 1989): 72–74. The author discusses the advantages and disadvantages of buffers and spoolers, two methods of operating a printer without tying up the microcomputer.

Roscoe, Tom. "Connecting this to that." *CD-ROM Enduser* 2 (March, 1990a): 24–29.

Roscoe, Tom. "More on 'connecting this to that.'" *CD-ROM Enduser* 2 (May, 1990b): 38–40. The technical side of connecting CD-ROM drives to microcomputers and making them work, for nontechnicians. These two articles provide a step-by-step plan of what, how, and why.

Rosenberg, Victor. "The scholar's workstation." *College and Research Libraries News* 46 (November, 1985): 546–549. An early description of a powerful, capacious microcomputer with integrated word processing and bibliographic database management software, and connections via networks, modems, and attached CD-ROM drives to multiple databases.

Rumsey, Eric. "The power of the new microcomputers: challenge and opportunity." *College and Research Libraries* 51 (March, 1990): 95–99. CD-ROM with its capacity to store vast volumes of text, the 386 microcomputer with its capacity to quickly manipulate vast amounts of data, and the graphic user interface that makes storing and manipulating easy for the average nonprogrammer, have the potential to make individuals independent of the library—their own information managers.

Schuyler, Michael and Jake Hoffman. *PC Management: A How-To-Do-It Manual for Selecting, Organizing, and Managing Personal Computers in Libraries*. New York: Neal-Schuman, 1990. Number six in the publisher's "How-To-Do-It Manuals for Libraries" series. This handy volume is indispensable for anyone who spends most of the workday making microcomputers do the work.

Walton, Robert. "Are PC fax boards good for libraries?" *Library Journal* 115 (March 15, 1990): 66–68. A review of fax technology and the type of PC needed to support a fax board. The author offers guidelines for when a fax board is appropriate for a library's applications.

Welsch, Erwin K. "Fax machines and microcomputers in libraries." *Computers in Libraries* 9 (November, 1989): 42–43. The author describes his adventures in installing a fax board. The first problem was finding a machine with enough empty expansion slots to accommodate the technology.

Wilson, Mark. "On-board faxes are worth a look: the complete PC fax board." *Online* 13 (March, 1989): 76–78. A product evaluation of THE COMPLETE FAX, an add-on board for PCs. The author suggests using a fax-board-equipped PC as a central node in a fax network, receiving and storing documents on its hard disk, then sorting and forwarding them to other points on the network.

Wright, Kieth. *Workstations and Local Area Networks for Libraries*. Chicago: American Library Association, 1990. An excellent guide through the issues of connectivity. Planning for networking, managing a networked environment, the technicalities of the human-machine interface, and networking protocols are thoroughly covered.

8

Planning for the Future

Mediated or end-user, fee or free, online or ondisk, CD-ROM or locally loaded tape—the availability of so many options and so many combinations of the options makes planning the correct configuration suitable for any individual library difficult. The fact that automated information retrieval is a dynamic and constantly changing business complicates the issue. For the decade from the mid-1970s to the mid-1980s the change was primarily one of growth, involving more databases, more vendors, and more computing power aimed largely at information professionals who found innovative ways to apply the automated information retrieval options. But then end-users entered, and changed, the picture. Producers and vendors are now aiming for an expanded end-user market, and libraries must find ways to incorporate the end-user products into library routines. The fact is, a good many end-users are introduced to these products in libraries and would not know of their existence or use if not for libraries.

Despite their musty, fusty image, libraries live in the future. Library staffs traditionally anticipate the future needs of their clientele—they select for purchase materials they predict will be used. They carve up the serials budget a year or two in advance in anticipation of changes in the serials market. Predicting the future, from predicting when the next issue will come in or the book will be returned, to predicting who will be assigned to desk duty next week or next month, are daily routines in libraries. The use of some types of technology in libraries has been ahead of the rest of the world. Libraries first made photocopiers available to the general public. Networking, the buzzword of this decade, is a very old hat in libraries. Librarians are database management systems; we "capture" data, index it, organize it, and retrieve it on demand, and librarians have been using computers to organize databases and to perform routine and repetitive tasks such as circulation for years. Online databases were accessed in libraries long before the general public saw the value of such access, and probably much of the general public saw and used it for the first time in a library. Seductive advertisements in computer magazines tout the virtues of encyclopedias on CD-ROM, but possibly more sales are clinched when an end-user uses one in a library.

"Proactive" is a buzzword among librarians, expressing a sense that it is better to act rather than react to the changing demands of the library's clientele. This is especially true in the automated information retrieval field, where changes are rapid and reach deep into the library's established routines. It is necessary to have the tools in place to provide the data upon which to anticipate the coming changes (Martin, 1989b). Librarians need to develop a "spreadsheet" mentality. Spreadsheet software allows one to change one or several variables to see how the change will affect the total operation—what would happen if serial prices rose an average of 12 percent and the serials budget dropped 5 percent? The difficulty for librarians is to figure out which variables to change and plug into the spreadsheet. The possible directions and the trends in automated information retrieval are the variables that need to be identified, or alternatively one can identify the problem areas and feel fairly certain that the trend will be to solve those problems. Options, trends, and problems have been mentioned in every chapter of this text. It is time to take a closer look at some of them to see how they might affect an automated information retrieval operation in the future.

INTEGRATING THE OPTIONS

As automated information retrieval is integrated into a library's operations it begins to impact on those operations. One impact is the shift of staff time and library funds to automated information retrieval operations. Automated resources increase access to the universe of knowledge; this causes increased usage of the local collection, a demand for more materials in the local collection, and an increased use of interlibrary loan. As funding tightens, libraries must choose between automated access and traditional print access, a choice that causes some libraries to drop subscriptions to print sources or to forego purchasing the print source in the first place if it is available as an automated resource, either online or ondisk. These impacts on the entire library operation point out trends that can be identified as the access over ownership problem, the bird-in-hand problem, and the scholarly publishing problem.

Access over Ownership

Traditionally, libraries are measured by the size of their collections, by how many hundreds or thousands or millions of volumes the library owns. It is a "recall ratio" measure; of the total number of volumes available, how many does the library have? Other libraries may boast a "precision ratio" measure, stating that they own nearly everything in a particular subject field. Librarians are increasingly aware that purchasing and owning "nearly everything," even in a finite field, is impossible because there is too much material, too little money and too little space. The trend is to consider the old measures to be a meaningless numbers game and to emphasize access instead. According to this new measure, the library that can provide access to any item its clientele demands serves the public better than the library with millions of volumes, 80 percent of which are never used. Access is provided by automated indexing and abstracting services that inform potential users of the existence of needed items, and by an interlibrary loan/document delivery network that borrows or otherwise acquires the items for the client. Automated information retrieval resources currently existing fulfill the first half of this equation; the interlibrary loan/document delivery network is the problem that remains to be solved.

The Bird-in-Hand Problem

Automated information retrieval resources provide instant access to a bibliographic citation. Interlibrary loan takes weeks and sometimes months, if it can provide the item at all. Once the researcher has the instant bibliography, he or she immediately searches and selects from and uses those items that are available in the local collection. To the researcher, interlibrary loan is a last resort. A book in the hand is worth two on the printout. More value is placed on the items in the local collection than the items "out there" in a nebulous and still largely theoretical library network.

Resource sharing is a lovely idea. A library chooses to spend its money and staff and building space on identifying, acquiring, and housing a comprehensive physics collection, and serves researchers in the modern languages by borrowing materials from the library that has chosen to specialize in modern languages. A network of libraries, each with its own specialization, can pool its members' resources and thus more effectively build a comprehensive and broad collection than can one library alone. The problem is that librarians are reluctant to rely heavily on each other's collections because, as of now, providing prompt exchange of materials is unreliable (Kibirige, 1988). The infrastructure for providing access to text as quickly and easily as providing access to the bibliographic citation does not exist, and until it does each library must build a local collection that provides the most materials to the most local users. In doing so, each library largely duplicates the collections of the others, and there is no pool of specialized materials to call upon. Telefacsimile and text-digitizing technologies are the possible solutions to the problem of accessing text stored in another library's collection. Even a handwritten manuscript can be delivered electronically by optically scanning the pages and sending the digitized image via telecommunications networks.

The Scholarly Publishing Problem

A migration from print to electronic information access has been predicted since the 1970s, when online access became widely available. It has not happened. However, CD-ROM may be the technological advance that makes the migration possible for certain publications. An index or abstract publication on CD-ROM provides the enhanced access points and speed and ease of access that characterize online access and yet provides a local copy with local control similar to a library's ownership of the printed version of the tool. Whereas libraries have not made wholesale cancellations of printed indexes in favor of online access due to unpredictable and high costs and the frequent need for an intermediary to operate the search engine, user-friendly indexes on CD-ROM can substitute for the print copy, and in fact end-users themselves have made this substitution by uniformly preferring the ondisk product to the print product. It is an easy experiment that any library can perform: provide a CD-ROM copy of ERIC or PSYCLIT alongside the print copy, and see which one gathers dust.

The migration from print to online access still has a chance if the publishers are willing to take the risk (Hudson, 1990; Smith, 1991). One copy of a scholarly article stored electronically in a clearinghouse accessible to libraries can take the place of hundreds of copies of the printed publications duplicated in hundreds of libraries. The advantage to libraries is obvious and enormous: rather than purchasing, processing, and storing the printed volumes of a publication in the hope that the local clientele will use it, the library purchases access to the individual articles on demand, knowing that they will be used. The advantage to the scholarly community is enormous; access to the text is as instant and reliable as access to the bibliographic citation has been in the past through online abstracting and indexing services. There may be other advantages to the scholarly community such as providing networks for communicating with author/researchers or for the peer review of articles.

Providing the machine-readable text is not a problem. The fact is, most modern publications are machine readable. This book was composed and written on a microcomputer; the text is stored on the microcomputer's hard disk as ASCII characters, the industry standard for machine-readable text. It is backed up on floppy disks, and it can be transmitted electronically over telephone lines. Most publishers use computers to prepare the copy ready for publishing, thus producing machine-readable text. The potential for electronic access to machine-readable text is enormous, as large as today's volume of printed publication.

The potential has not been realized because the publishers have yet to resolve issues of copyright and profit. Photocopiers were a new technology several years ago that produced a copyright crisis. Copyright clearinghouses have partially resolved the crisis. An electronic clearinghouse of machine-readable text provides a better solution because electronic access controlled by contracts and passwords leaves an unmistakable trail showing who accessed what and when. If libraries begin to show a clear preference for accessing the online full-text sources currently available, rather than purchasing the print copies, the migration will begin.

All of these issues relate to the access over ownership question, which is an increasingly important issue to libraries that are running out of money and space at the same time that they are running into increased demands from the local clientele for more materials. Access is the specialty of automated information retrieval techniques and technology. In a future when access to publications through an electronic clearinghouse becomes commonplace, which department of the library will specialize in providing the access? Will it be the automated information retrieval service that accesses any and all commercially available databases? Perhaps the task is better suited to interlibrary loan offices that provide access to any material not in the local collection, or the acquisitions department as part of its responsibility to acquire materials to meet the users' needs. Or possibly the circulation department will be responsible, since the material will be leaving the building. An interesting question. It will not be the first time that automation has forced a reexamination of the traditional divisions of labor and responsibilities in libraries (Brownrigg et al., 1984).

OPERATIONS OF AN AUTOMATED INFORMATION RETRIEVAL SERVICE

The unit of the library that manages the automated information retrieval options is naturally affected by all the trends described in this chapter, but certain trends immediately impact upon the day-to-day operations of the unit. The incorporation of end-users into the service drives both ends. One is the type of searches performed by the search analysts, and the other is the impact on the search analyst staff.

Mediated Searches

As the options available to end-users increase, the searches performed by search analysts undergo subtle changes. The databases currently available to end-users are the old standbys, the superdatabases intermediaries have been searching successfully for years, databases such as COMPENDEX, ERIC, AGRICOLA, PSYCINFO, MEDLINE, and INSPEC. Now end-users are searching these databases for themselves with varying degrees of success, but searching them nonetheless. Most end-users, having performed their own searches, will not recognize a need to continue the process of seeking additional information by requesting a mediated search, but those who do want something other than a repeat in the same old databases. Take, for example, the education doctoral candidate who has performed end-user searches in the ondisk version of ERIC, PSYCLIT and Dissertation Abstracts, and now approaches the mediated search service with a request for "anything else." The old standbys have been removed from the search analyst's repertoire, and what is left are those databases that are more complex to search or more expensive and thus not thought suitable for end-users, or the more specialized databases, or those that are peripheral to the subject and may be unfruitful unless approached very carefully. As a result, the mediated searches become longer, more complex, and more expensive. The average cost of mediated searches will rise as more databases are made available to end-users (Anders and Jackson, 1988; LePoer, 1989).

The Search Analysts

As more resources are made available to end-users, the demand for mediated searches will decline. This is alarming to the search analysts; they may have spent a good deal of time and money learning their skills; they may have built a career and a future based upon those skills. As with American automobile manufacturers watching the influx of Japanese cars, some search analysts look upon end-users as a threat to their livelihood.

Search analysts must find new ways to apply their specialized skills. Instructing end-users is an obvious alternative. Written instructions that end-users will actually read are desperately needed, as is one-on-one instruction as end-users perform their searches. A role as search strategy consultant is important and involves a level of professionalism that is appealing, but it will not happen automatically. It must be advertised and promoted aggressively, otherwise end-users will not know that such a service exists and will not recognize its value unless it can be proven to them that their own searches could be improved.

Search analysts can find new ways to use old resources. Online databases have been used in bibliometric research or as collection development tools. More extensive use of online sources as reference tools on demand, and increased use of full-text databases promise continued activity and involvement for search analysts. Eventually, however, the distinction between search analyst and reference librarian will dissolve as it becomes more and more likely that no reference librarian will be able to perform his or her duties without incorporating the skills of a search analyst. Until that time, search analysts can participate in and pioneer the trends discussed below in the section on "Staff".

FINANCES AND BUDGETS

There are more databases available from more vendors and in more formats today than ever before, and this trend will continue. The prospect for more full-text sources becoming available online is especially exciting. The clientele of academic libraries demand more access and so do the librarians who recognize the advantages of automated information retrieval. Not-for-profit libraries serving as intermediaries between the information consumers and the for-profit information database and equipment industries, driven by marketplace supply and demand issues, makes the matter of affording automated information retrieval less like a unidirectional trend and more like a whirlpool attempting to swallow itself (Martin, 1989a).

Fee or Free

Here it is again and it will not go away. What libraries do is expensive, from buying books and serials to erecting the buildings to house them, and an increasing amount of the total library budget is going to automation of one sort or another.

Should libraries acknowledge the fact and charge users big bucks for fancy services in an attempt to generate revenues to support expensive programs? Or should libraries continue to hide the costs from library users behind the philosophy of free libraries, while pinching pennies in an attempt to afford at least the minimum level of facilities the users demand? What value does the user place on library services when they cost the user nothing? When libraries forego subscriptions to serials in favor of online access either through a full-text database or an electronic clearinghouse, who should pay for an article delivered through the online source? Some might say that the library should pay, since it is saving money on subscription costs. Some might say that the user should pay, since libraries have traditionally charged back to the user the direct costs of online access. When online access to full-text sources becomes the routine replacement for paper copy purchase and this is not charged to the user, the issue of charging for online access to bibliographic databases will become muddier; the user will not recognize the distinction between full-text access for free and bibliographic database access for a fee.

The Pricing of Online Access

Two trends are affecting the way database producers and vendors charge for their products, and both are driven by the consumers of the products, that is, the end-users and the librarians. End-users simply will not accept traditional online connect fees. The vendors claim that an increasing number of end-users are setting up contracts with the vendors, but at the same time they admit that end-users seldom continue to use the online service after the initial free access period is over. Libraries have noticed the same thing; after investing considerable time and effort in learning to search in library-sponsored training programs, most end-users do not continue to search often enough on their own contracts to maintain their skills. The connect time pricing structure of the vendors is punitive to end-users, who are usually slow searchers and must stop to think through each command and seldom plan a search strategy before going online. End-users are exposed to automated information retrieval products in libraries that have tried, as much as possible, to make them available for free or at minimal cost, and they are astonished at the price when they try to obtain access through their own contracts or purchases.

Librarians are asking for a different kind of pricing structure, one that charges for the goods received rather than the time it takes to shop for them. However, the pricing structure that evolves in the future will not be designed to reduce the profits of vendors and producers, and the initial shakedown period may produce higher average costs than at present. Current experiments with new pricing structures involve charging for search terms and charging for hits. Trained search analysts can adjust and will find ways to reduce their overall costs, just as they have under present fee systems, but the new methods will still be punitive to end-users. Typically, end-users print more citations than trained search analysts, and they do not attempt to reduce a large set of hits by further refinement of the search strategy. Charging for search terms entered punishes casual mistakes and typing errors, and penalizes end-users who typically retype an entire search statement rather than reusing set numbers.

Both librarians and end-users favor the predictable costs of ondisk or locally loaded databases. The unpredictable costs of online access turn many people away, not because they cannot afford the actual bottom line but simply because it is unpredictable. Libraries must budget for a bottom line that will not be known until the last bill of the year comes in; end-users fear the absence of any sort of control over the cost of an online search. The producers and vendors will try to find a solution to this problem but the solution will most certainly favor the profit margin of the companies.

Equipment Costs

The cost of microcomputers and peripheral equipment has declined remarkably over the years, but there is always some new and therefore expensive item coming on the market that is just the right solution to an old information delivery problem. The microcomputers purchased just a few years ago are obsolete, too slow or too stupid to handle the tasks required of them today. Library budgets simply are not equipped to deal with the problem of expensive equipment that must constantly be upgraded or replaced. Libraries are geared to think in terms of permanent goods—books and serials stored on the shelves—rather than consumable goods which, frankly, exactly defines what computer technology is. Library budgets will have to be restructured and new methods of funding found to support the cost of automated information retrieval equipment.

The Library Budget

Every year, an increasing percentage of the total library budget goes to supporting the costs of automation. In the immediate future, libraries must expect to support traditional printed sources and increasing automated sources rather than replacing one with the other, and this will cost a great deal of money. As libraries are forced to cancel subscriptions to expensive serials, forego negotiating a contract with an interesting new vendor or service, and shift limited budget resources to cover increasing options for information storage and delivery, publishers and vendors are raising their prices to make up for lost revenue. As the library's OPAC becomes larger and more sophisticated, storage and processing costs leap skyward. Over the next few years, libraries will make hard choices regarding access over ownership, resource sharing and networking, print or electronic formats, and the trend will be to favor automation.

STAFF

The distinction between search analyst and reference librarian is dissolving. Using the OPAC, ready-reference searching, and assisting and advising end-users are tasks that all reference librarians must be able to perform, and all require the skills of a search analyst. As more automated information resources become available and begin to replace printed sources, all librarians will need the skills to deal with them (Molholt, 1990). In the meantime the distinction remains, and many librarians trained as search analysts are looking for ways to maintain the distinction.

Search Analysts as Teachers

The information industry is turning its attention to the development of products designed for end-users, and although search analysts may not use these products extensively, they must familiarize themselves with the products in order to teach end-users how to operate them. End-users prefer one-on-one instruction on demand. This is time-consuming and certainly will keep the search analyst busy for a good many hours of the day, but it is repetitive, it becomes boring, and the population of end-users needing instruction is growing faster than the library staff can handle. Librarians prepare written instructions and conduct classes in order to reach more people with the instruction they need. The end-users ignore the written instructions; they can always find something better to do with their time than attend a class. And yet, when they sit down to a keyboard and begin a search, they discover that they need help and they demand one-on-one instruction.

It is a vicious circle, and librarians have been trying for years to solve the problem of delivering library instruction when the patrons need it and in a form the patrons find acceptable. For a time, computer assisted instruction was seen as a solution to the problem, until librarians discovered that it takes between two hundred and three hundred hours of staff time to develop one hour of CAI, and CAI must be delivered by means of a microcomputer or terminal, expensive equipment that is rare enough in libraries and so heavily used that anyone monopolizing one for an hour or so of leisurely access to a CAI program will be resented by the other users trying to get their hands on it. Technological developments may solve the problem. Expert systems or knowledge-based programs and graphics software packages make the production of computer assisted instruction programs easier, such that a librarian can produce the package from start to finish, including graphics and sound effects, without the assistance of a programmer. The package can then be mounted on the campus mainframe and made available on the campus information network to the terminals and personal microcomputers increasingly available in offices, computer labs, and dormitories. Library resources will become more and more accessible to remote users, people who do not come into the library and therefore do not have the opportunity to request one-on-one instruction. CAI will be the only way to reach these users. Computers are perfectly happy to repeat instructions endlessly and patiently. Perhaps CAI's time has come around again, and this time the automated instructions are suited to the automated information resources the patron wants to use.

As the library's clientele becomes more adept at identifying sources using the library's databases, and as they acquire more of the information explosion's publications and data, either through purchase or photocopying or downloading from an online source, they will need help managing the accumulation of data. This is the librarian's domain, the librarian's area of expertise. Search analysts may perhaps become more involved in teaching bibliographic database management and instructing researchers in the techniques of record structure and indexing so that they can manage and control their growing collections of data (Hubbard and Wilson, 1986).

Value-Added Mediated Searches

In a typical mediated search, the patron meets with a search analyst by appointment, they discuss the topic and prepare a search strategy, the analyst performs the search and interacts with the database, and the patron walks away with a printout. When an end-user conducts a search, the end-user walks away with a printout, having cut out the hassle of making and keeping an appointment and explaining his or her topic to someone else who is then liable to make errors in translating the topic to a language the database can understand. Probably the end-user search costs far less than the mediated search. In both cases, the user ends up with a printout—the desired product. In the eyes of the end-user, the printout produced by a mediated search costs far more in time and effort and money than the printout produced by the end-user search.

Certainly, there are differences. The mediated search may access databases not available in an end-user format, and the search analyst is faster and more efficient than the end-user. But when the end product delivered into the hands of the patron looks very much the same regardless of its origin, the patron is likely to prefer the type of search that costs less in time, effort, and money. The patron is not likely to see the value of the mediated search product.

Search analysts are looking at postprocessing activities to make the product of a mediated search more attractive to patrons. Simply sorting a printout by journal or source publication title makes the bibliography immensely easier to handle; sorting capabilities are not available on most end-user systems. Downloading the results of a search and repackaging or reformatting it so that it is more attractive than the typical printout, easier to read and ready for the patron to use, can be done using Pro-Search or Sci-Mate software packages. The mediated search service can add call numbers for those items in the bibliography that are available in the local collection, items not in the local collection can be sorted out into a separate section, and items available through an online full-text or document delivery source can be indicated. Any of these steps adds immensely to the value of the product of a mediated search by saving the patrons the trouble of doing it for themselves. The next logical step is delivering the documents along with the printout. In fact, the product comes more and more to resemble the product delivered by the fee-based services of information brokers. It is an attractive product that patrons are willing to pay for, and it is a product that librarians can produce faster and better than even the most skillful end-user.

The Search Analyst as Information Professional

Packaging and delivering information products is the first step. Evaluating, interpreting, and filtering the information to be delivered is the next step. The information explosion in general and the proliferation of databases and database delivery systems make it impossible for the typical library patron to select the right resource to answer an information query. Search analysts with a wide knowledge of databases and their strengths and weaknesses already serve as information consultants when asked, and willingly advise end-users on appropriate databases. But now it is no longer sufficient to wait until the patrons asks. The freshman working on a term paper must be steered away from MEDLINE; the medical researcher must be steered away from MAGAZINE INDEX.

It is no longer a question of finding information. Information abounds. Articles on bulimia can be found in MEDLINE and in MAGAZINE INDEX and in a score or more other databases. The nutritionist, the physician, and the psychologist, each one researching the topic of bulimia, have different needs and none of them will be served by MAGAZINE INDEX; and yet academic faculty and professionals thought InfoTrac was the answer to their prayers when it first came out. Librarians are the information professionals; they must make professional level judgments and evaluations (Tenopir, 1990). It is no longer adequate to simply make information available and let the patron shop around. The physician does not offer a choice of pills; the psychologist does not offer a choice of therapies.

Does this sound radical? Academic librarians have long shied away from the idea of filtering or evaluating information before placing it in the hands of library users because this smacks of censorship. On the other hand, allowing a medical researcher to use an inappropriate database and hoping that he or she will eventually figure out that something is wrong smacks of "information malpractice." The trend is for librarians to be more assertive of their professionalism, to apply their specialized training and knowledge in evaluating and filtering information in order to present the library user with an appropriate product.

It still sounds radical, but consider this: a freshman approaches the reference desk and says that he needs ten good articles on bulimia. "Yes, of course," the librarian says, and checks a locally loaded database and the OPAC, prints out a list of fifteen to twenty citations with call numbers of magazines available in the library, and hands it to the freshman. Next, a medical researcher approaches the desk and says that she needs ten good articles on bulimia. "Yes, of course," the librarian says, "I'll have it ready for you in about an hour." The librarian goes online in appropriate databases, performs document-type searches and citation analyses, sorts the resulting bibliography and downloads it, checks for articles held locally and prints a list of articles to be photocopied by a student assistant while the librarian continues annotating and sorting the list for interlibrary loan or online document retrieval. The sorted list is printed and handed to the researcher with the photocopied documents.

What has happened in these transactions? Both patrons were presented with a selection of sources that in the librarian's professional judgment met their needs. The freshman and the medical researcher can examine the documents and accept them or reject them as they please. Information has not been withheld from them nor has it been forced down their throats with a take-it-or-leave-it attitude. They always have the option of returning to the reference desk with a revised or refined information request, perhaps with a request such as "Get me more articles just like this one," based on some worthwhile article produced in the original information product. Or they have the option of bypassing the librarian and striking out on their own search through databases and resources they consider appropriate. If they are satisfied with the product delivered, both have been saved considerable time and trouble.

"Yes," some readers are muttering to themselves now, "But that poor freshman hasn't learned anything about using the library." This is not entirely true. The freshman has learned that he will save himself considerable time and trouble if he asks an information professional for help in using the library. Furthermore, the medical professional does not teach patients how to prescribe for themselves.

An academic library is not a shopping mall where patrons can browse at a leisurely pace expecting to find something reasonably close to what they desire. Libraries are complex, complicated places and are becoming more so, and frankly, most patrons try to spend as little time as possible in them. The librarian's role, as it has been in the past, is to guide users to the information they need. The tools of information technology allow faster access to information and they allow more in-depth access to information. Should the librarian lay this mass of information and access technology out for the patron in one vast array and say, "Help yourself?" Or, should the librarian exercise some professional judgment and expertise and present the patron with a more reasonable, more appropriate array?

END-USERS

Database producers and vendors are concentrating much of their development energies on products designed for end-users. They have found, as have librarians, that end-users want simple and speedy access to relevant information, and they do not want to spend any time learning information management theories explaining the proliferation of databases and controlled vocabularies and search engines. The products being developed put the information management theories in the software and deliver information without troubling the user with details of where it came from or how it was found. A popular example currently available is Lotus OneSource, which presents information about companies to the user as a unified text although the information was extracted from several sources such as annual reports and 10-Ks and current Dow Jones News Service sources. The producers and vendors are reformatting and packaging information, then presenting the package to the user. This is the same trend mentioned above, wherein librarians evaluate, reformat, and package information they have gathered from several different sources and present the package to the patron. Both the information industry and librarians are thinking along the same lines, and both are responding to trends driven by the advent of the end-user.

End-User Population Dynamics

BRS/After Dark, Knowledge Index, and InfoTrac brought undergraduates into automated information retrieval in large numbers for the first time. Mediated searches were too expensive and perhaps too intimidating to appeal to undergraduates, but the do-it-yourself ease and low or no cost of the early end-user systems generated an enthusiasm that proved end-user searching was viable. InfoTrac brought library nonusers into the library, because it was fun to use.

An increasingly computer literate population expects to find automated information retrieval resources in a library. People who are reluctant to ask a librarian for help gladly take their information requests to a computer, confident that they will be able to understand the computer and the computer will be able to understand them. OPACs are welcomed. Libraries expected some resistance to this latest technology and of course there were some patrons who watched the card catalog go with sadness, but the resistance to automation is much less than the resistance to microfilm, as an earlier example of a new technology being introduced in libraries. Photocopiers were embraced immediately, and it looks like automation will receive the same enthusiastic welcome. As with photocopiers, the users complain when a malfunction takes the technology away.

The End-User's Mental Model

The information industry is trying to match the end-user's mental model of automated information retrieval with products such as Lotus OneSource mentioned above. The end-user does not understand the distinctions and relationships among databases, therefore in order to match the mental model the information product must blur that distinction by extracting information from various discrete databases and pulling the information together in a package presented to the user (O'Leary, 1990a).

End-users expect the database to present only "good" information, therefore programs are being developed that rank retrieved items according to word counts, word proximities, and the occurrence of words in weighted fields resulting in an ordered browsing list of items ranging from most relevant to least relevant in the "opinion" of the computer program. As end-users seldom use record structure to assist their searches and usually print browsing lists, such programs meet two other expectations in the end-user's mental model. DowQuest is a promising example of such a search engine (Weyer, 1989).

End-users expect the computer to understand what they want. When the user types in CAT the computer is supposed to understand that this means CATS, FELINE, FELINES, FELIS, and FELIDAE as well. The user should be able to type in an SIC number without having to tell the computer by means of codes and field indicators, "This is an SIC number." Automatic equivalencies, automatic plurals, and context-sensitive help systems that detect input needing clarification—such as an unidentified number—are some of the developments that will match future search engines to the end user's mental model.

End-users expect the database to be "just the right size," neither so large and comprehensive that hundreds of items are retrieved nor so small that nothing is retrieved in response to an information request. For most end-users, "just the right size" means available locally; in other words, the database should index only those items that are in the local collection, or at least indicate which items are in the local collection. The NOTIS system now incorporates the latter. Locally loaded database tapes such as the Wilson indexes can be searched on the OPAC, and those journals held by the local library will be indicated. This is not quite what the end-user expects, but it is coming close.

The elements needed to match the end-user's mental model exist in various products but they have not been brought together in one product yet. In order to meet the database size expectation of end-users, a library would have to compile its own database, and this may be the trend for the future. Librarians extract from various databases the records that match their local holdings, mount the records on a campus mainframe computer along with a ranking-algorithm search engine, and make this database available as the library's OPAC. Usage of the existing library collection would be increased dramatically. Those researchers who need material not held locally could be served, as they are now, by access to existing commercial databases. In fact, this marvelous access system already exists, but it is not a computer, it is a librarian. Extracting information from various databases and printed resources, evaluating the information, and correlating it to the local collection and local needs is what librarians do very well.

End-User Demands

As end-users are exposed to automated information resources, an orderly progression of responses occurs. First, end-users show a marked preference for automated information resources rather than their print equivalents. Even the patrons who complained about the loss of the card catalog will happily and quietly use the OPAC and only remind the library of their complaints when the OPAC computer crashes. End-users are driving the migration from print to automated.

End-users immediately demand more end-user access. As soon as the OPAC is up and providing access to the book collections, users expect it to index the journals as well. As soon as ERIC or MEDLINE is made available on CD-ROM, the engineers and the biologists want their special databases as well. Having Knowledge Index available at night is not enough; end-users want access around the clock.

End-users demand free access. If a library can afford to reduce or eliminate fees, usage statistics go through the roof. Even a nominal charge such as five cents for a page of references printed from an ondisk database will turn users away. Ondisk and locally loaded databases having fixed and predictable prices are making it possible for more libraries to provide free access. It is expensive for the library, but it is what the users want and expect.

End-users demand remote access (Bell, 1990). "Can I search this from my computer in the office/home/dormitory?" is a question that comes up every day and several times a day in reference to the OPAC, to ondisk databases, and to online databases. It is not unusual to find that significant numbers of the academic faculty have negotiated their own contracts with online vendors just for the convenience of searching from their offices and homes. When surveyed as to why they have online contracts they cite the convenience of being able to search when they want to and they frequently state that it "saves them the trouble of going to the library." In other words, they are willing to pay rather than come into the library (Clark and Gomez, 1990; Kupferberg, 1986). This is an alarming trend for two reasons. For one, it says something very negative regarding how users feel about libraries. Secondly, it indicates that librarians can very easily be squeezed out of the interface between the user and the information as remote access to the library's databases becomes commonplace in response to the users' demands. Librarians need to work on this. Consulting an information professional should be easy, profitable, and desirable rather than something to be avoided at any cost.

End-users demand access to the source publications. Electronic delivery of surrogate information—the bibliographic citations—is only the first step. End-users can recognize as well as librarians can that the next logical step is electronic access to the sources. They recognize the irony of instant access to a citation followed by long waits for interlibrary loan to deliver the full text if it can be delivered at all. For now, the burden and the complaints fall on the interlibrary loan offices but, as end-users have forced changes in search engines and pricing structures in the information industry, perhaps they will be the force that drives publishers to settle the issues that so far have prevented more widespread access to full-text sources online.

DATABASES AND VENDORS

Definitely end-users are driving the information industry marketplace. Libraries and information specialists are too limited a market (not to mention financially burdened) to allow the industry to expand, so it must develop products that are attractive to a different population. Most of the innovations in interfaces, graphics, and artificial intelligence applications have been developed in response to end-user demands and are aimed at end-users. What is good for the end-user is not necessarily good for the information professional, however (Basch, 1990a, 1990b, 1990c).

Pricing Policies

Online vendors are looking at various ways to change their pricing structures in order to eliminate or greatly reduce connect costs. Information professionals and end-users alike complain that they are being charged for merely looking, as if the shopping mall were to charge an entrance fee just to come inside, rather than being charged for using the databases (user input such as search terms) or for goods received (full citations or sources printed out). Fixed prices for ondisk databases look very good to librarians, in that they allow accurate budgeting for unlimited use, and they allow most libraries to eliminate charges to end-users. This will probably sound the death knell for online connect charges.

The prices of ondisk products have come down somewhat since they were first introduced. It is hoped that a larger volume of purchases by libraries and end-users will reduce prices further, but this hope was expressed in the past for online use and it did not happen there. Online usage increases every year and so do the prices. Libraries have managed to keep per-use prices at a fairly steady level by improvements in baud rate and improvements in techniques such as uploading and downloading. The pricing changes made by vendors are an attempt to keep profit margins up in response to the lower-cost searching performed by search analysts. If there is a widespread migration from print to ondisk products, the price of the ondisk products must rise as the producers make up the loss of revenue from their printed products. Libraries should not look for a significant break in the cost of automated information retrieval products.

User Interface Developments

End-users and search analysts alike would like to see a common command language that does away with the need to learn and memorize the commands of several different vendors. However, the vendors have invested considerable time and money in the development of their user interfaces so it is very unlikely that they will give them up. The user interface may be the most distinctive feature the vendor has to offer and to attract customers, since vendors make many of the same databases available. It is more likely that a common command language, when and if one is developed and agreed upon, will be a front-end system either widely available as a software package or mounted on the vendors' computers as an option the searcher can select rather than the vendor's native mode command system.

There is a problem with the idea of a common command language. An experienced search analyst searching the same topic in the same database through five different interfaces will get five different answers. It is a fascinating experiment to try. Take a topic with three or so concept groups and a date or language limit and perform a free-text search of the ERIC database in BRS, DIALOG, ORBIT, SilverPlatter, and a Pro-Search or Sci-Mate front-end interface. The more translating or interpreting the interface performs, the greater the variation in retrieval will be. The searcher loses control of the search. The experienced search analyst with a thorough and in-depth knowledge of the various interfaces will recognize what has happened and may be able to force the desired results from each search engine, but an end-user will not. The end-user will most likely accept whatever results are presented as the authoritative, final word.

Automatic equivalencies and cross-referenced thesauri are other improvements the vendors are developing. BRS's MEDSPELL is an example of an automatic equivalency feature that translates British spellings to American spellings and vice versa, and in this limited application it works quite well. But if automatic equivalency is expanded to include equivalent concepts—the "SEE" references in a thesaurus—once again the searcher has lost control over the database and the items retrieved from it. An end-user searching CIVIL WAR may be quite happy if the interface translates this to mean U.S.-HISTORY-CIVIL WAR-1860-1865, if that is what the user meant, but another searcher may wonder what happened to the English Civil War a couple of centuries earlier or to interdisciplinary studies of civil war in general.

What is good for the end-user is not necessarily good for the professional search analyst, and in the long run really may not be good for the end-user who does not realize that there are alternatives to whatever answer the computer supplies. Another development being considered involves the dissolution of the barriers among databases. End-users do have problems selecting appropriate databases and they are irritated by the task of switching from one database to another and sorting through the duplicate citations each produces. To them it looks like an extra step that should be eliminated. Lotus OneSource is a popular database that packages information drawn from different databases; DIALOG's ONESEARCH and duplicate removal features allow a searcher to select a category of databases, perform one input that searches all of them, and produce a unified output. The next step more closely matches the end-user's mental model of a superdatabase that covers everything. The end-user walks up to any terminal and types any subject request, ranging from a request for information on XYZ Company to information on the American Civil War. The interface analyzes the question and selects the appropriate database or databases. The interface knows that when an end-user types "American" the end-user actually means United States rather than Canadian or Mexican or Peruvian, because automatic equivalencies are programmed in. The interface performs the search using an algorithm other than Boolean that produces a ranked list of those items available in the local collection.

The interface just described is an expert system program that emulates what a librarian does now. When asked by a patron for information on the American Civil War, the reference librarian does not spew out a multipage list of every citation to every publication extant on the Civil War. Instead, after a few well-chosen questions, the librarian selects the appropriate database, an encyclopedia perhaps, or the OPAC, or a locally loaded or ondisk database, and directs the patron to the level of information needed. If the trend is indeed to match the end-user's mental model of automated information retrieval, then the trend is to develop expert systems using artificial intelligence that emulates librarians.

In the immediate future, what is more likely to develop is a system of multilevel interfaces, probably incorporating some kind of common command language at one or more levels that can be used by the novice who knows nothing of databases or database structure or Boolean operators, or by the experienced search analyst who must have a high level of control over the data in order to perform a complex search. Some vendors presently have multilevel interfaces, some presently allow concurrent searches of multiple databases, and some are working on the ranking algorithm type of search. Even so, user interfaces are proliferating at an alarming rate, and a librarian is still required to direct patrons to the correct database and to teach the patron how to use the interface.

Interacting with the Data

Search analysts talk about interacting with the database: the searcher inputs a query, the database responds by displaying items that match the query, the searcher revises the query in order to get a more precise response. Interacting with the data is something entirely different. Databases are full of errors such as typos, incomplete citations, and incorrect coding that is irritating at least and in some cases affects the searching such that a relevant item cannot be retrieved or irrelevant items pop up where they do not belong. If the author's name is SMITH but the database lists it as SIMTH an author search will miss the record. If the patron needs information on Jack the Ripper, does one type JACK or RIPPER, JACK or does one remember the correct Library of Congress subject heading and type WHITECHAPEL MURDERS? A searcher in the Southwest devises the perfect strategy guaranteed to find every citation on HEAVY METALS in the BIOSIS database and knows that it would be useful to other searchers everywhere. If the search strategy could be stored as a hedge in the database, it would become available to other searchers. It would be nice if searchers could interact with the data: change it or revise it or add to it in order to make it behave according to expectations. Changing a typo from SIMTH to SMITH is obvious and would be appreciated by everyone, but adding a descriptor for Jack the Ripper subtly changes the database, perhaps in a way that the database producer and copyright holder would not approve. If searchers could store hedges in the vendor's mainframe, hedges of varying quality could soon be eating up the storage capacity. Vendors probably will not allow online editing or additions to databases, but they are considering methods of allowing searchers to mark records that need correcting or editing. The producers are naturally concerned about the quality of the information in their databases and would like to see typos and errors disappear, but as the copyright holders they are more concerned about maintaining the copyrightability of the database, which would be jeopardized if individuals could change or add to the data.

Interacting with the data offers an exciting possibility in the world of scholarly publishing (Rogers and Hurt, 1989). Two academicians are coauthoring an article;

one is in California, the other is in Maine. Instead of mailing paper-copy drafts or floppy disks back and forth across the country, both go online to input their contributions to their publisher's electronic clearinghouse. The editor at the publishing house can get into the act as well and offer editorial suggestions and directions as the article is being written, and the editor can invite reviewers to critique the developing article at the same time, thus saving the delays and bother of extensive rewrites that now occur in the editing and peer review process. Once the article is completed to everyone's satisfaction, the publisher simply prints the text from the online file or, more likely, "publishes" it in an electronic journal format.

The Databases

Innovations like this may tip the balance in favor of electronic publishing and make the electronic clearinghouse of articles available on demand a reality. It seems so simple, so logical, an equitable solution to the problem of too many and too costly scholarly publications competing for severely limited library budgets and space.

Electronic publishing, when it comes, will greatly increase the number of databases available for access. At present, there is a type of database already available that is underutilized in libraries, and that is the numeric database—statistical data files and properties files, for example. The argument has been that such databases are not suited to the mediated search environment, that they are designed to be manipulated by the researcher instead of by a librarian intermediary who is more a barrier than a facilitator in this case; therefore the researchers should use, pay for, and maintain them, rather than libraries. The advent of end-user searching of databases maintained by the library negates this argument. Commercially published databases are now seen as the responsibility of libraries, and a library risks being squeezed out of the information delivery business entirely if it draws artificial lines limiting the type of information it is willing to deliver based on format. If the information in the database were published as a book the library would clearly see its responsibility, so why not the database itself? The *Physicians Desk Reference* and the *CRC Handbooks* are clearly of more immediate use to the professionals and researchers who use them in their laboratories and offices, but libraries have them and make good use of them too.

THE TECHNOLOGY: HARDWARE AND SOFTWARE

What made CD-ROM technology so immediately acceptable to libraries? It solved a number of information access and delivery problems that librarians had been combating for years. CD-ROM can store lots of data in a small, portable format. CD-ROM technology can be operated with a microcomputer rather than an expensive mainframe. The vendors put together packages of popular databases and user-friendly search engines, and sold the packages at a price that was moderate when compared to the same amount of online access, moderate enough so that most libraries can afford to allow no-fee access to end-users (Nicholls, 1990). CD-ROM does not appear to be a fad, a flash in the pan soon to be replaced by the next technological development. Even if some new technology provides a better way to access bibliographic databases, CD-ROM will still be useful for full-text reference tools and directories, especially as graphics are added, and for information packages that extract data from several discrete databases and reformat the data into reports for the user.

As for the bibliographic databases, the only thing that is likely to replace CD-ROM is local loading of the database tapes on a campus mainframe. Locally loaded databases can support more users accessing the same database at the same time, and they allow remote access. Unfortunately, they eat up mainframe storage and computing power, and they require far more technical support than CD-ROM databases mounted on microcomputers. If the vendors succeed in developing CD-ROM database markets outside of libraries, these new databases probably will not be bibliographic, since these have little appeal to office or home users who want access to data rather than the surrogate information provided by citations and abstracts. There will be demand to find these "data" databases in libraries as well as in offices, so CD-ROM is here to stay.

The technological innovation demonstrated in CD-ROM databases changed the way libraries do business; they forced reallocations of budgets and staff and changed the way librarians deal with patrons and the way patrons deal with the library. And they did it in less than five years. This is absolutely amazing. Innovations that solve existing problems or provide a new and better way to perform old chores have a way of taking over very quickly. Here are some other technological innovations or solutions that will change the way libraries do business.

Standardization

When someone says "I did an online search," it is now necessary to define what "online" means in this case. A conventional online search through a major vendor's native command mode comes immediately to mind, and one only needs to determine which vendor, and how many databases, and whether or not certain features—MEDSPELL, ONESEARCH, duplicate detection, field limiting, free-text, or descriptors—were used to get an idea of what the results might have been. But now, one might have used a gateway or user-friendly front-end software, or one might have searched a locally loaded database, or one might have searched an ondisk database from a remote location by means of a LAN. Each method of searching will produce different results. No one can ever be sure if an automated search is finding what it is supposed to find as long as this is true. A common command language may solve the problem, but there will be a long learning period as searchers try to achieve the same results that their favorite native mode provided in the new command structure. Furthermore, the common command language must have multilevel modes from neophyte to experienced, or some users will not use it. If it is too simple or uses an expert system interface to select databases or evaluate and rank the data retrieved, experienced searchers will not like it, and if it is too complicated and does not provide context-sensitive help, the neophytes will not like it. If the common command language does provide multilevel modes, how much language is in common among the modes?

Another area needing standardization is telecommunications, networks, and E-mail. Can my computer talk to your computer? If they can communicate, how do I find your BITNET address? What are the commands and protocols for leaving a message in your in-box? Much of the public is still surprised to discover that they can telephone the library and get an answer to a reference question. Unfortunately, many people on networked campuses are surprised to discover that they must still telephone the library or go there in person rather than using the E-mail network for something as simple as filling out an interlibrary loan request (Chang, 1991). Standardization is needed to facilitate communications not only on a campus, but among campuses. If indeed the library is the information center, perhaps it should be taking the lead role in the information network. Organizations investigating this trend are looking at the possibility of combining the library and the campus computing center into one unit. The OPAC of a large library can consume a great deal of computing power; if the two units are not working together closely, with a common vision of how the campus community will be served, the possibility for conflict and competition is great. Libraries that take the lead in developing a campus information network stand a chance of making themselves indispensable and thus drawing the computing center along with them rather than being swallowed up by, or at the mercy of, the computing center.

An area of standardization that would be nice but is not likely to happen soon is code standardization in existing, mainly bibliographic, databases. If one is searching for a publication published in 1988, does one code it as YR, PD, or PY? Is it 1988 or 88? Only a national or international standards organization has a chance of setting standards likely to be widely adopted, and once they are adopted producers and vendors will need to restructure their present practices and, it is hoped, revise and reload backfiles to conform to the standards. Such standards would make searching much easier for information professionals and end-users alike; it is a goal worth working for by campaigning for such an effort to be undertaken, and then working with the organization that will produce and enforce the standards.

Software Trends

Search analysts and end-users are always asking the vendors to make some major or minor improvements in the way a database or a search engine works. The ondisk vendors have been especially responsive to user demands and suggestions for better search engines, probably because the new search engine can be distributed on a floppy disk rather than requiring a major reconfiguration of a mainframe. Database producers and online vendors are less responsive because any change is a major undertaking, and the producers especially must be committed to a consistent product, one that looks and works the same over a span of many years. Perhaps the demands for change should be directed to software producers who can write programs that will meet the demands. In other words, don't ask the mainframe to do what the microcomputer can do. A common command language can be achieved by a front-end software package. Sorting and reformatting of downloaded citations can be accomplished by software loaded on the microcomputer. Viewing citations retrieved or typing ahead while the vendor's mainframe is processing a command is a feature of communications software allowing a simple type of multitasking, in which the computer performs one task while the operator goes on to another.

Other programming advances must be left to the vendors. One promising development does away with the barriers between databases by providing automatic links among them. A searcher finding an interesting citation in a bibliographic database marks the citation with a simple keystroke, and the text is retrieved from a full-text database. The searcher does not have to perform the link by printing out the citation from the bibliographic database, then switching to the full-text database where the text must be searched and retrieved. DIALOG's ONESEARCH feature already allows merged output from several databases and duplicate citation identification or removal. The feature needs to be refined and improved, and adopted by other vendors.

Artificial intelligence developments are needed if automated information retrieval is to match the end-users mental model. With no knowledge of database content or structure, or of information retrieval commands or techniques, a library patron approaches any terminal in the library or dials into the library information network from a remote location and types in an unstructured information request such as DAIRY BARNS SANITATION. The computer responds with a ranked list of citations, probably no more than twenty, which the patron examines. The patron marks the most promising citations and instructs the computer, "Get me more like this," and the computer obligingly evaluates the marked citations, interprets the patron's request, and produces another list of citations. The computer performs the tasks that librarians now perform, namely advising users on appropriate databases, instructing users on how to search that particular database with a particular search engine, and instructing users on how to evaluate the information retrieved and revise the search, except the computer with its artificial intelligence programming does not advise and teach, and leave the task to the user. The artificial intelligence program performs the task and presents the results to the patron. This is the direction that artificial intelligence applications will take in libraries, and who is better equipped to serve as the expert system's expert model than librarians who have worked with users, know how they phrase questions, and know how they interface with the information presented to them? If artificial intelligence programs are developed for use in libraries, librarians should be helping to develop them.

The Hardware

Speedier access is a trend that will continue. Multitasking is a development that will enhance speedy access; it would be nice if a search analyst could instruct the computer to download a retrieved set while continuing to search as the citations are being downloaded. Multitasking requires both hardware and software solutions to be fully realized.

Microcomputers will become faster and smarter with more capacious memories (Grosch, 1989). It is now possible to load a large database such as ERIC into the multigigabyte memories of existing microcomputers and search the data considerably faster than is possible with a CD-ROM, and it is possible to serve more networked users from the microcomputer than from a CD-ROM. This development may serve as an intermediate step between networked CD-ROM databases and locally loaded tapes. End-users have expressed interest in developing their own databases, possibly to manage reprint collections or personal libraries, possibly as SDI (selective dissemination of information) tools for a group of researchers working in the same or similar scholarly pursuits. Fast and capacious microcomputers make this increasingly possible as does WORM technology—the "write once read many" compact disk. Librarians should certainly volunteer their expertise to help those who are trying to develop their own databases, and librarians should be developing databases suited to their own needs and local collections. A reference desk expert system that remembers the answers to tricky or frequently asked questions and contains the answer to the latest freshman English class assignment is an exciting possibility.

The technology that promises to have the most far-reaching consequences for libraries involves document delivery. Telefacsimile, optical scanning, and fax boards installed in networked microcomputers and terminals are technologies currently available and being further developed with an eye toward solving the document delivery problem that presently fuels the access over ownership problem. In the future will be a text-digitizing machine that will be as common in libraries as photocopiers are now. The user places a document on the glass plate, feeds coins into one slot and a floppy diskette or its future equivalent into another slot, punches a button, and the document is scanned onto the diskette. What a marvelous opportunity for controversy this will be, as the copyright issues raised by the use of photocopiers in the past come alive and kicking once again.

THE FUTURE—PAST AND PRESENT

Past Predictions Not Yet Realized

Predicting the future is a tricky business. The "paperless society" has been expected for a few years now but has not arrived yet and probably will not before the twenty-first century dawns (Lancaster, 1978). Publishers must be willing to commit their livelihood to ephemeral electronic storage rather than tangible paper and ink. Moreover, users must be willing to sit for hours in front of a video display terminal in order to read the electronic publications, and the users may be more of a stumbling block than the publishers. Users demand printers on OPAC terminals and online or ondisk searching stations; they want paper, which is portable and can be taken back to the office where it can be marked on and cut into pieces for sorting, and filed away for future reference, and discarded when it is no longer needed. The proper programs exist for all this marking and filing and sorting; they are called database management systems, and most people print onto paper a copy of each record stored and print onto paper the results of the marking and sorting activities. The contents of full-text online files are printed out rather than read from the screen. If the electronic clearinghouse of publications becomes a reality, documents retrieved for users will probably be delivered as paper copies, and in fact it is possible that more paper will be consumed by making copies for users on demand rather than less paper than is now consumed by producing the multiple copies of the printed publications and the photocopies made from them. When the majority of the population is equipped with the electronic devices needed and the skills to manipulate electronic data, then the paperless society can begin to evolve.

The "library without walls" exists in the same future. At present, many libraries make remote access to their OPACs and some commercial databases possible, but very few are equipped to provide remote access to text either electronically stored or physically available in the local collection. The demand for such a service is growing, and the technologies to make it possible are coming together. An academic community probably has more computer equipment available to it and more computer literate inhabitants than any other population group, so it is quite likely that the library without walls and the paperless society will develop here. Since it is remote access to the library's resources that is being requested the most in the academic community, libraries have a good chance to shape the future. This is an exciting possibility.

Which Future

"The future ain't what it used to be," was a favorite theme of Arthur C. Clark, a science fiction author and the man who conceptualized the communications satellite. A bad guess or an overly ambitious prediction are some of the hazards of identifying trends and predicting what the future might look like even a few years down the road. In 1984, George Orwell's landmark year, how many librarians predicted that in just two years CD-ROM databases would be installed in their libraries and would be causing a revolution in the way automated information retrieval services are delivered to the library's users? How many of the trends identified in this chapter will evolve into standard practice in libraries, and how many will be looked upon as Neanderthal dead-ends a few years from now? Is there some new technology, a piece of hardware or a computer program now on the drawing board, that will revolutionize the way libraries do business?

Being proactive rather than reactive requires a look at the future and a plan for it, welcoming it rather than being surprised when it arrives on the doorstep. Listed below are some of the trends identified in this chapter. In order to plan a proactive future for automated information retrieval, the reader should examine the list and rate each item according to the following scales:

— The trend identified is (Probable; Possible; Unlikely).
— The trend will be realized in (2 years; 5 years; Next century).
— This is a trend I like and I am willing to make changes in current procedures to see it realized (Yes; Let someone else be the pioneer; Over my dead body).

The Trends

END-USERS are the driving force causing database producers, vendors, and librarians to make changes and developments that will meet their demands for:

—Access to more databases, including full-text source publications;
— More searching stations or LANs to provide more access in libraries;
— Remote access to library mounted and managed databases;
— Free access, meaning no cost to the end-user;
— Access that matches the user's mental model by incorporating artificial intelligence.

DATABASE PRODUCERS AND VENDORS respond to these demands by:

— Producing "packaged information" databases that extract data from several databases and repackage it according to the users' needs;
— Adopting electronic publishing and electronic clearinghouses of publications that will eventually replace the traditional print-and-paper format of scholarly publication;
— Developing user interfaces that incorporate artificial intelligence;
— Changing, but not reducing, the pricing structures for their products.

LIBRARIES will respond to these demands by:

— Favoring access over ownership, which will mean:
  — Developing interlibrary loan pools and networks;
  — Using all available means of electronic document delivery;
  — Not purchasing print-and-paper products when electronic access is available;
— Devoting more of the total library budget to a variety of automated information retrieval resources;
— Resolving once and for all the "fee or free" issue.

LIBRARIANS will respond to these demands as follows:

— Search analysts will perform fewer, more complex, and more expensive mediated searches;
— Search analysts will devote more of their time to teaching and consulting rather than performing mediated searches;
— Search analysts will deliver "value-added" products when mediated searches are performed;
— The distinction between search analyst and reference librarian will disappear as reference librarians incorporate more automated information retrieval resources into their work;
— Librarians, like producers and vendors, will package information that has been interpreted and analyzed for the user;
— Librarians will serve as models for and aid in the development of artificial intelligence as it applies to information retrieval;
— Librarians will produce and manage the campus information network.

Naturally, each one of these predictions could be sent down an alternate path by a slight change in emphasis or circumstances. For example, the last one could be recast: "Librarians will be squeezed out of the automated information retrieval picture as campus computing centers take over and manage the campus information network."

Some librarians may be saying, "Over my dead body," to each one of the trends, while others are cheering and wishing that tomorrow would hurry up and arrive. Each librarian must devise and revise his or her own list of possible futures and work for the ones that promise the best future for libraries and the people who use them.

"We are in a period of transition," people say. Well, of course we are. Only the dead are no longer in a period of transition from one state or time or activity to another, and we cannot be too sure about the dead. The trick is to figure out where we are transiting to, which has been the goal of this chapter. Only libraries that are stagnant and willing to remain inactive have no need to consider what tomorrow may be like, and for such places there may be no tomorrow.

The transition will be expensive, as libraries balance between traditional printed resources and developing electronic resources, as they retool for electronic access and delivery, and as they retrain the staff to use and interpret automated information retrieval resources. Whether as the model for an artificial intelligence interface, or in a continuing role as the human interface between users and the total library resources, librarians will continue to be the key to information in this latest period of transition.

REFERENCES

Anders, Vicki and Kathy Jackson. "Online vs. CD-ROM: the impact of CD-ROM databases upon a large online searching program." *Online* 12 (November, 1988): 24–32. Statistics from a mediated service and an end-user online service show decreased use of online databases only a few months after the ondisk products were purchased. End-user evaluation forms made it clear that free access—meaning no charge and no appointment necessary—was preferred by the users.

Basch, Reva. "Databank software for the 1990s and beyond, part 1: the user's wish list." *Online* 14 (March, 1990a): 17-24. Something better than Boolean is one of the desired features. Hypertext, graphical images, and cost schedules based on information retrieved rather than on connect time are among the others.

Basch, Reva. "Databank software for the 1990s and beyond, part 2: the online services respond." *Online* 14 (May, 1990b): 15-21. The author asked representatives of the major U.S. vendors and two European vendors to respond to the wish list presented in Part 1, and also invited the vendors to indicate the directions the online industry might be taking.

Basch, Reva. "Database reliability: the black box." In *National Online Meeting Proceedings 1990*. 31-36. Medford, N.J.: Learned Information, 1990c. The quality of a search is affected by the database structure, search engine features, and searcher behaviors, which can produce poor results from a good database. The author suggests that database producers need to put more effort into indexing, authority files, and so on to make database searching less like dipping into a black box.

Bell, Stephen. "Spreading CD-ROM technology beyond the library: applications for remote communications software." *Special Libraries* 81 (Summer, 1990): 189-195. RCS (remote communications software) links two modem-equipped microcomputers such that the remote user can perform any function mounted on the host micro; however, no one else can use the host micro while the remote user is connected. RCS is not a LAN, but it does make some form of remote access available at software costs.

Brownrigg, Edwin, Clifford Lynch and Mary Engle. "Technical services in the age of electronic publishing." *Library Resources and Technical Services* 28 (January/March, 1984): 59-67. Predicting a "long twilight" as libraries and publishers rearrange themselves in an electronic publishing evolution, the authors examine the overall nature of technical services in such an environment. The authors predict that the online catalog will become an online shopping guide.

Chang, Amy. "Developing an electronic information service in an academic library." *College and Research Libraries News* 52 (April, 1991): 237-239. An example of a campus E-mail system offering access to library services including interlibrary loan.

Clark, Katherine E. and Joni Gomez. "Faculty use of databases at Texas A&M University." *RQ* 30 (Winter, 1990): 241-248. Faculty were surveyed to see if they had their own contracts to online services. Many did, and cited convenience as the reason, especially the convenience of not having to go to the library.

Grosch, Audrey N. "Microcomputer decisions for the 1990s." *Online* 13 (July, 1989): 15-26. The author feels certain that IBM PC-type microcomputers will remain the system of choice in academic libraries, and gives sound advice for upgrading older machines and purchasing new ones. Definitions help the novice keep it all straight.

Hubbard, Abigail and Barbara Wilson. "An integrated information management program: defining a new role for librarians in helping end-users." *Online* 10 (March, 1986): 15-23. The library staff of a medical school library not only teach end-user database searching but other information management skills such as gateway or communications software, downloading, organizing reprint files, etc.

Hudson, Carvon. "Looking toward 2000: how the electronic publishing industry will evolve." In *National Online Meeting Proceedings 1990* 169-175. Medford, N.J.:

Learned Information, 1990. Downsizing, the birth of specialty vendors, development of global marketplaces, and the blurring of boundaries between producers and vendors are some of the trends the author identifies. Downsizing and specialization look like trends for libraries in the future as well, and Hudson predicts that the librarian's job is just going to get tougher.

Kibirige, Harry M. "Computer-assisted reference services: what the computer will not do." *RQ* 28 (Spring, 1988): 377-383. The author emphasizes that computer searching provides patrons with citations, not materials, and the local collection or interlibrary loan are inadequate to meet the patron's expectations once the citation is in hand. Artificial intelligence as it applies to automated information retrieval is another subject of this article.

Kupferberg, Natalie. "End-users: how are they doing? A librarian interviews six do it yourself searchers." *Online* 10 (March, 1986): 24-30. The end-users interviewed are working professionals in various fields. All agreed that online searching saves them considerable time, and most mentioned their appreciation of the fact that the time is no longer spent in the library.

Lancaster, F. Wilfrid. "Whither libraries? or, wither libraries." *College and Research Libraries* 39 (September, 1978): 345-357. A decade-old prediction of a paperless society that still sounds good and still lies in the future. The problems identified in scientific and academic publishing are true today and remain barriers yet to be overcome.

LePoer, Peter M. "CD-ROM's impact on libraries and users." *Laserdisk Professional* 2 (July, 1989): 39-45. After installing a CD-ROM version of MEDLINE at a health sciences library, the author made several observations: there are significant decreases in requests for mediated searches, most ondisk users are students rather than faculty, the searches performed are quick and do not use complicated search strategies, and the workload of the library staff is increased.

Martin, Susan K. "Information technology and libraries: toward the year 2000." *College and Research Libraries* 50 (July, 1989a): 397-405. The author identifies several trends in automation and its place in the library, including fiscal uncertainties as libraries slowly make the transition from ownership to access, and the tendency of the information industry to market directly to users, thus squeezing the library out of the picture.

Martin, Susan K. "Library management and emerging technology: the immovable force and the irresistible object." *Library Trends* 37 (Winter, 1989b): 374-382. The adoption of technologies provides a window of opportunity for planning the future of the library: what kind of institution it will be, how its users will relate to it, what its strengths will be, and what level of funding will be required. In fact, the author states, libraries should be planning for the future at all times.

Molholt, Pat. "A paradigm shift for information services." *College and Research Libraries News* 51 (December, 1990): 1045-1051. If libraries charged $100 per hour for access to the library building and $25 to check out a book, library users would be more interested in learning how to use libraries efficiently, and possibly, much more appreciative of librarians. Molholt looks at some future roles for librarians, which unfortunately do not include charging $100 per hour for consultation services.

Nicholls, Paul T. "CD-ROM in the library: implications, issues, sources." *Laserdisk Professional* 3 (March, 1990): 100-103. The costs of ondisk databases, their ready acceptance by users and the increased demand for them, and the changes they have created in reference work are among the implications and issues identified by the author. The bibliography is useful.

O'Leary, Mick. "Databases of the nineties: the age of access." *Database* 13 (April, 1990a): 15-21. The rise of end-users, long predicted in the 1980s, will become a reality in the 1990s as end-users demand more access and producers respond with the kinds of products they want. Access is the issue of the 1990s rather than more data.

O'Leary, Mick. "Local online: the genie is out of the bottle, part 1." *Online* 14 (January, 1990b): 15-18.

O'Leary, Mick. "Local online: the genie is out of the bottle, part 2." *Online* 14 (March, 1990c): 27-33. CD-ROMs on LANs and locally loaded databases are discussed in these two articles. The author notes the enthusiastic acceptance of local access by end-users who perceive the information to be free, and the librarians' perceptions of great expense and increased workload.

Rogers, Sharon J. and Charlene S. Hurt. "How scholarly communication should work in the 21st century." *Chronicle of Higher Education* 36 (October 18, 1989): A56. The author proposes a new environment for scholarly publishing in which electronic media provide the delivery of scholarly publications, changes in the reviewing process, and shifts in the responsibilities of editors.

Smith, Eldred. "Resolving the acquisitions dilemma: into the electronic information environment." *College and Research Libraries* 52 (May, 1991): 231-240. The advantages of electronic publishing and the electronic clearinghouse are detailed in this article. The heroic and historic struggle of libraries to acquire and preserve the records of scholarship is a losing battle that can be eliminated when electronic publishing allows libraries to become information centers stressing access over ownership.

Tenopir, Carol. "Online information anxiety." *Library Journal* 115 (August, 1990): 62-63. From the author's "Online Databases" column. Tenopir suggests that the information explosion causes information anxiety, which can be eased by knowledgeable librarians who act as filters applying professional level judgment to the selection of databases, sources, etc.

Weyer, Stephen A. "Questing for the 'DAO': DowQuest and intelligent text retrieval." *Online* 13 (September, 1989): 39-48. A description of DowQuest from Dow Jones, an online service that claims to use artificial intelligence and very fast word matching to process natural language queries, thus freeing the user from the chore of learning and applying Boolean operators and other search protocols. The author notes that it isn't quite what it claims to be, but it is getting close.

Woodsworth, Anne, Nancy Allen, Irene Hoadley, June Lester, Pat Moholt, Danuta Nitecki, and Lou Wetherbee. "The model research library: planning for the future." *Journal of Academic Librarianship* 15 (July, 1989): 132-138. A visionary view of the future role of libraries and librarians as integral and proactive parts of the research function of universities. Access and information technologies are major players in this vision. Reactions from five librarians (appearing in the September, 1989 issue on pages 196-203) are mostly positive and endorse a future in which librarians are true information professionals.

Index

ABI/INFORM (database), 175
Access vs. ownership, 33-34, 96-97, 216-219
AGRICOLA (database), 171
ALA Directory (database), 8
Appointments, scheduling, 16-17, 45, 115-116
Artificial intelligence, 231-232, 236, 240
Automatic equivalencies, 231

Beilstein Online (database), 176
Bibliographic databases, 7, 173
Bibliographic instruction, 25, 31, 35, 126, 138
BIOSIS (database), 3, 7
BITNET, 235
BRS, 3, 169, 186-187; CROS, 176; MEDSPELL, 182, 231; Occurence tables, 175
BRS/After Dark, 2, 84, 141-145, 183
BRS BRKTHRU, 142
BRS Colleague, 142
BRS Instructor, 24, 81, 126
Budgets, library: future trends, 221-222; reallocation, 32-34, 95-97
Buffers (printers), 209-210
Business Periodicals Ondisc, 150, 175

CA Search (database), 7, 170
CAI (Computer Assisted Instruction), 84, 157-158

CAN/OLE, 189
CAS Academic Accounts, 84
CD-ROM. *See* Ondisk
Cellular Data Communications, 211
Cendata (database), 171, 176
Chronolog, 8
CIS Index (database), 173
Collection development, 33-34
Common Command Language, 230-232, 234-235
Communications software, 206-207
Compact Disclosure (database), 151, 176
Compatibility of equipment, 48, 198-201
COMPENDEX (database), 173, 177, 190
Comprehensive Core Medical Library (database), 182
COMPUSERVE, 169
Computer and Control Abstracts, 7
Computer Assisted Instruction (CAI), 84, 157-158
Conference Papers Index (database), 173
Confidentiality, 46, 69, 119
Controlled vocabularies, 4, 135
Copyright, 44, 218
Cost recovery, 45, 52
Costs: direct, 82-83; end-user online services, 83-85, 88-89; indirect, 78-82; ondisk services, 85-86, 89-90; online services, 78-83, 87-88
Current Index to Journals in Education, 7, 28

Database Management System (DBMS), 6, 48, 60–62, 238
Database producers, 169, 171–173
Databases: definition, 6–7; directories of, 179–180; format choices, 190–192; types of, 173–177
DATATIMES Corp., 187
DBMS (Database Management System), 6, 48, 60–62, 238
Demonstration searches, 24, 56, 125, 157–158
Deprofessionalization, 117
DIALOG, 2, 185; BlueSheets, 178; Chronolog, 8; DIALINDEX, 177; duplicate detection, 177; OneSearch, 185, 231, 236
DIALOG Business Connection, 142
DIALOG Classmate, 24, 81, 84, 126
DIALOG OnTAP, 81, 126
DIALOGLINK, 80, 199
DIMDI, 189
Discretionary use, 22–26
Document delivery, 20, 237
Documentation, 48–49, 184; purchase, 179
DowQuest, 227

E-Mail, 1, 25, 31, 235
EASYNET, 26, 144–146, 169, 186
ECONBASE (database), 176
Electronic Encyclopedia (database), 150
End-user online services, 26–27, 141–149; effect of, 160–161; equipment for, 146; forms for, 146; management, 146–149; staff, 147–148
End-user searching, advantages of, 138–139
End-users: fees, 149; future trends, 226–229; mental models, 136–138, 227–228; misconceptions of, 132–134; preparation errors, 134–135; searching errors, 135–136; training, 154–160
Engineered Materials Abstracts (database), 177
EPIC, 25, 169
Equipment, 197–205; compatibility, 48, 198–201; inventories, 48, 203; location of, 47–48; maintenance, 202–205
ERIC (database), 7, 28, 31, 171
ESA-IRS, 189
Evaluation: of databases, 177–179; of search analysts, 117–120; of searches, 67–68; of the service, 67–72

FAPRS (Federal Assistance Program Retrieval Service), 171
Fax boards, 30, 210
"Fee or free," 91–93; future trends, 220–221
Fee structures, 93–95
Fee-based services, 20–22, 94
Fees, 18–19, 95–98, 149; future trends, 230; ondisk services, 154
FirstSearch, 169
Forms, 57–60
Front-end systems, 142
Full-text databases, 7, 173–176

Gateways, 144–146, 185–186
GEOREF (database), 171, 183
Graphic User Interfaces (GUI), 202

HAZARDLINE (database), 176
Help screens, 137–138, 184

Information Access Company (IAC), 7, 131–132, 225
Information industry, 169–171
Information malpractice, 116–117
InfoTrac, 7, 131–132, 225
INSPEC (database), 1, 7
Institute for Scientific Information (ISI), 183
Interlibrary loan, 1, 34, 175
Invoice monitoring, 52

Job descriptions, 43, 45, 114–115

Knight-Ridder, 169
Knowledge Index, 2, 84, 89, 141, 144–145

Large screen projectors, 210
LC-MARC BOOKS (database), 173

Index

LEXIS/NEXIS, 7, 176, 187
Local Area Network (LAN), 8, 29, 151–152, 201, 208–209
Locally loaded databases, 8, 30; future trends, 234
Lotus OneSource (database), 151, 176, 226–227, 231

MacSPIRS, 199
MAGAZINE INDEX (database), 225
MATHSCI (database), 171
Maxwell Online, 169, 185
Mead Data Central, 187
Mediated searching, 15–20, 105–110; advantages, 16; budget, 87–88; evaluation, 117–120; future trends, 210–220
MEDLINE (database) 2, 7, 173
Meridian Data, 209
MicroSoft CD Extensions (MSCDEX), 207
Mission statements, 42, 44

NeXT computer, 199
NOTIS, 228
NTIS, 171, 173
Numeric databases, 8, 176–177

OCLC, 25, 169
Ondisk, 8
Ondisk databases: equipment for, 201–202; prices, 170; replacing defective disks, 51
Ondisk services, 27–29, 150–154; costs, 85–86, 89–90; equipment, 207–209; fees, 154; staff, 152–153
Online, 8; equipment, 205–207; prices, 170
OPAC (Online Public Access Catalog), 30, 228
ORBIT, 169, 176, 182, 187–188
Organization charts, 45
Oxford English Dictionary (database), 150

Paperless society, 237–238
Passwords, 50–51
Performance standards, 46, 118–119
Pergamon InfoLine, 185

Pioneer 6-disk CD-ROM Mini-Changer, 151
Point-of-use instruction, 159–160
Policy and procedures manual, 23, 43–49, 63, 67, 154, 175
Postprocessing of searches, 224
Pro-Search, 142–145, 206
PRODIGY, 169
Promotion and advertising, 54–56
PTS databases, 7, 176

QUESTEL, 189

Ready-reference searching, 22–26
Record-keeping, 60–63
Remote access, 161
RLIN, 25

Scholarly publishing, future trends, 217–219, 232–233
Sci-Mate, 142–145, 199, 206
SDI (Selective Dissemination of Information), 12, 185, 237
Search analysts: characteristics, 105–107, 111–113; definition, 3; evaluation, 117–120; future trends, 220, 222–226; job descriptions, 114–115; management considerations, 113–120; scheduling, 115–116; selection, 112–113; training, 120–127
Search engines, 35, 181; definition, 6; future trends, 230–233
Search protocols, 6
Search strategies, 3–6, 107–110, 155
Searching, 3
Security: of access, 49–50; of equipment, 49
SilverPlatter, 155, 185, 188
Software, inventories, 203
Spoolers (for printing), 209–210
Spreadsheets, 216
Statistics: ondisk searches, 66; online searches, 63–67
STN International, 188

Text digitizing, 174–175
Training, 120–127; costs, 81; in-house programs, 122–127; of end-users,

154–160; vendor-sponsored, 121–122, 124, 183–184
TULSA (database), 183

Vendors, 8, 50–51, 80, 180–190
VGA (Video Graphics Array), 202
Viruses, 204, 208
VU/TEXT, 176, 188

WESTLAW, 7, 144, 176, 188
WILSEARCH, 84, 142, 144–145
WILSONDISC, 144
WILSONLINE, 8, 142, 182
Workstations, 49, 199
WORM (Write once, read many), 237

About the Author

VICKI ANDERS is Associate Professor, Sterling C. Evans Library, Texas A&M University. She is the author of several professional articles on automated library services.